DATE		

BROKEN WING, BROKEN PROMISE

A Season Inside the Philadelphia Eagles

Phil Anastasia

CAMINO BOOKS, INC
Philadelphia

Manufactured in the United States of America

1 2 3 4 5 96 95 94 93

Library of Congress Cataloging-in-Publication Data

Anastasia, Phil.
    Broken wing, broken promise : a season inside the Philadelphia Eagles / Phil Anastasia.
    p. m.
    ISBN 0-940159-20-1
    1. Philadelphia Eagles (Football team)—History. 2. Football—United States—History. 3. Brown, Jerome, d. 1992. 4. Football players—United States—Biography. I. Title
GV956.P44A53 1993
796.332'64'0974811—dc20   93-5211

Photos courtesy of Glen Scroggy

This book is available at a special discount on bulk purchases for educational, business, and promotional purposes.

For information write:

Publisher
Camino Books, Inc.
P.O. Box 59026
Philadelphia, PA 19102

ACKNOWLEGMENTS

In one way or another, a great many people helped make this book possible. I am grateful to all of them.

My thanks go to Edward Jutkowitz at Camino Books for believing in the potential of this project and in my ability to produce it. I also want to acknowledge the support I received from everyone at the *Courier-Post*, including executive editor Ev Landers, sports editor Bob Kenney, fellow pro football writer Kevin Callahan and the dozens of other people at the newspaper who have been helpful both in this project and in my writing career.

I've been on a crowded beat for too long to mention all the Eagles writers who have been a help to me. An abbreviated list of those who have shared insights, information and good times with me over the years would include Kevin Noonan, Mark Eckel, Reuben Frank, Ed Hilt, Kevin Mulligan, Tim Kawakami, Bill Ordine, Greg Greenday, Phil Sheridan, Rich Hofmann, Jack McCaffery, Paul Domowitch, Angelo Cataldi, Steve Hubbard and Jere Longman. There were many others. I am grateful to Glenn Scroggy for his generous assistance and enthusiastic support. Finally, special thanks go to my brother George and to Sal Paolantonio for their advice and encouragement at the start of this project.

CONTENTS

PRESEASON

· 1 ·

TIES THAT BIND

Through his tears, Reggie White looked far into the future. His eyes were red and puffy, but his vision was clear. He saw a football team that had rallied around the memory of a fallen star. He saw a Philadelphia Eagles team that had won the Super Bowl for Jerome Brown.

"I play for Jesus and I want my teammates to play for Jesus," said White, a Baptist minister, a Pro Bowl defensive end, a huge, outspoken man whose life has been built around faith, family and football. "But this year, we have to win a championship for Jerome."

The 1992 season had promised to be the most memorable in recent Eagles history. With star quarterback Randall Cunningham returning from injury to join forces with the NFL's best defense, the Eagles were poised to finally realize their vast potential. A sense of great excitement and urgency enveloped the entire franchise.

For four seasons, this team had stood on the brink of greatness. The Eagles were National Football Conference Eastern Division champions in 1988. They won 41 regular-season games from 1988 through 1991—more than all but three other NFL teams. But they never finished the job. They had teased their fans and themselves but they had never delivered on their promise. They never won a playoff game, much less made a run at the Super Bowl. This season was going to be different. They could sense it. The time was right. An aging, unfulfilled team was determined to break through in 1992.

Then came the shattering night of June 25.

Jerome Brown, the Eagles' Pro Bowl defensive tackle and irrepressible team leader, was killed in a car accident in his hometown of Brooksville, Florida. Suddenly, this wasn't just another football season. Suddenly, the stakes were higher. As word of Brown's death spread among his teammates, as shock and grief spread through the entire organization, White was wiping tears from his eyes and vowing to win the Super Bowl for his friend. Later that night, safety Andre Waters made a promise: "Whatever it takes, that's what we do. Whatever we have to do to win this season for Jerome, we'll do it. This season is for him. This season is for No. 99. I'm not going to let anybody forget that."

Brown, the boisterous, fearless athlete who embodied the spirit of the NFL's loudest, loosest team, was killed when his 1992 Corvette flipped over, nicked a palm tree and crashed into a utility pole. His 12-year-old nephew Augusta Westley Brown, the son of his sister Gloria, also was killed in the crash.

Brown was the heart of the Eagles' defense and the soul of their locker room. He had the foulest mouth and the brightest smile on the team. He was a terrific player and a remarkable person. "I never knew anyone like him, but who ever did?" asked Eagles defensive tackle Mike Golic. "Jerome was the spirit of the Eagles. His personality became our personality. It just became infectious. He would always kid around and make jokes but he was a leader of this team." According to former Eagles coach Buddy Ryan, "Jerome was the one who got the defense started. He was the leader of that group. He led the way and they all followed him." Free safety Wes Hopkins added: "Forget about Jerome the football player. We all loved Jerome the person. He was something special, the kind of person that you don't meet very often in life. He had a heart of gold."

He often described himself as a "big, old kid," but Brown became a leader of proud, ambitious men. In a locker room filled with great players and powerful personalities, Brown romped around with utter abandon. Brown was absolutely fearless. He was a ferocious competitor, an athlete who despised losing. But just as no opponent ever cowed him, no game ever overwhelmed him.

That attitude was contagious. With Brown in the locker room—laughing, joking, scheming, playing pranks, his high-pitched voice commenting on anything and everything, from a reporter's attire to a teammate's girlfriend to an opponent's quarterback—the Eagles never were nervous before any game, never were intimidated by any foe. "Jerome was the type of guy who always kept the locker room loose," Waters noted. "In the week before a big game, he would keep everybody going. He would keep people laughing. He loved to play but he always kept us from taking the game too seriously."

On a defensive line that included Pro Bowlers such as the deeply religious White and soft-spoken Clyde Simmons, as well as role players such as Golic and Mike Pitts, Brown was the bad boy. He reveled in that image. He had his reputation to protect and he guarded it as ferociously as he defended the Eagles' goal-line.

Brown always was the first guy off the sideline in the event of a fight on the field, the first guy to join the festivities in the event of a training camp melee. He loved it. He would yell, scream, curse, then laugh when it was over. In the last football game he ever played, at the Pro Bowl in Hawaii in February, Brown got in a scrap with Houston guard Bruce Matthews and Los Angeles Raiders guard Steve Wisnewski.

"That was Jerome," said Golic, reminiscing. "My best memories of him off the field are at meetings we would have on Friday or Saturday morning, after Jerome had been out the night before. You'd hear what he did, or just the way he would describe it, and you had to laugh. He'd make you laugh out loud every other minute."

Brown loved to eat and drink and laugh. He stood 6-foot-2 and weighed around 300 pounds. He fought a constant battle to keep his weight under control. He hated to diet and he wasn't too crazy about exercise, but he brought a boundless energy and enthusiasm to everything he did. "He loved life," said Eagles president Harry Gamble. "That's what I'll always remember. He lived life to the fullest. I'll remember that, and I'll always remember that smile. He could light up a room with that smile."

Brown wasn't too impressed with London during the team's week there for an exhibition game in the summer of 1989. He didn't like the food and he couldn't get a handle on the exchange rate from American dollars to British pounds. "I saw a sign that said I could get a hamburger and fries for four-fifty," Brown said one day in London. "Then I find out it's four pounds, fifty. Then I find out that's almost nine dollars. You know how many Big Macs I could get for nine dollars? Nine of 'em."

Brown also grew concerned about the personal hygiene of female Londoners. Never one to keep his thoughts to himself, Brown couldn't help but comment on the aroma of body odor on a dance floor one night at the Hippodrome, a popular London nightclub: "Man, I couldn't believe it. I didn't know they don't use deodorant. I thought we came all the way to London and ran into a bad batch of women."

Eagles running back Keith Byars said Brown used to stroll in the locker room about 9:15 every morning during the football season. Byars would be at his locker, reading the paper. "He would slap the paper out of my hands every day," Byars recalled. "I mean, every day. So one time he walked past and didn't do anything. I said, 'You sick?' He said, 'Oh, I forgot.' That was Jerome. If he didn't do something or say something to you, you would look at him like something was wrong. He meant so much to us. Words really can't describe it."

Brown was the guy who backed up his truck to lock Ryan in a Spot-a-Pot at practice one day at JFK Stadium. Brown was the guy who commandeered one of those little carts and sped around the Superdome during a practice before the Eagles played a Monday night game in New Orleans in 1989. Brown was the guy who yelled across the locker room at the team's tall, thin player personnel director, "Hey, Joe Woolley. I just talked to Sears. They got our rear end on order." And Brown was the guy who got out of his truck in front of the players' dorm on the first day of training camp in 1990 and screamed, "F--- West Chester!"

That attitude sometimes got Brown in trouble. He was leader of the infamous walk-out by University of Miami players before the 1987 Fiesta Bowl game against Penn State. It was a bold, audacious move—pure Brown—but the Hurricanes failed to back it up and lost the national championship game to the Nittany Lions. "That was all Jerome," said Alonzo Highsmith, a star fullback on that Miami team and one of Brown's closest friends. "I was eating my steak. Somebody said, 'Jerome says we're walking out.' I said, 'Well, if Jerome says so, I guess we're all going.' So we all followed him out."

Once, a reporter asked players in the Eagles' locker room what person from history they would most like to meet. Some mentioned Dr. Martin Luther King Jr. Some said Jesus. "Janet Jackson," Brown yelled in his high-pitched voice. "Buck naked."

In the NFL, Brown found the perfect coach in Ryan, who made him the Eagles' No. 1 draft pick in 1987. Ryan loved Brown as much for his cocky attitude and feisty demeanor as for his ability to play defensive tackle. "This is the kind of guy who takes you to the Big Game," said Ryan, who always referred to the Super Bowl in that way. A few days after the 1987 draft, New York Giants coach Bill Parcells walked into the weight room at Giants Stadium and told some of the offensive linemen for the reigning Super Bowl champions, "You guys better get your chains out. You've got to deal with Jerome Brown now as well as Reggie White."

The Eagles never had a losing season with Brown on the roster. They went from 7-5 (in games played by union players) in 1987 to 10-6 in 1988 to 11-5 in 1989 to 10-6 in 1990 and again in 1991. Their defense always was regarded as one of the most physical and intimidating in the NFL.

Brown was slowed by injuries and weight problems early in his career. He always was nagged by a sore knee, a sore shoulder or a sore elbow. He missed a lot of practices—and a lot of post-practice conditioning runs—but he always played on game days. Brown never missed a game in his NFL career.

That attitude endeared Brown to Ryan and to most of his teammates. He was inconsistent—a great game, then a fair one, a dominating play, then a rest period. But he was a powerful force on a powerful team, and his weight and practice routines seemed less of an issue as he developed into a Pro Bowl player by the 1990 season.

Or so it seemed. But shortly after Ryan was dismissed as head coach—three days after a 20-6 playoff loss to Washington, a game before which Brown took six injections of pain-killing drugs so he could play despite a torn right rotator cuff that would require surgery—Eagles owner Norman Braman made clear his feelings about his football team and about a certain defensive tackle with a big mouth and a nasty attitude.

Braman, a man of immense wealth, a man who collected art and fine wine, clearly was embarrassed by the Eagles' bad-boy image and he just as clearly felt that Brown was the symbol of a football team out of control. Citing high-stakes card games on plane trips, poor practice habits and an openly disrespectful attitude toward some assistant coaches, Braman painted a picture of Brown as a loud, undisciplined, spoiled, disruptive athlete.

"That story really hurt Jerome," said Ryan, who felt a little sting from the article as well. "I mean, what did they expect from the guy? He was a great player who laid it on the line for them. He was there on Sunday. Nobody ever played harder than Jerome."

Braman's comments came in conjunction with the promotion to head coach of former offensive coordinator Rich Kotite, with whom Brown had an uneasy relationship stemming in part from a brief but fierce training-camp argument back in the summer of 1990. Also, Brown's contract would expire on February 1, and he would need to negotiate a new deal before reporting to the team the next summer. His career with the Eagles seemed over.

But Brown was nothing if not unpredictable. He hired a nutritionist to help him control his weight. He worked out diligently. He rehabilitated his shoulder and knee. He said nothing controversial. "He was determined," said linebacker Seth Joyner, one of Brown's closest friends on the team. "Jerome felt he needed to lose some weight and play a little more consistently. He knew it. He started to change his attitude a little bit. We used to have to get on him about working out but not anymore. I never saw him work harder."

Cortez Kennedy, an All-America defensive tackle at the University of Miami, spent much of that off-season with Brown. Kennedy was preparing for his rookie season with the Seattle Seahawks and he shared a house outside of Orlando, Florida, with Brown.

Kennedy had met Brown during the former's junior season at the University of Miami. At the time, Brown was a third-year NFL player and one of the most famous products of the Miami program. Kennedy remembered Brown storming into the weight room at Miami one day, looking for the player they were comparing to him. "He said, 'Where's this guy whose supposed to be just like me?' " Kennedy recalled. "Then he just gave me a big hug."

Kennedy said his friendship with Brown grew over the next three years, especially during the spring of 1991, when the two players—both of whom had a tendency to become overweight—worked out together under the supervision of a nutritionist. "That's when we became close, close friends," Kennedy noted. "We lived together. We did everything together, go on boat rides, rent jet skis. We had a great time, just trying to get in shape, going to movies, going bowling, things like that. It was fun because we would eat light for a couple of days then just say, 'Forget it.' We didn't care. We didn't care about our weight."

Kennedy laughed aloud when he recalled the time he caught his friend sneaking a late-night snack. "We had eaten one of the nutritionist's meals that day and early that night," Kennedy explained. "So we came in at about 1 o'clock in the morning and a friend had brought some chicken over. So I came in the house and I saw Jerome eating the chicken and I said, 'What are you doing eating that?' I was chasing him around and he was chewing on the chicken and spitting it out. We laughed so hard that night. We laughed so hard. We always had times like that."

Brown's contract negotiations were long and difficult but not acrimonious. When he was named to the Pro Bowl near the end of the 1990 season, Brown said the honor meant "More money, more money, more money, more money." But he was professional during the negotiations, which were handled by his agent, Robert Fraley. Brown didn't rip management. He didn't request a trade. He signed a new contract, a three-year deal for $3.3 million, four days before the season-opener in Green Bay. He took care of one final piece of business in the Lambeau Field locker room just before that September 1, 1991 game. "It was just before we went on the field," Kotite said, a sense of wonder still in his voice. "I was in the coaches' room and he grabbed me and said, 'Come here for a second.' It was in the bathroom. He actually picked me up. He said, 'Let's go out and have a hell of a year.' "

They did just that. Despite losing Cunningham to a knee injury on the first play of the second quarter in Green Bay, despite losing reserve quarterback Jim McMahon to assorted injuries for all or part of eight games, the Eagles won 10 and stayed in playoff contention until the last week of the season. They did it with defense. In 1991 the Eagles became the first team in 16 years to lead the NFL in total defense, run defense and pass defense. It was an incredible triple crown. They also led the league in quarterback sacks, in forced turnovers and in general mayhem and intimidation.

Brown was a big part of it, maybe the biggest part. He was peerless as a run defender, fighting off two blockers, tying up the middle, chasing runners from sideline to sideline. He finished second on the team with 150 tackles, an amazing total for a player at his position. He also was a master of the inside pass rush, a pocket-collapsing force who sent quarterbacks into the waiting arms of White and Simmons and Joyner. Brown managed nine quarterback sacks of his own, more than any other inside pass rusher in the NFL. "He would make three or four plays every game that nobody else could make," said Golic. "He was a remarkable athlete, a guy that big and strong but also so quick. There really wasn't anybody else like him."

Beyond all that, Brown was a leader. Eagles defensive coordinator Bud Carson, a 20-year veteran as an NFL coach, a man who helped build the famous Steel Curtain in Pittsburgh in the mid 1970s, thought Brown had the best game-day disposition he had ever seen."He hated to lose and would do whatever it took to win," said Carson. "That rubbed off on everyone around him."

On December 2, 1991, the Eagles played the Houston Oilers on a Monday night in the Astrodome. The Oilers were one of the American Football Conference's best teams, with a high-powered offense and a homefield advantage from playing in a place they had dubbed "The House of Pain." On this occasion, however, the Eagles dominated the Oilers on national television. Their defense forced five turnovers and administered a brutal beating to the small, finesse-oriented Houston team. Walking up the tunnel to the locker room after the game, Brown started sing-songing, "They brought the house, we brought the pain. They brought the house, we brought the pain." His teammates picked up the cheer.

With Cunningham expected back to join forces with the NFL's best defense, 1992 looked good for Brown and the Eagles. Brown was 27. He had made more than $3 million in his first five seasons in the NFL. He was scheduled to make another $1.1 million in his sixth season. Cunningham's progress from reconstructive knee surgery was good. He was expected back at full strength by the middle of training camp. On June 22, the Eagles signed running back Herschel Walker, another potential game-breaker, another piece to the puzzle.

Three days later, everything changed.

Brown pulled into the driveway in front of the service shop of Register Chevrolet in his hometown of Brooksville, Florida late in the afternoon of Thursday June 25. It had rained a little earlier in the day. It was hot and humid. Brown's little nephew Gus, his sister Gloria's son, was with him. Brown talked for a while with some friends in the service area. He mentioned a fish fry he wanted to host before heading up to Philadelphia for voluntary camp, which was scheduled to begin July 6.

Brown pulled away. He turned onto Hale Avenue, hit the accelerator and lost control of the sleek, low-slung sports car. They heard the crash in the service shop. A few of Brown's friends ran down the street, but there was nothing they could do. Brown and his nephew had died instantly.

"He accelerated rapidly on the wrong side of the street, went into an erratic slide pattern and slid off the road," Brooksville police captain Ray Schumacher said at a press conference the next day. After an investigation, the police ruled out the possibility that the accident was drug- or alcohol-related. "There was no sign of impaired driving," Schumacher said. "We didn't find anything that would suggest that. We're not sure what caused the accident."

White didn't want to believe it. He was in a little dressing room in Veterans Stadium, preparing to preach at the Billy Graham Crusade, when Eagles vice-president Bob Wallace and public relations director Ron Howard walked in and said that Brown had been in a car accident, that there were reports that he was dead.

White went into Billy Graham's dressing room. A telephone was brought in. White called the hospital in Brooksville. He asked for a member of Brown's family. A nurse came on the line. "She told me he was gone," White said. "I put down the phone and cried. He was like my younger brother and now he was gone." Howard said Billy Graham came in the room, along with his son and another of the leaders of the crusade. They formed a circle and said a prayer for Brown and for his family.

Word spread quickly among members of the Eagles organization. Howard got his public relations staff together and divided up responsibility for calling players and relaying the news. "We just didn't want them to hear about it on the radio or on television," he said. Defensive tackle Mike Pitts called and got Howard on the phone. "He just broke down sobbing and he must have said 10 times, 'No, Ron, it didn't happen. No, Ron, it didn't happen,' " Howard said.

Mike Golic got the word from the public relations staff and volunteered to call Clyde Simmons, another of Brown's closest friends. Golic said he told Simmons and heard nothing on the other end of the line. He didn't know what else to say. He hung up. Many shared Kotite's view: "When you were around Jerome, you always felt he was indestructible. You just had that feeling. He was indestructible. But his life got snuffed out and that's hard to deal with."

Joyner was in Los Angeles, filming an appearance on the "American Gladiators," a made-for-television competition. During a break in the filming, Joyner was resting on one of the mats when Miami Dolphins wide receiver Mark Clayton told him that Brown was dead. "I was frantic," Joyner recalled. "I kind of lost it there. I'm usually good with numbers and I started calling some people and nobody was home. Now I was losing it. I couldn't think. I couldn't remember anybody else's phone number."

A week later, most of Brown's teammates gathered in Brooksville, a small town in rural north-central Florida, for the double funeral. On the hot and muggy night of July 1, a public viewing was held at the Josephine Street Church of the Living God. It was a tiny white building at the end of a dead-end street in a run-down section of Brooksville known as "The Sub"—short for Negro Sub-Division, which is what they used to call places like this back in the 1940s and 1950s. This was where Brown grew up, the second youngest of 14 children of Willie and Annie Bell Brown. His father was a mechanic, his mother worked at a local hospital. Brown was known as a mischievous but good-hearted child. He was a choir boy in this same 20-pew church, and he was renowned for his bongo playing, wide smile and infectious laughter.

Brown was a remarkable athlete at Hernando High School. He was a star in football, basketball and baseball. He once scored 41 points in a high school basketball game. His favorite sport might have been baseball, which he learned to play in the nearby Kennedy Little League. In his senior year in high school, Brown hit .385 and stole 24 bases as a right-fielder for a district championship team.

Brown was remembered in his hometown for his generosity and dedication to the community as well as for his athletic exploits. He was the kind of guy who would wave and yell "Hi, Brooksville" when the television cameras found him on the sidelines. Just one month earlier, Brown had hosted his first football camp for Brooksville area youth, inviting down many of his professional teammates, convincing White to preach at the Josephine Street Church.

In January 1991, Brown rented two buses to transport 70 Brooks-ville-area youths to a football clinic prior to the Super Bowl in Tampa. He once broke up a Ku Klux Klan rally in his hometown by blasting rap music from the oversized speakers in his truck, drowning out the sound of the rally's organizers.

Brown's public viewing drew hundreds of callers from every part of Brooksville society—black and white, rich and poor, men in dark suits and ties, women in flowery dresses, others in shorts and softball uniforms and basketball jerseys. "Words can't describe Jerome Brown," said Johnny Roberts, a physical education teacher at the local middle school. "He had a heart of gold. He was a special young man for this whole community." Lorenzo Hamilton, an assistant principal at Brooksville Central High School, added his thoughts: "Jerome did more than any person in this community to bring people together. He did more than anyone ever did to mend relationships between races. I never met anyone that he met that didn't come to love him. He was so unselfish. Even after everything he accomplished, he never put himself up there. He always came back and shared with the home folk. That was a trait that most people don't have but that was Jerome."

Brown lay in a black coffin surrounded by flowers. He wore a gray suit and his gold "Jerome 99" necklace. A bed of white roses with an NFL football on top lay on his lap. Next to Brown lay his nephew. Augusta Westley Brown lay in a blue coffin with the words "Going Home" stitched on the lining on the inside of the lid. Outside, standing in the sweltering heat in the church's gravel parking lot, Alonzo Highsmith said, "It's the most devastating thing that ever happened in my life. Jerome was the brother I never had. You only meet a few people in your lifetime that touch you a certain way. That was Jerome."

The next day, the scene shifted across town to the First Baptist Church of Brooksville, a large brick building with white pillars and wide green lawns. About 2,000 people were in attendance for the funeral service. Most of them were forced to stay outside in 92-degree heat and oppressive humidity to listen to the service on loudspeakers. Inside, the lives of Brown and his nephew were celebrated by their family and close friends. With the 110-member Community Mass Choir belting out such gospel songs as "Pass Me Not" and "We're Going to Make It," the service became a truly moving experience that echoed Brown's upbringing. More than once, members of Brown's immediate family—including his parents, Willie and Annie Brown, and his sister, Gloria—rose from their seats to sing, dance, clap and lead the congregation in celebration.

"It was the most uplifting funeral service I've ever seen," Andre Waters remarked. "If Jerome had designed a funeral service, that's the way it would have been—uplifting, joyous, and filled with a lot of singing." Tight end Keith Jackson agreed: "That was Jerome's kind of service. He would have liked that, all that singing and dancing, just a joyous feeling. I guess that's what we should take away."

Less than an hour later, after a short service at the gravesite in Fort Taylor Cemetery on the outskirts of Brooksville, White removed his colorful silk tie and draped it across Brown's black casket. Silently, dozens of others—Brown's brothers, his college and professional teammates, his friends from the neighborhood—did the same. Seth Joyner and Clyde Simmons, Brown's closest friends on the Eagles, removed their ties and wrapped them around the handles of the casket. They made knots and pulled them tight. They used the sleeves of their sweat-soaked shirts to try to wipe the tears from their eyes.

It was July 2, 1992, a hot, humid day in north-central Florida. Four days later, the Eagles would open their annual pre-camp on the grassy fields outside Veterans Stadium. Ready or not, the football season was upon them.

━━━━ ▪ 2 ▪ ━━━━

NOW OR NEVER

Time flies in the fast-paced, violent world of the NFL. In the NFL, the clock can outrun any wide receiver. In the NFL, a 27-year-old is a grizzled veteran and a 30-year-old is an old-timer. In the NFL, four years is a generation.

Four years . . . that's how long it had been since a young, cocky Eagles team had captured the NFC Eastern Division title. Back then, the Eagles' star quarterback was 25. Their superstar defensive end was 26. They had a 23-year-old rookie tight end who made the Pro Bowl.

The nucleus of the team—the quarterback, defensive end and tight end, the starting running backs, the future Pro Bowlers at defensive tackle, defensive end and linebacker—was young and vibrant. The head coach was in his third season. The Eagles were a gathering storm.

Four years later, as the Eagles began training camp at West Chester University in the summer of 1992, the quarterback was 29 and coming off reconstructive knee surgery. He was 0 and 3 as a starter in the playoffs. The superstar defensive end was 30. The Pro Bowl tight end was locked in another bitter contract dispute with the team's management. He would never play another down in an Eagles uniform. The nucleus of the team— the running backs, most of the defense—had entered athletic middle age.

The boisterous Pro Bowl defensive tackle was dead. He had been killed in a tragic car accident just a month before the opening of training camp. Both starting safeties were past 30. The old coach was long gone, living on a horse farm in Lawrenceburg, Kentucky.

Time waits for no NFL team. For the Eagles—aging, unfulfilled, frustrated, rocked by the recent death of team leader Jerome Brown—the time was now. Or never.

"It's time to give it a go," Eagles coach Rich Kotite said as the team gathered for the start of another training camp. "Even with the loss of Jerome, as big a loss as he was, we're still formidable. We're experienced. We've got guys that have been there. It's time. This is the year to make a push for it."

A sense of urgency filled the air around West Chester, a pretty little college town nestled in a hilly, rural area about 30 miles from Philadelphia. For the Eagles, this wasn't just the beginning of another season. This was the start of a mission. For reasons ranging from Brown's death to frustrations of the past to the accomplishments of their hated division rivals, the Eagles were desperate to make something special of this season. This was a team that had been on the brink of greatness since 1988. They were determined to break through in 1992.

"We have to win it this year," said defensive end Reggie White, whose uncertain status contributed to the heightened sense of urgency around the team. Not only was White going to turn 31 in December and not only was he playing his ninth professional season, he also was in the last year of his contract. In September, he would file a class-action lawsuit against the NFL in hopes of becoming an unrestricted free agent after the season. "I think it's that urgent," White said. "We have to win this year and then maybe we can build on that. But if we don't get it done . . . we may never get an opportunity again."

With star quarterback Randall Cunningham returning from injury to join forces with the NFL's best defense, the Eagles were convinced they could finally realize their vast potential. It was time for them to step up to another level. For years, they were a swaggering, cocky team that failed to back up their boasts. They had talked the talk. It was time for them to walk the walk.

"I'm tired of waiting for something good to happen with this team," said Pro Bowl linebacker Seth Joyner, a fiercely competitive athlete who was often outspoken in his criticism of his teammates and the entire organization. "You can only wait so long. This team has to make a move or we're going to regret it the rest of our lives. We've got a lot of great players. Are we going to be remembered as a team with great players that never won anything?"

This was a team that had shocked the NFL by winning the division title back in 1988. This was a team that won 41 regular-season games from 1988 through 1991, more than all but three other NFL teams. This was a team that was widely regarded as one of the toughest and most talented in all of football. This also was a team that never finished what it started. This was a team that had not won a playoff game since the 1980 season, much less made a serious run at the Super Bowl.

In the Eagles' biggest game in each of the last four seasons, they had played their worst football. They were flat and mistake-prone in playoff losses to Chicago, the Los Angeles Rams and Washington following the 1988, 1989 and 1990 seasons, respectively. They were thoroughly outplayed by the young, upstart Dallas Cowboys in the biggest regular-season game in 1991, a loss that cost the Eagles a berth in the playoffs.

"I think definitely they are on the verge, but they've been on the verge for a while," observed former New York Giants coach Bill Parcells, winner of two Super Bowls, now an analyst for NBC-TV. "My experience is that you can only knock at the door for so long. Sometimes there's a step backward. This may well be the last chance they'll have." Said Eagles safety Andre Waters: "I believe we can go to the Super Bowl. I just believe that. We have the talent, the experience, everything it takes. We've been a very good team for a long time. It's time for us to become a great team."

The team's sense of urgency was only heightened by the pressure felt by some of its more prominent players. Reggie White wasn't the only athlete to sense the passage of time, the intruding twilight of his own career. His status as one of the NFL's greatest defensive linemen was established. He was a certain future Hall of Famer. But White didn't want to be remembered as the greatest defensive player never to have won a playoff game. And after seven NFL seasons, six Pro Bowls, 105 games and 110 quarterback sacks, White's number of playoff victories still stood at zero.

The same went for Randall Cunningham, the gifted quarterback who also was at a crucial point in his career. Cunningham had missed all but the first quarter of the first game of the 1991 season with a knee injury. Now, after months of difficult rehabilitation, Cunningham was back to join up with the NFL's best defense. He, too, was feeling frustrated and unfulfilled.

More than players at any other positions, quarterbacks tend to be measured by the success of their teams. And while Cunningham's own regular-season statistics were spectacular, and while he had been named to three Pro Bowls, his fortunes in the playoffs mirrored those of his team. The Eagles were 0-3 in the playoffs under Cunningham. It was an ugly 0-3, too. Their most lopsided losses in both 1989 and 1990 had been in the playoffs. Cunningham had yet to throw a touchdown pass in the post-season. But he had thrown five interceptions.

Cunningham was 29 in March. Uncertain of his own place in NFL history—was he a trend-setter, the quarterback of the 1990s, or an underachiever, a guy who couldn't win the big game?—Cunningham didn't want to hit 30 before taking his team to some post-season success. "The other day I was riding down the road and I said, 'These times are going fast,'" Cunningham remarked midway through training camp. "I just want to sit and look at things and appreciate them more. Because it's going by so quick."

Herschel Walker was at a crossroads, too. Released on May 29 by a Minnesota team that had traded eight draft picks and five players for him less than three years earlier, Walker was ignored by most NFL teams. Unnamed personnel men ripped him in national publications, questioned his heart, his commitment. "The biggest fraud in football," an unnamed NFC personnel source called Walker in an article in *Sports Illustrated* magazine. "Nobody has ever made more money and done less."

The Eagles took a chance on Walker and signed him to a big contract. But if this was a new lease on NFL life, it probably was his last. Walker had turned 30 in March. This was his third NFL team, his fourth professional team. His first three never won a championship. He probably wasn't going to get another chance.

"People talk about us going 14-2 or 13-3, but my philosophy is why don't we just go 16-0?" Walker said in training camp. "It can be done. Somebody's going to win and somebody's going to lose on Sunday, so why don't we win? This team is going to be very good. There's no doubt I want to win. I want to win at everything. That may be my problem."

Age was catching up with other Eagles, too. Keith Byars was entering his seventh NFL season. Not many NFL running backs lasted much longer than that. The average career for players at that position was fewer than five years.

This was season No. 7 for Seth Joyner and Clyde Simmons, too. And if they weren't already noting the advancement of time, the passing of Brown, their close friend, certainly heightened their sense of urgency. Joyner, a brooding, emotional athlete, had lashed himself and his teammates for the lost opportunity at the end of the 1991 season. Sure, the Eagles had been No. 1 across the board in defense. Sure, they had been heroic in their efforts in spite of the loss of Cunningham and reserve quarterback Jim McMahon, both of whom went down with injuries. But the bottom line was another season without any real success. No playoffs. No chance at the Super Bowl. Nothing. Another year gone. Another chance—and how many would they get?—gone.

"We're not getting any younger," Joyner said at the end of the 1991 season. "We better hurry up and get something done around here or we're going to spent the rest of our lives saying, 'Woulda, Coulda, Shoulda.' Every year it's the same thing. You wonder how many times you have to go through this situation before guys start realizing you only get so many opportunities. It's like a child putting his hand on the hot stove. Do you have to get burned before you realize what's at stake?"

The Eagles' starting safeties, Andre Waters and Wes Hopkins, were near the end of their careers, too. Hopkins would turn 31 in September. Waters had turned 30 in March.

They were two of just four players left on the team (White and Cunningham were the others) that had played under former coach Marion Campbell, who had replaced Dick Vermeil in 1983 and lasted until the last week of the 1985 season. No player had been with the team longer than Hopkins, who arrived in 1983. Next on the list was Waters, who arrived in 1984.

Could the Eagles make the Super Bowl with thirty-something safeties? That kind of talk bothered Hopkins, who wasn't so sure it was now or never for the Eagles. Proud and sensitive, Hopkins believed he had two or three good years left and believed the team did, too. "It's like, you hit 30 and all of a sudden you lose a step in people's minds," Hopkins said. "I don't believe it. I feel like I'm as fast as I ever was."

Kotite agreed with Hopkins: "We have some players who have been in the league for a while but we don't have an old football team. I think the timing is right for us to make a run for it. But this team is not going to disintegrate this year. This isn't it and all of a sudden it's over. I know people have said this is the year. If we don't do it this year, we're never going to do it. I don't know if I agree with that. But I do believe this is the year to make a push for it."

Waters was less optimistic about his long-term prospects. Although he was a year younger than Hopkins, both had played eight seasons (Hopkins sat out the 1987 season because of a knee injury). Waters was just 5-foot-11, 195 pounds, not a big man by NFL standards. He had played the game hard for eight seasons. He had delivered resounding hits on almost every play. He knew that his time was running out: "I feel like we have to make a run for it this year. It's tough in this league to keep being a contender year after year after year. You've got a lot of guys in this locker room who have been around for a long time. You have to wonder how much longer it can last."

Brown's death also contributed to the urgency surrounding the team. For one thing, it added another layer of emotion and importance to the season. What were the Eagles going to do, dedicate 1993 to Brown, too? Kotite called Brown's memory an "emotional driving force." But there was little hope that force would remain behind the Eagles in the future. There were plans for an opening-day tribute, to leave Brown's locker as he left it, to wear patches on the uniform. But those would be 1992 touches, and everybody knew it. Everybody also knew that whatever emotion Brown's death had stirred would dissipate a little following the season, that time would dull the pain but also take the edge off the Eagles' motivation. "For me, there's a lot more feeling of urgency," said Simmons, one of Brown's closest friends. "I don't think we can stop this season until we reach our ultimate goal, which is the Super Bowl. Nobody wanted to win more than Jerome. We have to win it for him."

Expectations were high among the Eagles fans. For quite a few years, the Eagles had been the most popular professional franchise in Philadelphia, thanks both to their own success and colorful nature and to the struggles of the other professional teams in town. The Phillies, Sixers and Flyers were all in down periods, far removed from contention for their respective titles.

The team had long stirred the passion of their fans. The franchise was formed in 1933 and christened the "Eagles" in honor of the symbol of President Franklin Delano Roosevelt's New Deal. In the heady, romantic days following the end of the Second World War, the Eagles were the best team in the NFL. Behind running back Steve Van Buren, a future inductee in the Pro Football Hall of Fame, the Eagles made the NFL title game three years in a row and won the league championship in 1948 and 1949. The Eagles' 14-0 victory over the Los Angeles Rams in 1949 ended that golden era in their history. They would go through four coaches and seven non-winning seasons before they emerged again as the class of the NFL in 1960. Led by coach Buck Shaw, quarterback Norm Van Brocklin and two-way star "Concrete" Chuck Bednarik—a future Hall of Famer who played both center and linebacker—the Eagles compiled a 10-2 record and won the NFL title with a 17-13 victory over the Green Bay Packers in Philadelphia's Franklin Field. But both Van Brocklin, a fiery leader who had been the league's Most Valuable Player, and Shaw announced their retirement at the end of that championship season. The Eagles would enter a long, frustrating period in which they posted losing records in 12 of the next 15 seasons.

Things began to change when Dick Vermeil, a charismatic 39-year-old who had led UCLA to the Rose Bowl title, was hired as head coach in 1976. Behind Vermeil, quarterback Ron Jaworski, running back Wilbert Montgomery and a gritty defense, the Eagles became an NFL power in the late 1970s. In 1979, they went 11-5 and won their first playoff game since 1960. In 1980, they went 12-4, won the NFC Eastern Division title and made their only appearance in the Super Bowl following a thrilling 20-7 NFC title game victory over the Dallas Cowboys on a frigid afternoon in Veterans Stadium. The Eagles lost the Super Bowl to the Oakland Raiders by a 27-10 score. Jaworski threw three interceptions and the defense couldn't contain Raiders' quarterback Jim Plunkett, who passed for 261 yards and three touchdowns in the Louisiana Superdome in New Orleans.

After a first-round playoff loss in 1981, the Eagles slid to the middle of the NFL pack. They posted six consecutive losing seasons but their identity began to change when Buddy Ryan, the crusty, controversial defensive coordinator for the Chicago Bears, was hired as Philadelphia's head coach in 1986. By 1988, Ryan's Eagles were NFC Eastern Division champions again. But Ryan's team never won a playoff game in three tries, and his uncompromising manner and stubborn refusal to negotiate the diplomatic differences between himself and his bosses—a stance that earned him loyal supporters both in the locker room and among many of the team's fans—led to his dismissal by team owner Norman Braman following the 1990 season.

Ryan was replaced by Rich Kotite, who had been the team's offensive coordinator in 1990. Kotite led the Eagles to a 10-6 record in 1991, but injuries to Cunningham and McMahon kept the team from qualifying for the playoffs. Yet Ryan's mark was still very much on the team, which led to another reason for the urgency in 1992. The Eagles' recent drafts had done little to restock the team with impact players or future stars.

Ryan had built this team through shrewd personnel moves, although his job was made a lot easier by the presence of White and Cunningham. Remarkably, seven seasons after their arrival in 1985, White and Cunningham still were regarded as the two most important players on the team. Still, Ryan had done an impressive job of stocking the franchise with talented players. But the large majority of his best moves were made in his first three seasons, from 1986 through 1988.

From the entire 1989 draft, the Eagles had two remaining players: reserve linebacker Britt Hager and reserve running back Heath Sherman. From 1990, the Eagles got a pair of starting wide receivers in Fred Barnett and Calvin Williams. But the No. 1 pick, cornerback Ben Smith, had been sidelined since November of 1991 with a severe knee injury and his return was in serious doubt. Smith would sit out the entire 1992 season and in November of 1992 would learn that he needed additional surgery and that his return by the start of the 1993 season was in question.

In his first season, Kotite had kept the team together through adversity. He was regarded as a proven offensive coordinator and strategist. But Kotite was unestablished as a judge of NFL talent. That was Ryan's strength and his departure created a void in that area. Kotite's first draft was marked by his bold move to use two No. 1 picks to get Tennessee tackle Antone Davis, who had struggled as a rookie in 1991. Linebacker William Thomas looked like a solid pick in the fourth round in 1991 and sixth-rounder Andy Harmon, a defensive lineman, was showing some potential. But the remaining players from that draft were looking like a collection of future journeymen.

Without a No. 1 pick in April of 1992, the Eagles had used their first selection to take Alabama running back Siran Stacy in the second round. Stacy struggled in training camp, as did the rest of the class of 1992. By opening day, the Eagles had six drafted rookies on the active roster, but none were expected to make much of an impact in 1992. The legacy of bad No. 2 picks was starting to catch up with the Eagles, too. Two days before the 1992 season opener, Kotite cut safety Jesse Campbell, his No. 2 pick in 1991. Who could forget that Kotite had sworn that the Eagles would have used their No. 1 in 1991—the 21st overall selection—to take Campbell if they hadn't been able to swing the deal to move up in the selection order and take Davis?

Now Campbell was cut. The No. 2 pick in 1990, wide receiver Mike Bellamy, had been cut at the end of the next year's training camp. And the No. 2 pick in 1989, linebacker Jessie Small, had been left unprotected during the Plan B free-agency period and was signed by Phoenix. Brown was the No. 1 pick in 1987. He was gone. Jackson was the No. 1 pick in 1988 and his future with the team looked questionable. In fact, he would be gone by way of court-ordered, unfettered free agency by the end of September. The No. 1 in 1989 was traded for guard Ron Solt, who had been a bust. The No. 1 in 1990 was Smith, whose career was on hold. The No. 1 picks in 1991 and 1992 were both used to acquire Davis, who had yet to develop into a dependable player, much less a Pro Bowler.

The bottom line was ominous. The Eagles' 1992 opening day roster would have just three players gleaned from the 12 first- and second-round picks in the previous six drafts. The prime picks of the drafts from 1987 through 1992 had left the Eagles, on September 6, with just three players—Eric Allen (No. 2 in 1988), Davis (Nos. 1 in 1991 and 1992) and Stacy (No. 2 in 1992). "This isn't an exact science," said Joe Woolley, the Eagles' player personnel director. "Jerome and Keith Jackson, those were pretty damn good picks."

Kotite also dismissed suggestions that bad drafts were catching up with the Eagles. He called the 1991 draft, "the best I've ever been around." He said the previous drafts would sustain the Eagles in the future. "I don't think many teams, maybe one or two, in the last four or five years have done as well in the draft as this team," Kotite said. "This team has done very well building through the draft."

But the winds of change were blowing through the NFL. It was possible that the draft wouldn't be so important in the future. The summer headlines were dominated by testimony in the long-awaited antitrust trial in Minnesota. Eight players, led by New York Jets running back Freeman McNeil, were suing the NFL, charging antitrust violations as a result of the league's restrictive system of free agency. Since 1977, the NFL had operated under a system in which a player whose contract expired was able to sign with another team only if his new team was willing to surrender compensation to his old team, usually in the form of two No. 1 draft choices. Only two players had ever changed teams that way.

The NFL's system was far more restrictive than the ones used in professional baseball and basketball. Although they varied in detail, both major league baseball and the National Basketball Association had systems that allowed players to test the open market and sign with any team after five seasons of service.

In 1987, after the expiration of a five-year collective bargaining agreement that had been signed in 1982, the NFL players had struck for 24 days in the hopes of forcing the owners to change the league's restrictions on player movement. But the owners had broken that strike with a brilliant, ruthless strategy of staging "replacement games," using nonunion players. The strategy of keeping the league in operation convinced many union players to cross the picket line and return to work, and ultimately led union leaders to call off the strike. At that point, the NFL Players Association changed its strategy and began to attack the NFL through the courts. The culmination of a long legal fight was the *McNeil v. NFL* case.

Times were changing. On September 10, the jury in Minneapolis would rule that the NFL's system was too restrictive and a violation of antitrust laws. A new form of free agency was coming to the NFL. It was inevitable. And the Eagles were likely to feel the impact because 25 of the 47 players on the opening-day roster had contracts that expired at the end of the season. "If NFL players get free agency, it could be terrible for the Eagles," Reggie White had said early in the summer of 1992. "Just about everybody in this locker room has had a problem with management when it's time for them to negotiate a contract. That could be a big problem for this team." '

Would they all walk? Would some? Surely a team with that many potential free agents was likely to undergo massive disruption in the offseason. And just to underscore the stakes in 1992, White would serve on September 21 as the lead plaintiff in a class-action lawsuit in Minneapolis that sought freedom for himself and the 300 or so other NFL players whose contracts would expire February 1, 1993. White called his lawsuit, "The football equivalent of the Emancipation Proclamation."

Time was flying. Four years earlier, the Eagles were a young, talented team filled with promise. They were a rising NFL power, a team ready to make its mark. It never happened. And adding to the Eagles' frustration was the sight of their fierce division rivals, who were growing and changing and accomplishing feats beyond their reach.

The New York Giants won the Super Bowl after the 1990 season. Washington was next to win. Dallas went from 1-15 in 1989 to 11-5 in 1991. And the hated Cowboys had won a playoff game after the 1991 season and were regarded by many as the rising power in the NFL. "That's what hurts," Byars said in training camp. "Every year at the end of January, it seems like I talk to Reggie on the phone, and we talk about how some team from our division just won the Super Bowl. Some team that we beat in the regular season. And it hurts. We ask each other, 'When is it going to be our turn?' "

The Eagles had their chances. They lost their first playoff game in 1988, 1989 and 1990. They lost the infamous Fog Bowl playoff game in Chicago after the 1988 season. They lost at home to the Los Angeles Rams after the 1989 season. And they lost at home to Washington after the 1990 season.

Three strikes. In 1991, they were out. They missed the playoffs because of injuries and questionable personnel choices—like Kotite's decision to sign retired 36-year-old quarterback Pat Ryan to take Cunningham's roster spot. Ryan's struggles forced the Eagles to start a rookie free-agent named Brad Goebel at quarterback, and his limitations cost the team crucial games against Tampa Bay and New Orleans.

It was a quiet summer, a stillness before the storm. The Eagles went 2-3 in exhibition games. They lost their opener 41-14 to the New York Jets in the Hall of Fame game on August 1 in Canton, Ohio. They beat Pittsburgh and Cincinnati, then lost to Atlanta in the first game ever played in the new Georgia Dome and again to the Jets in the exhibition finale on August 27 in Veterans Stadium.

The Eagles spent 29 days in West Chester. The players slept, two in a room, in a student dormitory named Schmidt Hall. They rode in cars or vans across campus every day to the athletic complex and practice fields. Meals were served in the college cafeteria. Kotite stressed conditioning, weight-lifting and mental preparation. Unlike previous training camps under coaches such as Ryan, Campbell and Vermeil, this one was short on two-a-day practices and heavy hitting.

The Eagles would lift weights every third morning. During a typical week, the team would have just two days of double sessions—practices in both the morning and afternoon—and just two practices where the hitting approached their pre-1991 ferocity. "Easiest camp I've ever been a part of," said Joyner, who had missed Kotite's 1991 training camp because of a contract dispute.

Ryan loved double sessions and hard hitting during training camp. He felt it toughened his team. On the first day of Ryan's first training camp in 1986, 11 players were sent to the hospital for dehydration. Kotite had another approach. From August 5 to August 12, a Wednesday-to-Wednesday stretch smack dab in the middle of training camp, the Eagles wore pads only once—in the August 8 exhibition game in Pittsburgh. "The mental mistakes are what gets you beat," Kotite said in training camp. "This team practices hard. They work. But I want them to be in shape and I want them sharp mentally and durable for the whole season. It's a long season. I don't want them worn down."

The Eagles avoided major injuries in training camp. They whittled away at their list of veteran free agents, unsigned players who could not report to the team until they signed new contracts. They opened training camp without 15 veterans. By the time they played their final exhibition game, only cornerback Eric Allen and tight end Keith Jackson were unsigned players.

David Archer, a refugee from the World League and one of reserve quarterback Jim McMahon's closest friends, beat out Jeff Kemp for the No. 3 quarterback position. Cunningham's progress was good. A 310-pound tackle from San Diego named Eric Floyd, who was signed during the Plan B free-agency period, emerged as the starting right guard. Heath Sherman was the team's best runner, far more impressive than Herschel Walker, who was nursing sore ribs.

It was an uneventful training camp, just another training camp. But when the Eagles packed their bags and left West Chester, they knew they weren't about to begin just another season. "It seems like we go into every season and say, 'Well, maybe we'll win it this year but if not, there's always next season,' " White reflected. "I just don't think we can do that anymore. We have to bank on this season."

REGULAR
SEASON

· 3 ·

REBORN RUNNING BACK

Herschel Walker got hurt on the second day of the 1992 training camp. He tried to score during a goal-line drill, a nasty little border war that matched the first-team offense against the first-team defense, and he ended up with bruised ribs. And no touchdown.

Was this any way to make a good first impression? Was this any way to ease the doubts of some of his new teammates? In a word, no. And make no mistake, Walker's new teammates needed to be impressed by him. Many of them were skeptical when the Eagles began their pursuit of the famous free-agent running back in early June. Still more were upset when they learned that the Eagles had made him the team's third highest paid player, behind only Randall Cunningham and Reggie White.

Walker was regarded by some of his new teammates as an eccentric, by others as an outright kook. Some of them thought he was a talented underachiever, a muscle man lacking in football instincts and competitive drive. Some of them weren't sure what to make of him, but they wondered why the Eagles front office would agree to pay $2.8 million over two years to a player who had attracted little interest from any other NFL team.

"All these guys care about is performance," Eagles coach Rich Kotite said early in training camp, whistling past the graveyard of disgruntled veteran players. "Herschel has done everything we've asked him. He's worked hard and he will continue to work hard. I don't see a problem. I honestly don't. This guy just wants to play football. This is the perfect situation for him."

Walker was released on May 29 by the Minnesota Vikings, who had tried for five months to trade him. But they couldn't find a taker, at any price. So the Vikings cut Walker loose, closing the book on the most disastrous transaction in their history. They had traded eight draft picks and five players to the Dallas Cowboys for Walker on October 12, 1989, thinking he was the final piece in solving their Super Bowl puzzle. Instead, he was merely puzzling, a great talent who seemed at times to lack focus and desire, a gifted athlete who seemed ill-suited to their offensive system.

Walker played in 42 games for the Vikings. He ran for 2,264 yards on 551 carries, a respectable 4.1-yard average. He scored 20 touchdowns, including 10 during the 1991 season. But it wasn't enough for the Vikings. They had invested their future in Walker. They were thinking Super Bowl. Instead, they went from 10-6 in 1989 to 6-10 in 1990 and 8-8 in 1991.

Walker never seemed comfortable in Minnesota coach Jerry Burns' running-back rotation. He was split out as a wide receiver at times, used as a decoy at times, jerked in and out of the lineup. He was a running back who needed the football, but he averaged just 13.1 carries per game with the Vikings.

"It was an OK season," Walker said during his first training camp with the Eagles, looking back on his last year with the Vikings. "I can only do what I'm told. I'm not paid to coach. I'm only paid to play, so whatever they tell me to do, I'm going to do it." Kotite had a different view: "I don't think the coaching staff there was ever really comfortable with him there. The front office wanted him there, but I'm not so sure that the coaching staff did. It just seemed like the situation was never right for him." Walker stated that Vikings' coach Dennis Green, who replaced Burns in January, had asked him to stay in Minnesota. Walker was intrigued. He was impressed by Green. But he wanted out. "It was time for a change," Walker said.

The Eagles were the only team seriously interested in Walker, the free agent. And they were only interested because they had failed to sign Cincinnati's James Brooks during the Plan B free agency period in the spring (having been outbid by Cleveland) and had failed to trade for New Orleans' Reuben Mayes (having been outbid by Seattle). In retrospect, the Eagles were correct to avoid a bidding war in both cases. Neither Brooks nor Mayes made much of an impact with their respective teams in 1992.

Back in June, however, the Eagles were feeling a little desperate. They were determined to upgrade the running back position, but their only new guys were draft choices Siran Stacy and Tony Brooks, neither of whom could be counted upon to make an impact as a rookie. So there was Walker, free and clear, a once-great player derided in some NFL circles, a strange, enigmatic athlete, an Olympic bobsledder, ballet dancer, martial arts expert. Also a running back with speed and strength, plus two Pro Bowl appearances and a Heisman Trophy on his mantle.

The media was in full roar. "Sign Herschel" columns appeared in several newspapers. The morning guys at WIP-AM, the local all-sports radio station, began a "Honk for Herschel" campaign. Eagles officials were cautious. Three days after Walker was released, Eagles president Harry Gamble issued a statement noting that "running backs aren't put on the street for no reason." But Gamble admitted that the Eagles were interested and would investigate the situation.

Wes Hopkins cringed. So did Andre Waters. The Eagles' two veteran safeties, hard-hitting, uncompromising players, both thought Walker was something of a fraud. "You trying to get us Herschel?" Hopkins asked a newspaper reporter on the practice fields before the start of the Eagles' rookie camp on June 2. Hopkins was working out on his own. He sneered at the mention of Walker's name. "Herschel can't play anymore," Hopkins remarked. "He hasn't been able to play since he was with the Generals."

Hopkins was referring to the New Jersey Generals of the United States Football League. Walker was a legendary figure in the USFL, rushing for 5,562 yards in three seasons, including a pro-football single-season record 2,411 in 1985. He produced fourteen 100-yard games that season.

But that was 1985 and that was the USFL. Walker had played three-plus seasons in Dallas and two-plus seasons in Minnesota, each time arriving to great expectations, each time leaving a team mired in disappointment. The Cowboys never managed a winning season during Walker's time with them, and they were on their way to a 1-15 record when he left midway in the 1989 season. The Vikings were winners in 1989 but went a combined 14-18 in Walker's two full seasons with them. "The problems I have come from watching film of Vikings games," Hopkins said. "I'd see one play when he looked great, the next play when he'd take a couple of steps and fall down instead of helping protect his quarterback."

If anything, Waters' feelings were even stronger. A former free agent who worked his way up from the absolute bottom, Waters was suspicious of big-name guys who don't appear to play as hard as he does. To him, Walker was nothing more than a guy with great speed but little heart, a running back who looked for a soft place to land. "Herschel disappears in big games," Waters was quoted as saying the day the Eagles signed Walker. "I have a problem with that. I really don't see where he's going to help us that much."

Many other veteran Eagles shared Waters' opinion. Who could forget Walker's last game in Veterans Stadium? That was October 15, 1990, a wild Monday night game in which the Eagles rallied for a 32-24 victory over the Vikings. Walker was nothing short of atrocious. He fumbled three times, losing two. He tiptoed around, falling at the sight of an approaching Eagle. He looked confused, listless, disinterested. At one point, ABC-TV analyst Dan Dierdorf watched a replay of Walker going down and commented, "There wasn't much contact there." After the game, Walker attributed his performance to a "cold" he had caught while trying out for the Olympic bobsledding team earlier that week in Lake Placid, New York.

Gamble and Kotite had their own doubts. They saw the films, the plays where Walker would turn his back or dive to the ground, and generally fail to "pour it up there," to use the NFL's hot phrase for running backs who lay it on the line. They had read the articles, heard the whispers. Nobody ever questioned Walker's athletic ability. The guy was 6-foot-1, 225 pounds, with a body that looked like a suit of armor. He was strong. He could run. He could catch. But what about his heart? His dedication? His commitment?

Gamble and Kotite drove to Verona, New Jersey on June 10. They met Walker at the home of his wife Cindy's parents. They spent two hours with him, talking football, talking life, and they came away convinced he was right for the Eagles and the Eagles were right for him. "I had drawn some semi-conclusions and frankly they were erroneous," Gamble said. Kotite added: "I looked him in the eye and I became convinced that he was committed to playing football for us. I could just tell. This guy is determined."

The Eagles signed Walker to a two-year deal on Monday, June 22, three days before star defensive tackle Jerome Brown died in a car accident. They held a big press conference and showed off Walker's new No. 34 Eagles jersey. "He's going to help us make a run for it," Kotite said of Walker's impact on the Eagles' Super Bowl aspirations. "This guy is a great football player, and he's going to help us. I couldn't be happier. We talked about Brooks and Mayes, but we really made out a lot better by not getting either of those guys. This guy is really going to help us."

Hopkins and Waters weren't impressed. Neither were many of Walker's new teammates. And another problem arose when word leaked out that Walker's contract was for $1.3 million in 1992 and $1.5 million in 1993. It was a slight cut from the $1.7 million salary Walker had earned in Minnesota in 1991, but it still was an incredible amount of money for an athlete who had never played a down for the Eagles and was not sought by any other NFL team.

Pro Bowl linebacker Seth Joyner, who fought the Eagles long and hard in the summer of 1991 for a contract that would pay him more than $300,000 less than Walker in base salary, was incensed. Joyner seriously considered boycotting voluntary camp in protest of the Eagles' decision to give Walker that kind of money—after hard-lining so many veterans—

but changed his mind after Brown's death. "What the hell has Herschel Walker ever done?" Joyner asked in training camp.

Then Walker was hurt two days into training camp. Players were looking at each other sideways. Eyes were rolled. Doubts arose.

Things only got worse during the exhibition season. Walker's first carry as an Eagle produced minus one yard. He carried four times that August 1 day in Canton, Ohio, in the Hall of Fame game against the New York Jets. He ended up with minus three yards. His five-game exhibition totals: 43 carries, 111 yards, a paltry 2.6 average. He didn't have a single carry that produced double-digit yardage. In the final exhibition game, against the Jets again, Walker carried 12 times for 12 yards.

Walker also was being his typical self off the field. He was regarded as a loner, a quiet man who preferred to spend his free time with his wife. He didn't smoke or drink or hang out with the guys. He spent a lot of time in his dorm room, studying the playbook, keeping to himself. "One thing people don't understand about me is that I'm not going to try and be something that I'm not," Walker said in training camp. "You're not going to see me driving a Ferrari because it's expensive. I'm not the kind of guy that hangs out in bars. I don't drink. I'm going to be myself. I'm not going to be someone that people want me to be. One question that someone asked me and they got upset over my answer was, 'Who was your favorite football player when you were a little kid?' I said I didn't have one. The people I admired when I was a kid were God and my mother and father. I didn't know anything about sports and I never even thought about them. People see something like that and they think it's strange."

Walker met the media three times a week, around lunchtime on Tuesdays, Wednesdays and Thursdays. He was cooperative, even cordial, but there was no sense that he was enjoying himself. He seemed at times to be supplying programmed answers to stock questions, never revealing his feelings or himself. Walker kept his recent past stored in an old trunk with thick chains and double locks. He would talk about growing up in Wrightsville, Georgia, about his success at the University of Georgia, but he was reluctant to discuss his time with Dallas and Minnesota. If he had something to prove, he wasn't going to admit it.

"I never look back," Walker stated. "I don't look back at anything. Why look back in life? You've got to keep moving forward because that's what life is all about. I've learned that you have to be happy with yourself. As long as you're happy with yourself, you don't worry about what people say or people do." That was typical Walker. Placid. Satisfied. Not a ripple of concern about his play in training camp, his teammates' skepticism, the criticism in Minnesota, the whispers around the league that he was a shot running back.

Walker loved to appear impervious to the opinions of others. Only occasionally would he display his feelings. "Those people that have questions about me, let them step up on the line," Walker said at one point during an interview in training camp. "They don't have the guts to step on the line." Walker always was a little different. A sportswriter once asked him to name the four people he would most like to invite to dinner. He said Donald Trump, Prince, the Pope and Clint Eastwood, in that order.

Walker was like Eagles quarterback Randall Cunningham in one respect: stardom in the NFL wasn't enough for him. He wanted to branch out. So he talked about joining the FBI. He appeared with the Fort Worth Ballet during his time in Dallas. He made the U.S. Olympic Bobsledding Team that competed in Albertville, France in February 1992.

"People make such a big deal out of what I do in the off-season," Walker remarked. "People don't know that I used to compete in karate tournaments on Sunday after playing in a [college] game on Saturday. No one made a big deal out of that. People don't know I was running track when I was at Georgia, and spending my summers in Europe. I've been playing more than one sport ever since I was a little kid. My life is competing. I started out in high school with a speech impediment and I couldn't put a sentence together. I had to work and compete in the classroom to overcome that. I think life is competition for me."

Walker was a legend in Georgia. He had run for 6,317 yards and 86 touchdowns in his career at Johnson County High School in Wrightsville. He was the most famous high school athlete in America in 1979, when he ran for 3,167 yards and 45 touchdowns. It was more of the same at the University of Georgia. He was a three-time, consensus All-America selection. He led the Bulldogs to the national title as a freshman. He ran for 5,259 yards in just three seasons and won the Heisman Trophy as a junior.

Walker was a superstar in the USFL and a two-time Pro Bowler for the Dallas Cowboys. He once ran for an 84-yard touchdown and caught an 84-yard touchdown pass in the same game against the Eagles in 1986. He led the NFC in rushing with 1,514 yards in 1988. But in 1992 he was 30. He hadn't been to the Pro Bowl since 1988. He was coming off two-plus solid but unspectacular seasons in Minnesota.

Walker was saying all the right things but many of his teammates were skeptical. This was a guy who said he ate nothing but bread and water as a training regimen before the Winter Olympics in France. "He's a picky eater, and he didn't like the French food," explained Peter Johnson, Walker's agent.

The ballet, the bobsledding, the FBI talk, the karate, the incident in 1990, when Walker nearly asphyxiated himself after falling asleep in his garage with the car running—all created the image of an odd character, a weirdo, a guy who might not fit in with a team filled with proud players and powerful personalities. "If you play for this team you have to be committed to football," running back Keith Byars said in training camp. "What you do in the off-season is your business. But we expect you to concentrate just on football for six months. It's all business. No bobsledding or anything else to distract you. Just football." Reggie White, one of Walker's few close friends on the team, felt that the criticism and doubt that followed Walker to Philadelphia "bothers his wife a lot more than it bothers him. He lets it go in one ear and out the other. He knows he doesn't have to please."

Inside, though, Walker was keeping something secret. He was as motivated, as excited about playing football, as at any time in his professional career. He felt his time in Minnesota had been wasted. The fit just wasn't right. He wasn't really wanted by the coaches, wasn't really accepted by his teammates. He retreated into himself, which was easy to do in a locker room filled with self-centered underachievers.

Now he had another chance. "A new life," he called it the day he signed with the Eagles. He was with a good team, a potentially great team. And he was just a piece of the puzzle. Lower expectations, less pressure. Plus, in contrast to the Vikings, the Eagles were a loose, close, upbeat team filled with a collection of strong leaders. "I just feel like the timing is right for him to be here," Kotite remarked. "He's right for us and this is the right team for him. The timing is perfect." Peter Johnson, Walker's long-time agent, added: "Herschel has plenty of money. He has saved everything he's earned. He's accomplished so much but now he wants to play with a great team and have a chance to get to the Super Bowl. That's what's driving him. He's 30 years old and he wants to play for a winner. He's absolutely driven after what happened to him in Minnesota." Three days before the season opener, Walker told Cunningham to expect to see something special. He said his ribs were healed. He said he felt strong and ready to bust loose. "I'm going to turn it up," Walker assured him.

The Eagles opened the 1992 season at home against New Orleans. The Saints were a tough team, the defending NFC Western Division champions. They had one of the NFL's best defenses, having finished second to the Eagles in most categories in 1991. They were especially sturdy against the run.

It was an emotional day. Thirty minutes before the game, the Eagles held a tribute to Jerome Brown, showing a touching video on the gigantic Phan-O-Vision screen at the top of Veterans Stadium, honoring his parents, retiring his jersey. But the game belonged to Walker. On the first play, he gained eight yards. On his fifth carry, he broke free over the left side, sprung by a fabulous block by guard Mike Schad, and gained 32 yards. On the eleventh play of the first drive of the season, Walker caught a two-yard touchdown pass from Cunningham.

The Eagles won by a 15-13 score, thanks to a punishing ground game and typically strong defense. The Philadelphia defense held the Saints to eight first downs and 55 rushing yards. New Orleans quarterback Bobby Hebert completed just 12 of 30 passes and Philadelphia's veteran safeties, Hopkins and Waters, both made interceptions. Walker ran for 112 of the Eagles' 186 rushing yards. That was more rushing yards than the team had managed in any game in 1991. Walker carried the football 26 times from scrimmage and caught four passes for another 28 yards. Seven of his carries produced first downs. "I never questioned myself," Walker said in his Georgia drawl after the game. "That's one thing I've never done. I knew I could still run, that I was still strong. So I never questioned myself. But running for 300 yards doesn't mean anything if you don't win. This is just the first game, and we have a bunch more. This is just one game."

But one game became two games, and one great performance became two great performances. A week later, on a 100-degree night in Tempe, Arizona, Walker helped the Eagles to victory No. 2 by a lopsided 31-14 score over the Phoenix Cardinals in steamy Sun Devil Stadium. Walker gained 115 yards on 28 carries. The Eagles spent much of the game in a power formation that featured Keith Byars, Pat Beach and converted guard Rob Selby all playing tight end. Walker pounded away at the Cardinals' defense, a sledgehammer on a crumbling wall. His running opened up the passing game. The Cardinals were confused, off-balance, on their heels. They sent their strong safety, Tim McDonald, close to the line and that cleared the passing lanes for Cunningham and the Eagles' wide receivers. Cunningham completed 17 of 22 passes for 267 yards and three touchdowns without an interception. Wide receiver Fred Barnett caught eight passes for 193 yards, a career-high, and two touchdowns.

The Philadelphia defense was strong again. Rested for long periods by Walker and the offense, the Eagles allowed just 54 rushing yards. They shut out the Cardinals in the second half. They registered six quarterback sacks, and they scored their first defensive touchdown of the season when Reggie White caught a Chris Chandler fumble in the air and rumbled 37 yards into the end zone in the fourth quarter.

Walker got stronger as the game got longer. He carried nine times, including six times in a row, in a fourth-quarter drive that consumed nearly 10 minutes off the clock. The Cardinals couldn't stop him, and some of his teammates couldn't believe him. "We're tired and he's walking back to the huddle like nothing ever happened," Eagles tackle Ron Heller commented after the game. "I know he's carried the ball and taken shots. It's an inspiration. You win football games when you're tired, when it's on the line, when you're fighting, when you've got to make something happen. You win by your desire to go on. You're hurting, your legs are sore, you're tired, you just got your fingers caught between two guys and you see him walk back to the huddle like it's a walk in the park. So you think, 'Geez, if he can do it and he's running all over the place and getting hit all over the place, I can suck it up and go.' "

The Eagles were 2-0. Walker was the third leading rusher in the NFL with 227 yards. He was the first Eagle to run for more than 100 yards in the first two games of the season. Ever. "Look at him," Wes Hopkins reflected a few days later in the locker room. "I don't know what happened in Minnesota. But he's got the fire back."

▪ **4** ▪

DOUBLE TROUBLE

It was a performance as perfect as the weather. On a cloud-free day, the Eagles played mistake-free football.

It was a good day for sending and receiving messages. On a clear afternoon, Wes Hopkins and Andre Waters sent a clear signal across the Veterans Stadium field. "Sometimes you have to send a message," Waters remarked after the Eagles had dismantled the Denver Broncos by a 30-0 score on a sunny September 20 afternoon. "Sometimes you have to let people know what you're all about. Sometimes you have to let them know what the day is going to be like for them."

When it was over, when the soft late summer sun began to set over the edge of the stadium, the Eagles were 3-0 and there was a supercharged air of excitement and anticipation around the team. Following their dominating victory over the Broncos, the Eagles would be off for 15 days before hosting Dallas on Monday night, October 5, in a matchup of the last two unbeaten teams in the National Football Conference.

The Denver Broncos were an unbeaten American Football Conference power when they arrived in Philadelphia. They were a pile of orange pulp by the time they left town. Talk about "Orange Crush."

Fact: The Broncos managed just 82 total yards and four first downs. The yardage total was their lowest in 25 years. Fact: Denver quarterback John Elway suffered through one of the worst performances of his illustrious career. Elway was 8-for-18 passing for a measly 59 yards and was sacked three times.

Fact: The Eagles' offense generated 388 yards and 20 first downs and controlled the football for 39:18 of the game's 60 minutes.

Fact: Philadelphia quarterback Randall Cunningham completed 18 of 25 passes for 270 yards and three touchdowns without an interception.

"A stress-free day," Eagles linebacker Seth Joyner called it. "About the only problem was that everyone wanted to make a big play. Guys were running into each other a little bit because everybody wanted to get a piece of it." Added defensive tackle Mike Golic: "It was one of those days where the game plan just seems to come to life. That doesn't happen very often, so you have to savor it."

It was a special day for Hopkins and Waters, the Eagles' thirty-something safeties. They had played a game within a game, winning a private little war with Dennis Smith and Steve Atwater, the Broncos' big-hitting safeties. "They're the two best safeties in the AFC," Waters said after the game in the locker room. "I think me and Wes rate right up there with them. I'm not going to say who's the better two, but we sure didn't want them to outdo us." Hopkins felt the same way: "We know they play very aggressive defense. We know what the other team's safeties are like. Those guys are good. We had to make sure we didn't get out-hit by them. That was very important to us."

The threat from Smith and Atwater, real or imagined, was enough to motivate Hopkins and Waters. The Eagles' elder statesmen were proud and competitive. They enjoyed a good fight. They were a flinty, fierce combination, sensitive to slights, quick to answer any challenge.

Hopkins grew up in Birmingham, Alabama. He attended Catholic grammar school, and he remembered the fear that spread through his fourth-grade football team when they played a scrimmage against a rough-and-tumble outfit they had dubbed "The Country Boys." "We had uniforms and they were in jeans and ripped shirts, and some of them didn't even have shoes on," Hopkins recalled. "Our quarterback, he was so nervous that when he called the signals, his voice went way up. You couldn't even understand him."

Hopkins said his team got crushed by "The Country Boys," but he learned a lesson about courage and persistence that day. It was well he did, too, because obstacles would keep springing up through his football career. Hopkins hardly played as a senior at Carroll High School in Birmingham because of injuries. He was lightly recruited by colleges. At the urging of his uncle, Jim Lee, a Dallas businessman, Hopkins attended Southern Methodist University and tried out for the football team as a walk-on, a non-scholarship player just trying to impress the coaches.

SMU was a Southwest Conference power at the time. Just that year, the Mustangs had recruited a running back from Sealy, Texas, named Eric Dickerson. Hopkins was a no-name kid with little to recommend him other than desire in his heart and the chip on his shoulder. One day, though, Dickerson came through the line of scrimmage, running in that high, haughty style of his. Hopkins introduced himself with a hit that resounded through the practice field. He was accepted.

Hopkins was a starter by his sophomore season. By his senior season, he was leading the Southwest Conference in interceptions with seven and winning the defensive MVP award in the Mustangs' 7-6 Cotton Bowl victory over a Pittsburgh team that included a quarterback named Dan Marino. "This kid will stick his head into the herd of turtles," Eagles coach Marion Campbell said after the team selected Hopkins in the second round of the 1983 draft.

Campbell loved Hopkins' style and made him a featured player in his defensive system. Playing deep centerfield, Hopkins became one of the best free safeties in the NFL. At 6-foot-1, 212 pounds, with good speed and instincts and a tenacious style of tackling, Hopkins would roam around the Eagles' secondary like a patrolman on a beat. By 1985, Hopkins was a Pro Bowler.

But the good times didn't last for Hopkins. Adversity was coming in the form of a devastating injury and a difficult coach named Buddy Ryan. They should have been a great match: the hard-hitting free safety and the tough, defensive-minded coach. But Hopkins never really got along with Ryan. Their relationship was uneasy at best, antagonistic at worst. "I had a hamstring pull during the first minicamp and I also was unsigned, so I never really met him at first," Hopkins once said. "All I knew was what I read and I couldn't understand what I was reading. He was saying that I pulled my hamstring because my wallet was so heavy. We just didn't hit it off."

Things only got worse for Hopkins. In the second game of the 1986 season, a 6-3 overtime loss in Chicago, he hurt his left knee. It was sore and weak, but Hopkins kept playing. Two weeks later, in a home game against the Los Angeles Rams, he planted his left foot and felt the knee give way. Ironically, Hopkins was trying to tackle Dickerson, his old college teammate, on the play.

The injury was bad: torn cartilage, severe ligament damage. He would miss the rest of the 1986 season and all of 1987 following reconstructive surgery. He felt like a ghost in the locker room—a once-great player who was still a part of the team, but somehow separate.

Meanwhile, the team got better and better. Hopkins was on the outside, looking in. A bond was forming between Ryan and many of the young players the coach had brought to the team. The Eagles were a competitive team by the end of the 1986 season and a rising power by the end of the next. "Buddy and I had no relationship," Hopkins once said. "I don't remember him saying anything to me until he knew I was going to come back."

Hopkins did come back. After nearly two years of rehabilitation, Hopkins started all 16 games in 1988 as the Eagles won the NFC Eastern Division with a 10-6 record. He made two interceptions in the 23-7 victory in the season finale in Dallas, the game that clinched the Eagles' first title since 1980. "I actually shed a tear that day," Hopkins recalled.

Not that everything was perfect. Hopkins was sharing time in the secondary with Terry Hoage, who often replaced him in passing situations. The platoon continued in 1989, when Hopkins went the entire season without an interception. And then, with his first pick in the 1990 draft, Ryan selected defensive back Ben Smith from the University of Georgia. Smith, Ryan told everyone that day, was his new starting free safety. Hopkins was out. "It hit me like a ton of bricks," Hopkins recalled. "Buddy had told me at the end of the previous season how well I had played, how he was looking to me for leadership, and then he does this. I had been having a good training camp and Ben was holding out and Terry had just come in. One morning I'm sitting in the training room and I read that Buddy has said something about me making the team. Making the team! That was it. All the stuff that had happened to that point just sent me over the edge. I got in my car, drove to the dorm and packed my bags. I was going home to call my agent and tell him to get me out of here. I couldn't take it anymore. Coach [Tom] Bettis saw me and talked me out of leaving. He told me to go talk with Buddy." Hopkins went to see Ryan. He said Ryan told him he had no intention of cutting him. "I didn't believe him," Hopkins said.

Hopkins started the season on the bench. It was a frustrating time for him, and he lost his cool on a couple of occasions. He took a few menacing steps toward an abusive fan in Veterans Stadium during a wild Monday night game against Minnesota. Six days later, he came off the sideline and earned a 15-yard unsportsmanlike conduct penalty in a game in Washington. But a week later, Hopkins returned to the starting lineup. Smith was switched to left cornerback to replace the struggling Izel Jenkins. Hopkins would start the rest of the season and finish with 138 tackles and five interceptions. "The coaches were wrong and I think I proved that," Hopkins said.

Ryan's relationship with Hopkins was one of the oddest aspects of the coach's five-year stay in Philadelphia. Ryan rarely praised Hopkins, not in the same way he praised players that he had drafted or discovered. He seemed to resent the fact that Hopkins was an established star before his arrival in Philadelphia, unlike others such as Reggie White and Randall Cunningham, who blossomed after Ryan took over the Eagles.

The Eagles lost their third consecutive playoff game on January 5, 1991. Three days later, Hopkins was driving to Veterans Stadium. He heard on the car radio that Ryan had been fired. "I turned around and went back home," Hopkins recalled. "In a sense, there was a weight off my back."

Waters' reaction was different. A little-known free agent from nearby Cheyney State University, Waters had made the team as a special-teams player as a rookie in 1984 and again in 1985. But Ryan had other plans for Waters. He saw a fast, aggressive, hungry young hitter. He cut a veteran named Ray Ellis, who had been the starter for three seasons and was one of Hopkins' closest friends, and made Waters his starting strong safety. "Andre's my kind of guy," Ryan remarked during his first training camp in the summer of 1986. "He turns them upside down and laughs at them."

Waters never lost his hunger after making the starting lineup. He had come too far, beaten too many odds, to ever take anything for granted. Waters was one of six children raised by his mother, Willioah Perry, in the tiny, rural town of Pahokee, Florida. He was working in the fields by the age of 10. After he returned a kickoff for a touchdown against Washington in his rookie season of 1984, Waters told reporters crowded around his locker that he got his speed and moves from "chasing rabbits back home." "I told myself back then, if I ever got any money, I was going to use it to help people," Waters once said. "My mom always told me, 'You can do what you want to do. Nothing can stop you. If you want to help people, you can help people.' "

Waters might have been one of the most misunderstood athletes in professional sports. He was regarded by many as a villain, a cheap-shot artist, a mean-spirited athlete deserving of the nickname "Dirty Waters." Waters admitted that he played the game with reckless abandon. He hit hard. He hit low. "I'm an animal, a beast," he once said in describing his temperament on the field.

Waters' reputation came as a result of some well-publicized late, low hits. It all began in 1986, his first season as a starter, when he leveled Atlanta quarterback David Archer out of bounds. He was penalized for the late hit, and fined by the NFL. Two years later, Waters hit Los Angeles Rams quarterback Jim Everett on a blitz. Taking "the shortest route to the quarterback," Waters left his feet and dove in the direction of Everett's knees. No penalty was called. But after a complaint by the Rams and a review by the NFL office, Waters was hit with another fine. Then in the same Monday night game in 1990 in which Hopkins got into a squabble with some fans, Waters' reputation was cemented. Coming again on a blitz, Waters dove and hit Minnesota quarterback Rich Gannon around the knees. He earned a penalty and a label from ABC-TV commentator Dan Dierdorf, who called Waters "the cheap-shot artist of the NFL."

Waters usually shrugged off the criticism. But the Dierdorf comments stung him. "It hurts me that people judge me that way and they don't even know me," Waters said a few days after the incident. "I've always believed: don't judge a man unless you get to know him. What would this world be like if all we did was judge people from the outside?"

Waters had another side, a softer, gentler side. But he was reluctant to promote himself. He had chastised his agent, Jim Solano, and even the Eagles' public relations staff for promoting his community service and charity work. "I don't do things for publicity," Waters once said. "That's doing something for the wrong reason. I help people because they need help not because I want people to know that Andre Waters is out there trying to be some big man."

Waters donated much of his free time to Philadelphia-area Special Olympics programs. He was honored as Philadelphia's Special Olympics Athlete of the Year in 1988. Waters also supported a rehabilitation center in Reading, Pennsylvania, for drug and alcohol abusers. His help had been so instrumental that the facility was renamed "The Andre Waters Light House." Waters made countless speaking appearances at schools and on behalf of the Fellowship of Christian Athletes. He had been an active participant in the "Say No to Drugs" campaign of the New Jersey State Police.

In the summer of 1990, Waters met a 9-year-old boy from Chester, Pennsylvania, named Shawn Hawkins. Shawn had heart and lung disorders. When Hawkins died on Halloween, Waters served as a pallbearer and paid for the funeral. "Shawn was a diehard Eagles fan," said Mildred Anderson, one of Hawkins' teachers at William Penn Elementary School. "He had a hero to look up to in Andre, and Andre, in turn, called Shawn his hero." That was the side that Waters rarely showed to the public. He was better known as the tenacious, tightly wound athlete who attacked New Orleans wide receiver Eric Martin following a game in Veterans Stadium in 1991, earning still another fine from the NFL office.

Waters also was among the more superstitious athletes in the Eagles' locker room. He would sometimes sprinkle himself with holy water before games. He taped motivational slogans—such as "Let's Get Started" and "I'm for Real"—to his forehead. He worried about the impact of his choice of undershirts. Once, Waters made the mistake of wearing one of cornerback Eric Allen's long-sleeve undershirts during a 1991 game against Pittsburgh. Waters was assigned to cover Pittsburgh's Eric Green, but the big tight end had several long receptions and an 8-yard touchdown catch in the first quarter. So there was Waters, on the sideline after Green's touchdown, stripping off his jersey and his shoulder pads, ripping off Allen's undershirt, spiking it to the ground. Waters changed shirts. Green was quiet the rest of the day. The Eagles won going away. "It was the shirt," Waters said after the game. "It was bad luck. I should have known better." While Hopkins was struggling through his injury rehabilitation in 1986 and 1987, Waters was establishing himself as a starter for the Eagles. Although just 5-foot-11 and 195 pounds, small by NFL standards, Waters was renowned for his aggressive play and sure tackling. With his shaved head and goatee, he was a menacing, intimidating sight. "Andre lays them out," linebacker Seth Joyner once said. "People know if they get through the line that Andre's going to be there waiting for them. They don't want to deal with him."

By 1988, Waters and Hopkins were set as the Eagles' safeties. Over the next four seasons, they combined for 949 tackles, 20 interceptions and 13 fumble recoveries. They also earned a reputation as two of the hardest hitters at their position, a tenacious tandem. "They're very, very physical," Eagles coach Rich Kotite said during training camp before the 1992 season. "They make people pay. I think we probably have more dropped balls against us because of those two guys. People are waiting to get hit. I think 'persuasive' is a good word to describe them."

The Broncos found that out the hard way on the afternoon of September 20. On the fourth play of the game, a third and eight from the Broncos' 38, wide receiver Mark Jackson caught a short pass from Elway. Jackson turned upfield and into a green-helmeted missile with menace in mind. It was Waters. "I kind of zoomed in on him," Waters recalled. "I just put the beams on him. I wanted them to know they were in for a war." Defensive tackle Mike Golic agreed: "A hit like that sets the tone. It's got to make receivers nervous. Those guys have a 'rep' anyway, then these guys come in here and get tagged right away. It's got to make them think."

Thinking was something the Eagles defenders were doing all week before the Broncos game. Thinking and seething and waiting for their chance. They had read the quotes in a Philadelphia newspaper early in the week from Denver cornerback Tyrone Braxton, who had the audacity to suggest that the Broncos' defense was the equal of the Eagles' defense. Braxton also mentioned that the Eagles play against low-powered NFC offenses, while the Broncos regularly face turbo-charged teams from the AFC. "He needs to get real," Joyner said after the game. "I mean, they face those big offenses from San Diego and Seattle, right? I noticed he was the first one toasted up for a touchdown. So maybe he learned a lesson."

Braxton wasn't the only Bronco burned by the Eagles' passing game. Cunningham was sensational, effortlessly tossing perfect passes to wide receivers Fred Barnett and Calvin Williams, who combined to cut through that orange secondary for 210 yards and three touchdowns. Time and again, the Broncos' highly touted safeties, Smith and Atwater, who had been to a combined seven Pro Bowls, were caught out of position and forced to give futile chase. "A very, very frustrating day," Smith said after the game. "They kept us off-balance the whole game. We would move up to stop the run and they would beat us deep."

Meanwhile, Denver's wide receivers caught just four passes for 44 yards. Jackson's only catch was that six-yarder that ended with Waters' thunderous hit. Later in the first quarter, Waters submarined tight end Shannon Sharpe two yards short of a first down. Hopkins got in the act, too. On the Broncos' final drive of the first quarter, Hopkins circled wide and threw the stunned Sharpe for a three-yard loss. The first player to reach him and offer congratulations—in the form of several hard, happy slaps on the top of his helmet—was Waters. "Yeah, Wes, yeah," Waters yelled.

It was a romp, just the Eagles' second home shutout in 11 seasons. Elway called it "an old-fashioned butt-kicking." Two weeks later, after engineering another of his patented late rallies for victory, Elway would say, "We never feel like we're out of the game, unless we're playing in Philly."

The Eagles were smooth on offense, solid on special teams, sensational on defense. It was a complete victory, a team victory, but it was extra special to the team's set of thirty-something safeties. They had sent the signal, loud and clear. The Broncos had gotten the message.

"If one of us don't get you, the other one will," Waters declared. "If you're running away from one of us, you're running into the other one. And you're going to get hit."

■ 5 ■

FREEDOM FIGHTER

The Eagles were 3-0 and living large. They were No. 1 across the board in the NFL rankings in defense. They were gathering strength on offense, gaining confidence and momentum from the performances of running back Herschel Walker, quarterback Randall Cunningham, wide receiver Fred Barnett and the revamped front line.

Things were looking good for the Eagles. Washington, the defending Super Bowl champion, was 2-1 but moving with a lumbering, awkward gait. One season after cruising to a 17-2 record, the Redskins were looking old and a little overrated. Plus, one of their best defensive players, cornerback Darrell Green, had a busted forearm that would force him to miss 12 games.

The young powers in the National Football Conference, Atlanta and Detroit, were in serious trouble. Both the Falcons and Lions had made the playoffs in 1991. Both were regarded as contenders for the conference title in 1992. But both were sporting 1-3 records. In the NFC's Western Division, San Francisco was looking strong at 3-1. But the Eagles' most immediate threat seemed to come from Dallas, another NFC Eastern Division team that also was 3-0. Because of the bye in the schedule, the Eagles and the Cowboys would take 15 days off before meeting in a Monday night showdown on October 5 in Veterans Stadium.

It should have been a quiet, confident time for the Eagles. It should have been a time of excitement and anticipation, a time to sit back and relax and ponder the possibilities of a season filled with promise. Instead, it was a time of tumult. Without playing a game, the Eagles suffered a loss that would haunt them for the rest of the season.

Three months earlier, the long-awaited, much-anticipated antitrust court case, pitting eight veteran players against the NFL, had begun in Minneapolis. In *McNeil v. NFL*, the plaintiffs, led by New York Jets running back Freeman McNeil, had charged that the NFL's system of free agency was too restrictive and a violation of federal antitrust laws. It was a trial that would dramatically change the NFL, and the Eagles, much to their chagrin, would be one of the first teams to realize it.

For those players without contracts, the trial held special importance. All summer, negotiations with veteran players moved slowly for all NFL teams. Many players were reluctant to sign new contracts and report to their teams before the resolution of the court case. What if the jury ruled for the players? Would that mean free agency for all players, or just for the unsigned players? "It's having an effect on us and on every other team," Eagles president Harry Gamble had noted early in training camp. "It's been expressed to us and to other teams that some of these players and agents just want to wait and see what happens in the trial. Nobody seems to know for sure what's going to happen and that has slowed some of the negotiations down."

The trial cast a long shadow over every NFL training camp. The Eagles opened camp without 15 veteran players. Under NFL rules, players without contracts could not report to their teams until they signed new deals. But as the pressure began to build, as the trial dragged on and veterans watched other players take their places on the field, the Eagles and every other NFL team gradually began to sign their veterans.

Testimony from the trial filled the newspapers almost every day. But the pressure of the coming season—and the concern that no matter what the outcome, the case would be tied up in appeals for months, even years—led most veterans to finally sign contracts.

"I could have waited," said Eagles cornerback Eric Allen, who signed on September 2, four days before the opener against New Orleans. "But this is the best place for me. If I made a list of what I was looking for in a team—a great defense, great defensive line, great system, chance to go to the Super Bowl—this team probably would be at the top."

By the time the case went to the jury, the regular season had begun. And by the time the jury ruled in favor of the players, on the afternoon of Thursday, September 10, just 10 veterans around the league remained unsigned. One of them was Eagles tight end Keith Jackson. "We could have signed last week," Jackson's agent, Gary Wichard, said when the jury of eight women in Minneapolis ruled that the NFL's system of free agency was too restrictive and a violation of federal antitrust laws. "But what would we be telling ourselves now? That we should have waited? That we blew our chances? This was the piece of the puzzle I was waiting for. I could talk to the Eagles about Keith Jackson, about his catches, about him being a first-team All-Pro three years in a row. But what did it matter? It was take-it-or-leave-it from them because that was the NFL's system. Well, that system has been struck down in the courts."

On the night the jury in Minneapolis ruled in favor of the players, Jackson was in his mother Gladys' house in Little Rock, Arkansas. "I'm not completely free yet," Jackson said that night. "But I'm in a good position. What this means is that I'm going to be free someday in the near future and so is every other NFL player. The future looks good. Change is finally coming to this league." There were reasons why Jackson suddenly found himself as the NFL players' foremost freedom fighter, and a lot of them had nothing to do with his feelings about the NFL's restrictive system. He was out there, on the front line of the legal battle, because of his past problems with Eagles management.

Under ideal circumstances, Jackson would have been content to play in Philadelphia. The Eagles were a good team, with a legitimate chance to make the Super Bowl. Their offensive system featured the tight end. He had a good rapport with quarterback Randall Cunningham. He had some close friends in the locker room such as Keith Byars and Reggie White. But Jackson's hard feelings toward Eagles management ran deep. So did Wichard's. This was more than the case of a player trying to change the system in the NFL. This was an employee trying to cut his ties with a despised employer. "The Eagles could have signed Keith Jackson a long time ago if they just showed him some respect," Wichard said after the verdict in the antitrust trial. "But they don't do that. They don't treat their players that way. Their players are employees. It's take-it-or-leave-it. 'It's our ball and we set the rules.' That's their approach. Well, this kid [Jackson] is not going to be pushed around by them."

On the night the jury ruled for the players, Jackson had this comment: "I've stayed out of the negotiations this year because I've learned that if you get too involved, you develop a hate for management, and you bring that back to the field with you. I don't want to do that again. I don't want to go through that again. So I stay out of it." After the season, Jackson said, "I learned a lesson back in 1990. I had to keep my emotions out of it, because I know the things they say, the way they handle business. They had promised me some things, told me that things would be different when my time came to negotiate a new contract. But then they started changing their story. They started bagging out on me. I wasn't surprised. I knew who I was dealing with. I kind of figured it would happen."

Jackson had joined the Eagles in 1988. He was a No. 1 draft pick out of the University of Oklahoma. Confident and outspoken, Jackson was a favorite of Eagles coach Buddy Ryan, who drafted him with the thirteenth overall selection in the first round. At 6-foot-2, 250 pounds, with great speed, agility and soft, sure hands, Jackson made an immediate impact in the NFL. At Oklahoma, Jackson had caught 13 passes as a senior, just 62 in his career. He would top that in one season in the NFL.

It was kind of a joke. The Sooners had the best receiving tight end in college football, but they also had an overpowering ground game. Their wishbone offense had little use for a tight end with deep speed and great hands. "When I was being recruited, they had [running back] Marcus Dupree," Jackson once said. "They told me they were going to switch to an 'I' [formation] and throw the ball. They lied."

Jackson used to laugh when he told that story. He had been a Mercedes surrounded by bulldozers at Oklahoma, but he had found his place with the Eagles. He caught 81 passes, a team record, as a rookie. He made the Pro Bowl after that season and again after the 1989 season. "The best tight end in football," Ryan called him when Jackson failed to show up for the start of training camp in 1990.

With two Pro Bowl appearances under his belt, Jackson had decided that his contract needed some sprucing up. A year earlier, on the morning before a game in Washington, the Eagles had signed Cunningham to a five-year contract extension worth close to $18 million, including a $3 million signing bonus. That day, September 17, 1989, Cunningham passed for 447 yards and five touchdowns in leading the Eagles to a remarkable 42-37 comeback victory over the Redskins in RFK Stadium. Jackson caught 12 passes for 126 yards and three touchdowns, all career-bests. He caught the game-winning touchdown pass with 52 seconds left to play.

It was a memorable day for Jackson in more ways than one. The next summer, armed with the knowledge that the Eagles had given Cunningham a contract extension, Jackson decided to try to get one. He held out of training camp, drawing fines of $1,500 per day. He stayed out through the first two games of the 1990 season, both losses. "All we want the Eagles to do for Keith Jackson is what they did for Randall Cunningham," Wichard said at the time. Jackson was seeking a three-year, $5 million contract extension, including a $1.5 million signing bonus. It was an ugly, bitter standoff, an unblinking test of wills between Wichard, a confident, militant agent, and Gamble, the Eagles' stubborn team president.

The Eagles never budged. Ryan clearly took Jackson's side, praising him at every chance, never criticizing him for hurting the team. It was the kind of stance that earned Ryan a lot of loyalty in the locker room and cost him a lot of points with management. Eventually, it would cost him his job.

Jackson finally ended his 1990 holdout on September 19. Ryan told reporters who gathered around him after practice that Wednesday afternoon that they should be outside the Eagles' entrance to the stadium at 4:30. "You might get a story," Ryan reported. Ryan sent a limousine to pick up Jackson at the airport. Then, in one of the more bizarre scenes in Eagles history, Ryan presided over a wild press conference downstairs in one of the meeting rooms off the coaches' offices.

Normally, every Eagles press conference was run by the team's public relations department. They would notify the newspapers, the radio stations, the television stations. They would set up the room. They would handle things. This was the image-conscious NFL after all. This press conference was different. Ryan ran this one. Nobody from the public relations staff was around. But there were dozens of reporters, camera crews, microphones, tape recorders.

And what a press conference it was. Jackson made no secret of his bitterness toward Eagles management. And he said he was back for one reason—because he heard of a "front-office conspiracy" against Ryan, who was in the last year of his original five-year contract.

Not surprisingly, Gamble and Eagles owner Norman Braman were livid. It was all Gamble could do to maintain his composure at a press conference the next day when he denied the existence of a conspiracy against Ryan. "Ridiculous," Gamble said. "But I was right," Jackson claimed after the 1992 season. "I said then that I came back to help my teammates and to keep them from firing Buddy. But we lost that playoff game [to Washington] and they got rid of him just like I said they would. People looked at me like I was crazy, but I was as right as daylight on that one."

Back in 1990, after Jackson returned to the team, Wichard was ripping Eagles management in the press, calling Braman a "fish peddler." Jackson further fueled the controversy when he said that Braman told him "I own you" during a short, bitter conversation immediately after his return. According to Jackson, he had told Braman to trade him and Braman replied, "You're playing here or nowhere. I own you." "That was the one that Keith never forgot," Wichard stated. Braman denied making the comment.

Jackson made the Pro Bowl again after the 1990 season. But after a third straight loss in the team's first playoff game, Ryan was dismissed by Braman, who promoted offensive coordinator Rich Kotite. Jackson was outraged. He called Braman "an idiot" and said he planned to "cause a lot of trouble" in hopes of forcing the Eagles to deal him to another team. "I don't care if they got Bill Cosby as head coach," Jackson said at the time. "It doesn't change the fact that me and the owner aren't the best of friends."

Jackson wasn't traded and he didn't hold out. He decided to play out the last year of his contract and then make his move. But the 1991 season wasn't a pleasant one for Jackson. He vowed during training camp to avoid controversy. "I learned my lesson," he said. Jackson maintained he was older, more mature. He told reporters he would only talk with them on Wednesdays.

Jackson had his worst NFL season, statistically speaking. Injuries to Cunningham and reserve quarterback Jim McMahon created an unsettled offense that was unable to take full advantage of Jackson's receiving skills. And struggles by rookie right tackle Antone Davis forced the Eagles to keep Jackson in to block almost as often as he went out on pass patterns.

Jackson finished the season with just 48 receptions, his career low. He caught five touchdown passes in the second half of the season, when the Eagles went 7-1, and his 73-yard catch-and-run against the Giants in a November 4 Monday night game probably was the turning point of the season. On the play, Jackson caught a pass from McMahon and ran away from legendary linebacker Lawrence Taylor on his way to the end zone. But Jackson also dropped a lot of passes. In one memorable miscue, he dropped a perfect deep pass from McMahon in a November 17 game against Cincinnati. He missed the Pro Bowl for the first time in his NFL career. "I didn't deserve to make it," Jackson said when the Pro Bowl voting was disclosed late in the 1991 season. "I didn't have the numbers this year. But they can't take away the fact that I did make the Pro Bowl three years in a row." Asked if he still felt he was the best tight end in the NFC, Jackson smiled and replied, "In the NFL."

Confidence was never a problem for Jackson. He was born and raised in a tough neighborhood in Little Rock. His favorite sport was basketball, but he was an All-America selection as a tight end for the Parkview High School football team. Jackson was smart, tough and different. He joined the orchestra in high school, learning to play the cello. He was a good student and earned his degree in communications from Oklahoma in just three and a half years.

Jackson had interests outside football. He made a music video entitled "Coming Back Hard" during the off-season in 1990. He released a rap album filled with positive messages entitled "K-Jack In America" in 1991. He opened a clothing store in South Jersey called "Keith Jackson's Silk, Leather and You." Jackson also was active in community service. He began a project in 1991 called P.A.R.K. (Positive Atmosphere Reaches Kids) that sought to create a safe recreation center for street-tough youth in his hometown of Little Rock. He spent much of the spring and summer of 1992 raising money for the project.

"Just prior to Jerome's death, we all went down to Keith Jackson's charity benefit in Little Rock," recalled Keith Byars, reminiscing about events just before the June 25, 1992 death of Jerome Brown. "We had a great time. Who would have thought it would be the last time we were all just sitting around, being ourselves?"

It was no surprise when Jackson didn't show up at the Eagles' voluntary camp on July 6. It was no surprise when his contract negotiation, such as it was, dragged through training camp. One by one, the Eagles signed their veteran players. But not Jackson. Four days before the season opener against New Orleans, the Eagles signed cornerback Eric Allen to a three-year, $3.6 million deal. That left Jackson as their only unsigned player. The Eagles were offering Jackson roughly the same deal as they gave Allen, $3.6 million over three years, with salaries of $1.075 million in 1992, $1.2 million in 1993 and $1.325 million in 1994. He wanted a three-year deal for $6 million, including a $1.5 million signing bonus, and he wanted the contract to be guaranteed. The Eagles had just two players with guarantees in their contracts, Cunningham and White, and they weren't willing to let Jackson join that exclusive company. "We're offering to make him the highest-paid tight end in the NFL," Gamble said late in training camp. "We're comfortable with our offer."

Everything changed on September 10, four days after the New Orleans game. The jury in the antitrust trial in Minneapolis struck down Plan B, the NFL's system of free agency, and kicked open a door for Keith Jackson to run through. On September 14, Jackson was the lead plaintiff as the 10 remaining unsigned veteran players filed suit before U.S. District Court Judge David Doty, who had presided over the antitrust trial. The 10 players were seeking to become unrestricted free agents. "It was new territory," Jackson said after the season. "I didn't know what was happening, nobody knew what was happening. But it was like, 'Hmmmmn, we might have something interesting here. Let's check it out.'"

It was a weird time for the Eagles. The night before Jackson's legal action, they whipped Phoenix by a 31-14 score to improve their record to 2-0. Six days after Jackson filed suit, the Eagles crushed Denver by a 30-0 score to improve to 3-0. They were scoring points. They were running the football, thanks in part to strong blocking by tight end Pat Beach. They didn't seem to need Jackson. "We miss him," Eagles safety Andre Waters said, however, a few days after the Denver game. "We're a great team but we need players like him. You can never have enough great players, not in this league. If they know what's good for us, they'll sign him."

Jackson was unique. He wasn't a great blocker, but he had the speed, hands and moves of a wide receiver. His ability to get open and get deep down the middle forced defenses to double-cover him on many occasions. That opened up the flats for running back Keith Byars, and the deep outside for the Eagles' wide receivers. In a 1990 book about his preparation the week before a 1989 game against the Eagles, New York Giants coach Bill Parcells and defensive coordinator Bill Belichick both were quoted as describing Jackson as the most dangerous weapon on the Eagles' offense.

The Eagles were still hoping to sign Jackson. But there were no real negotiations—the team was sticking to its three-year, $3.6 million offer, and Jackson and Wichard were waiting to see the outcome of their legal action. "That's when things really got nerve-racking," Jackson said after the season. "I really thought I was going to end up back in Philadelphia. I really thought so. I knew they wouldn't make the decision until they were forced to. But when free agency came up, I really thought they would step up to bat and hit a home run. I thought they would change their offer, do something. But they did nothing."

For the players in the Eagles' locker room, it was a sensitive issue. On one hand, as NFL players, most of them wanted to see free agency. A ruling by the judge in favor of Jackson could help make that happen for all of them. On the other hand, as Eagles, they knew their best interests in 1992 probably would be served by a ruling against Jackson. That would increase the chance of his returning to their team.

"I want the ruling to go in his favor," Eagles linebacker Seth Joyner said at the time. "As a player, I look at this differently. I just want him to be happy. I want players to be able to decide where they want to play." Guard Mike Schad admitted to another view: "I don't want to see him set free. That means he'll probably hit the road. I want him here. He's a great player. We're a lot better with him here."

"It's like a double-edged sword," defensive tackle Mike Golic commented. "I'm rooting for him but at the same time I want to see him come back with us."

On September 24, Doty issued a temporary restraining order against the NFL, making Jackson and the three remaining plaintiffs—the other six had been released by their teams—free agents for five days. The door was wide open. "Freedom is what it's all about," Wichard said that night. "Now we'll see what a player like Keith Jackson is worth on the open market."

Gamble wasn't happy. He had given Jackson and Wichard permission to investigate the possibility of trade in late August. Gamble said he talked to officials from a few teams, but there didn't seem to be any interest in Jackson at his asking price. The Dallas Cowboys had expressed some interest, but the Eagles were reluctant to deal Jackson to a team in their own division. Elsewhere in the NFL, there was little interest, according to Gamble. "I even had guys tell me, 'No way anybody will pay him that kind of money,' " he added.

But now Jackson was free. That meant the Eagles could lose a three-time Pro Bowl player, a 27-year-old star, without any compensation in the form of draft picks or other players. That's the kind of thing that can cripple a franchise.

Gamble still wanted to sign Jackson, but he didn't want to get into a bidding war for his own player. He was hoping Jackson wouldn't get any offers better than the one he had on the table. But Gamble also felt that Jackson's limitations as a blocker had hurt the Eagles' running game in the past. He remembered the bitterness of the 1990 holdout, the things that Jackson and Wichard had said in public. Plus, the Eagles were 3-0 and veteran tight end Pat Beach, who had been claimed on waivers September 1, was impressing everyone with his blocking. "We still hope to sign him," Gamble said of Jackson. "That's always been our hope. Keith Jackson is a good football player and we want him on our football team. Our position hasn't changed."

On Monday night, September 21, three days before Doty's order, Gamble had restructured the Eagles' offer. Working with the same dollar amount, Gamble moved some money into the first year and sweetened the incentive package. Wichard rejected it. "A feeble, half-hearted attempt," he called it after the season. "What was I going to do, come all this way and then sign my guy to basically the same deal just as we were waiting for the ruling? Are you kidding? The Eagles had their chance. They blew it."

Wichard was a powerful, confident agent. A native New Yorker, he has a brash air about him. And he was a man on the move. During Jackson's 1990 holdout, Wichard had spent much of his time in Biloxi, Mississippi, where he was serving as executive producer of the movie debut of another of his clients, former Oklahoma linebacker Brian "The Boz" Bosworth. The movie, entitled *Stone Cold*, is an action-packed shoot-'em-up featuring Bosworth as a police officer who infiltrates an outlaw motorcycle gang. Ironically, the movie was in regular rotation on cable television channels in the Philadelphia area late in the summer of 1992, just as Wichard was trying to spring Jackson free from the Eagles.

Wichard said his first phone call as the representative of Keith Jackson, unfettered free agent, went to Don Shula, the Dolphins' coach and primary decision-maker. Two days later, Wichard and Eddie Jones, the Dolphins' general manager, were haggling over contract details. "Don Shula is the greatest coach in the history of the NFL for tight ends," Wichard declared after the season. "Going all the way back to Baltimore and the John Mackey days [in the 1960s]. We knew how much Shula likes to throw the football to the tight end."

"You can't go wrong with Miami," Jackson had said that Saturday, September 26, as he drove around Malibu in Wichard's car. "Don Shula, [quarterback] Dan Marino, great weather. I love Miami. I was down there for the Orange Bowl four years in a row when I was at Oklahoma. It's a great place." Two days later, Jackson agreed to Miami's offer: a four-year contract for $6 million, including a $1.5 million signing bonus. The kicker: the first year of the contract was guaranteed, assuring Jackson of $2.625 million.

Appearing at halftime on ABC-TV's "Monday Night Football," Jackson said the Dolphins' contract offer "blew Philadelphia out of the water. It wasn't even close." Wichard claimed the Eagles never made a legitimate counter-offer. He said he called Gamble on Monday morning and told him that Jackson was signing with Miami. "He moved some numbers around but it was over," Wichard concluded. Gamble released a statement that he was "comfortable" with the Eagles' offer to Jackson and felt it was "fair."

Reaction was mixed in the Eagles' locker room. On one hand, most players were happy to see another player beat the system. Jackson was a pioneer, a leader in the fight for freedom. "We'll miss him," defensive end Reggie White commented. "But what happened to Keith Jackson is good for all NFL players."

Eric Allen, who wore a Miami Dolphins baseball cap in the locker room in honor of his departed friend, had this to say: "Twenty years from now, the only people from this team that people are going to remember are Randall Cunningham and Reggie White and Jerome [Brown] and Keith Jackson. They'll remember them for different reasons. Keith, he's going to be remembered as the one who started it."

The Eagles still were 3-0. They were still tied with Dallas for first place in the NFC Eastern Division. They still were a serious Super Bowl contender. But things were adding up. Jackson's departure created a nagging sense of worry in some corners of the locker room. First, Brown was killed. Now, Jackson had left. Two 27-year-olds, two Pro Bowlers in the prime of their careers, gone. "I thought Keith would be back," Cunningham said two days after Jackson signed with the Dolphins. "He was my main target. I really thought he was coming back. I thought he would be in here for the Monday night game against Dallas. I'm happy for him, and it's good for the NFL players but, man, he was a big part of our team."

Keith Byars sat in front of his locker and tried to put Jackson's departure in perspective. The development would dramatically affect him, since by the end of the season he would no longer be a running back. He would be a tight end. Byars didn't know that then. He only knew that the Eagles, in this most special, most urgent of seasons, had lost a three-time Pro Bowl player. "It's business and people sometimes make hard decisions in business," Byars said. "Sometimes they look back and realize they made a mistake. I talked to Keith and his mouth was saying one thing but his heart was saying another. I know that he would like to have come back here. I really believe that he belongs back here with this team. I know Keith Jackson and I know the Eagles and, to me, it shouldn't have happened. It just never should have come to this."

■ 6 ■

EAGLES FEVER

The morning crew from WIP arrived under the big top at 5:30 a.m. It was cold. It was dark. It was less than 16 hours before the kickoff of the Eagles' Monday night game against the Dallas Cowboys.

The sun wasn't up yet. The city was still and silent, but there were about 25 people—wearing green hats and sweatshirts, waving pennants, screaming about the Cowboys—waiting for Angelo Cataldi and the rest of the morning sports-talk radio crew in the WIP tent across the street from Veterans Stadium. "My first thought was, 'These people are crazy,'" Cataldi said. "It was 5:30 in the morning and they were ready to go. They were ready for the game to start."

The buildup for the October 5 game between the Eagles and Cowboys had been incredible. Because of the bye in the NFL schedule, both the Eagles and Cowboys had been off for 15 days. Both teams were 3-0, the last remaining unbeaten teams in the National Football Conference. For two weeks, Cataldi and the rest of the regulars on WIP sports radio, as well as the newspapers that cover the Eagles and the local television stations, had beat the drum of expectations for this game. It was a dream matchup: the rugged, blue-collar Eagles against the glitzy, pretentious Cowboys. "I've done some shameless things," said Cataldi, a former Eagles beat writer for the *Philadelphia Inquirer* who now was the host of a raucous, irreverent morning show on WIP. "But this was an all-timer. We goosed that game for two weeks, and people just loved it. We couldn't do enough. We couldn't talk about it enough. People just became obsessed with it."

Such was the supercharged atmosphere around the 1992 Eagles. Philadelphia was a major-league city with professional franchises in baseball, basketball and hockey and with established college teams. But the Eagles dominated the sports scene. Eagles coach Rich Kotite spent seven seasons as an assistant coach with the New York Jets, but Kotite said he never remembered the kind of media interest and saturation coverage of the Jets that was routine with the Eagles. "When I came here, I was in shock," said Kotite, who was hired as offensive coordinator by then-coach Buddy Ryan in February of 1990. "I'd never seen an offensive coordinator have a press conference. That was a first for me." Kotite noted that in New York, fan interest is spread among the professional teams and the colleges. There's also more national interest. The same seemed true in places such as Los Angeles and Chicago.

Philadelphia was different. Fan interest and media coverage seemed to focus more on the local teams, sometimes to the exclusion of national events. On the day after a game, the *Philadelphia Daily News* routinely devoted eight to ten stories to the Eagles, and a paragraph or two each to the rest of the games in the NFL. In 1992, the Eagles were covered on the road by more newspapers than any other NFL team. During a typical road game, 11 different newspapers would send reporters to cover it. "Teams are absolutely shocked when we tell them how many credentials we need," said Eagles public relations man Ron Howard. When the Eagles played at Kansas City on October 11, Chiefs public relations head Bob Moore claimed he never remembered issuing more credentials for visiting media. When the Eagles played the Green Bay Packers in Milwaukee on November 15, Packers public relations man Lee Remmell said the same thing.

A comparison: on November 8, the Eagles hosted the Los Angeles Raiders and there were 14 requests for credentials for visiting media. The next week the Eagles played the Packers in Milwaukee and there were 32 requests. Remmell ran out of room in the press box and had to sit one visiting newspaper reporter and two radio reporters outside, in the 28-degree cold. "Nobody else is even close," said Howard. "When we play the Giants, we'll request 50-55 credentials. They aren't even sure if they'll get that many for their home media. And that's New York."

The Eagles were smack dab in the middle of a media circus. Eight different newspapers—the *Philadelphia Daily News*, the *Philadelphia Inquirer*, the *Courier-Post* in South Jersey, the *Trenton Times*, the *Burlington County* (N.J.) *Times*, the *Atlantic City Press*, the *Delaware County* (Pa.) *Times* and the *Wilmington News-Journal*—covered the Eagles on a daily basis. That meant they had at least one reporter with the team nearly every day and a story in the paper just as often. On most days during the football season there were two or three stories on the Eagles in every local paper. In addition, reporters from the *West Chester Daily Local,* the *Norristown Times Herald,* the *Reading Eagle-Times,* the *Easton Express,* the *Allentown Morning Call,* and the *Gloucester County* (N.J.) *Times* covered the team on Sundays, Mondays and Wednesdays. The Associated Press' venerable Ralph Bernstein, who had covered the Eagles since 1948, was in the locker room on Sundays and Mondays and sometimes on Wednesdays.

Camera crews, producers and reporters from the four television stations in Philadelphia were in the locker room on a regular basis. When the Eagles opened the locker room from 11 a.m. to noon on a typical day during their practice week, it wasn't unusual to find 20 or 25 media representatives on hand, turning most interviews into crowded sessions with the athlete buried deep in his locker stalls surrounded by a straining, shoving pack. "I've never seen anything like it," Kotite said. "In New York, it just seemed like there were other interests. The reporters covered other things besides the Jets. You guys are always here."

The media presence was only a reflection of the fan interest. The Eagles were the hottest team in town, towering over the Phillies, the Sixers, the Flyers and the college teams. "The Eagles always have been the team that generated the most interest, but this year it hasn't even been close," Cataldi said during the 1992 season. "The Sixers and Phillies, there's total apathy. We would go weeks during the baseball season without a single call on the Phillies. The Eagles hadn't played an exhibition game yet this season and we were getting five calls on them for every one call on the Phillies. This was in June and July!"

Why the intense interest in the Eagles? For one thing, the Phillies were the only team in baseball that had a losing record every year at the all-star break since 1984. Not coincidentally, NFL training camps start to open soon after the all-star game. The Phillies were a boring, losing team again in 1992. They would finish in last place, 26 games behind the Pittsburgh Pirates. The Flyers were another losing team. Along with the Quebec Nordiques, the Flyers were one of only two National Hockey League teams to miss the playoffs in 1989, 1990 and 1991. They made big news in June when they traded for superstar-in-waiting Eric Lindros, but they still seemed years away from serious Stanley Cup contention. The Sixers were perennial non-contenders, too. They were nine seasons removed from their last championship, and they had missed the playoffs in 1991. Finally, in June 1992, the Sixers had traded away all-star forward Charles Barkley, Philadelphia's most colorful, controversial athlete.

Philadelphia wasn't a college football town, either. Temple, the only Division I program in the city, was locked in a downward cycle of losses and modest fan support. Penn and Villanova were Division I-AA programs that drew a faithful but small following. The closest national power was Penn State, a four-hour car ride away in rural State College.

As Angelo Cataldi put it, "The Eagles are the only show in town," "They've been the only show in town for three or four years. But now, it's such total domination that it's like we don't have any other franchises. It's just the Eagles." Veteran *Daily News* columnist Stan Hochman agreed: "This town is desperate for a successful athletic team. The Flyers have missed the playoffs three years in a row. The Sixers are rubble. The Phillies are horseshit. All the passion is poured into the Eagles. They are people's best hope." Rich Kotite added another perspective: "I think people around here think their only shot at a winner is the Eagles. So they're tough on us."

Eagles fans were unique. The Dallas game would be the nineteenth consecutive home sellout. Veterans Stadium was known across the country as a rough, rowdy place, with fans that sometimes seemed to reflect the tough mentality of their football team. When he retired in May 1991, former New York Giants coach Bill Parcells said one of the things he would miss was walking down the tunnel from the visiting locker room to the field at Veterans Stadium. "They called me things that I never heard before," Parcells said. In an interview with NFL Films, Parcells once remarked, "I came to love those fans for how much they hated me. They call it the city of brotherly love. It's a banana republic, a communist country."

In some ways, current Eagles fans were just upholding a tradition that was established by previous generations. Philadelphia's fans had first made their reputation by throwing snowballs at Santa Claus during the halftime of a December 15, 1968 game at Franklin Field. "It was a horrible Santa Claus," said former Eagles defensive back Tom Brookshier, who was at that infamous game as a broadcaster for CBS. "He was a skinny guy with sunken cheeks and a five o'clock shadow. He had a bad suit on, too." Stan Hochman added: "I remember it was a bad sled. But I don't think they were complaining about the sled or the Santa Claus as much as the football team. They were saying, 'Don't give us this halftime garbage. Give us a winning football team.'" Booing was something of a Philadelphia tradition. Hard-edged, insecure and demanding, fans in Philadelphia had booed Mike Schmidt, probably the best Phillies player ever. They had booed every Eagles quarterback, especially Ron Jaworski, their only Super Bowl quarterback. Jaworski was a tough, gritty player who set just about every Eagles passing record in his 10 seasons with the team. According to team trainer Otho Davis, Jaworski sustained about three concussions a season, or 30 in his Eagles career. But he was remarkably durable, setting an unofficial NFL record by starting 116 consecutive games as quarterback. The fans booed him anyway. Once, Jaworski was knocked out during a 1983 game against the St. Louis Cardinals. He was carried off the field by two assistant trainers, blood pouring off his cut lip. He was booed. "Booing is the thing to do in

Philadelphia," Dr. Joel Fish of the Philadelphia Center for Sports Psychology once said. "It's passed down when kids see their fathers boo."

Veterans Stadium was known as a rough place filled with a lot of profane, passionate fans. Of the stadium's 700 level, the upper section of the stands, a caller to WIP once remarked, "It's not so bad. It's just not a place where you'd want to bring women or children." Of the atmosphere in Veterans Stadium, Hochman said, "It has a rowdy tone to it. I think it's been cut down some lately by the tailgating policy and the limited amount of drinking in the stadium. That has cut some of the drunkenness that gives the place a bad name. But it's still a tough place to be wearing the other team's colors. You still might get assaulted or at least verbally abused if you try that."

Over the past several seasons, the Eagles front office had taken steps to curb fan violence in Veterans Stadium. First, they petitioned the NFL office to eliminate 4 o'clock home games against the New York Giants and the Washington Redskins, since the few fans of those teams that entered the stadium often found themselves in violent confrontations with Eagles fans. An Eagles-Giants game in 1984 was the scene of more than 20 arrests or police interventions. Once, in full view of the press box, a Redskins fan in full Indian garb was attacked and beaten. The front office felt that 1 o'clock starts would reduce the number of pregame tailgate parties and the alcohol consumption that led to fan violence.

The Eagles also cut off the sale of beer in the stadium at the end of the third quarter in 1986. They changed that to halftime in 1987 in hopes of curbing the drunken behavior of some spectators. They also instituted a "family section," a segment of the 700 level where alcohol was not served.

"I thought I saw everything until I got here," Kotite commented. "Philadelphia fans are known all over the country. They booed Santa Claus. They booed the Pope. That's their nature."

Some Eagles fans were even beginning to take their show on the road. It wasn't unusual for Saturday afternoon plane flights to the site of the next Eagles game to include small groups of fans wearing green sweatshirts and striped Eagles hats, sitting in the back of the plane, chanting "E-A-G-L-E-S." Another common sight on those flights was a harried stewardess swearing that the plane really was out of vodka. On December 2, 1990, the Eagles played an important game in Buffalo. On the day before the game, a crew of four Eagles fans wearing the latest fad—plastic hard hats designed to resemble Eagles helmets—were loudly enjoying themselves on a flight to Buffalo. The next day, those same four fans, still wearing their hard hats, were seen being escorted out of Rich Stadium by security personnel. It was a half-hour before kickoff.

In November 1989, the Eagles played a rare game in San Diego against the Chargers. The game was attended by a large number of green-clad Eagles fans, many of whom had made the trip as part of one of the package deals offered by area travel agencies. The next day, the *Los Angeles Times* ran a story recounting the unusual amount of fan violence at Jack Murphy Stadium. According to Stadium Manager Bill Wilson, the total of 10 arrests and 55 police "contacts" was the highest at the stadium in "recent memory." Wilson blamed alcohol and the Eagles fans. He said the "mentality" of the Eagles fans in attendance was a factor in the violence. "I'm not putting their fans down," Wilson added. "But the mindset is that 'We're the rough, tough, can't-beat-our-guys type of fan.' It's starting to be a real problem. You have this whole mystique of the rough, tough, Buddy Ryan Eagles."

All these factors appeared to come together in the two weeks before the Dallas game. Most Eagles fans seemed to regard Dallas as their most hated rival, a haughty team that they wanted to see knocked off its high horse. "It's the whole America's Team image," said Jaworski, who still lived in the area. "We always wanted to beat the Cowboys. You could sense how the people in those areas, a blue-collar kind of area, just wanted us to knock them off." Current Eagles' defensive tackle Mike Golic agreed: "These people just hate Dallas. They hate the Cowboys. They're nuts and that's good for us."

Hating the Cowboys was another Philadelphia tradition. There seemed to be a kind of inferiority complex among the Philadelphia faithful, perhaps rooted in the fact that the Cowboys had been to five Super Bowls and the Eagles to just one. Or perhaps it had to do with the fact that the Cowboys had beaten the Eagles 21 of 23 times between 1967 and 1978. Dallas was good back then. Philadelphia was bad. The games held no real significance for the Eagles, who always missed the playoffs in those days. But that didn't diminish their animosity for the Cowboys.

The situation was reversed in the late 1980s. From 1986 through 1991, the Eagles beat the Cowboys nine times in a row in games not involving strike-replacement players. Philadelphia was good. Dallas was bad. The games held no real significance for the Cowboys, but they never failed to work up a good hate for the Eagles. "I think it stems from Buddy," Golic said of former Eagles coach Buddy Ryan. "We sort of embodied Buddy's personality to them, and they didn't like Buddy. They hated him in fact."

What the rivalry historically lacked in playoff significance, it made up for in controversy. In the late 1960s, there was Leroy Jordan's clothesline of Timmy Brown, a hit that knocked out some of the Philadelphia running back's teeth. Ryan brought all the bad blood back to the surface during the 1987 players' strike, when he ripped Dallas coach Tom Landry for using his picket line-crossing regulars in a rout of the Eagles' replacement team. Ryan got his revenge in the first game after the union players returned to work. He ordered quarterback Randall Cunningham to fake a kneel-down at the end of the game and fire a long pass to Mike Quick, who drew a pass interference penalty from Ron Francis in the end zone. That gave the Eagles the football at the 1-yard line, and Keith Byars scored on the final play of the game in a lopsided 37-20 victory. "F--- 'em," Ryan screamed to reporters as he ran up the tunnel for the locker room even before the Eagles had kicked the extra point.

Two years later, on Thanksgiving Day in Dallas, first-year Cowboys coach Jimmy Johnson accused Ryan of placing bounties on the heads of quarterback Troy Aikman and kicker Luis Zendejas, a former Eagle. Ryan denied the charge, but it did seem awfully suspicious when Eagles line-backer Jessie Small went out of his way to "seek and destroy" Zendejas on a kickoff. Two weeks later, the teams played the so-called Bounty Bowl in Veterans Stadium. It wasn't much of a game—the Eagles won 20-10, one day after quarterback coach Doug Scovil collapsed in the locker room and died of a heart attack—but Johnson remembers it as the day he was pounded with snowballs by unruly fans.

The Bounty Bowl was merely the second bowl to be played between the Eagles and Cowboys in that rich period in the rivalry. In the final game of 1988, the teams played the Pork Chop Bowl, so named by Dallas president Tex Schramm because Ryan had nearly choked to death on a piece of pork three weeks earlier. The Eagles won that game 23-7 and clinched the NFC Eastern Division title when the New York Giants were upset by the New York Jets. The Dallas fans' only revenge was a master-piece of minimalistic sign-making that read "Buddy Is Fat."

"When we play the Cowboys, you can always hear a crowd a lot more," Eagles safety Andre Waters said a few days before the big Monday night game. "They get vocal. They don't like the Cowboys too much around here." When WIP polled fans in 1990 about their biggest sports thrill, the overwhelming winner was the Eagles' 20-7 victory over the Cowboys in the 1980 NFC championship game. That victory secured the Eagles' one and only trip to the Super Bowl, where they were trounced by the Los Angeles Raiders by a 27-10 score.

The 1992 Eagles were seen by many fans as the best hope since that 1980 team to make it back to the Super Bowl. Expectations were great and so was the pressure on the team to produce. "They don't want honest effort from this team, they want results," said Stan Hochman of the Eagles fans.

Adding to the anticipation for the October 5 game was the strength of both teams. They were generally regarded as two of the top five teams in the NFL. The Eagles were a little older, a little stronger, a little more frustrated by their past failures. The Cowboys were a little younger, a little faster, a little more wide-eyed and anxious.

For 15 days, the excitement built. The city newspapers and television stations sent reporters to Dallas for breathless updates on the anticipation in North Texas. The *Daily News* ran a "Countdown To Dallas," a daily recap of the 10 best games in the rich, bitter rivalry between the Eagles and Cowboys. Over at WIP, the morning crew was incessantly hyping the game. "We beat the drum like we never beat it before," Cataldi admitted. "We found all the street signs in the area with 'Dallas' on them and got people to put 'Dump Dallas' stickers over them. We asked businesses with Dallas in their names to change their names. We told the mayor of Dallas, Pennsylvania, to change the name of the town or he wouldn't be re-elected. We just kept pumping this game and pumping this game. People just went bonkers."

Sports-talk radio on the scale projected by WIP was a fairly new phenomenon in Philadelphia. The station went to an all-sports format in 1988, just as the Eagles were about to win their first division title since 1980. "It's hard to gauge just what role we play," said Cataldi, a Columbia University-educated journalist. "Sports stations are still brand new. I've heard people who hate us say that all we do is enhance the negative stuff. I've heard other people say we're the columnists of the 21st century, that the things we say are what the athletes react to first. I think we focus interest. We go to the big story, and the Eagles are almost always the big story."

What was unclear is what role, if any, sports radio played in enhancing public pressure to the point of influencing coaching or front-office decisions. Take the Herschel Walker case. The Eagles were luke-warm in their interest in Walker when the veteran running back was released by Minnesota on May 29. Their position would change, and they would sign him to a two-year, $2.8 million contract on June 22. Eagles president Harry Gamble and Kotite said they took their time in evaluating Walker. They studied film. They talked with his old coaches. They met with Walker. They said they were not pressured or influenced by public sentiment. "I never listen to WIP," Gamble once remarked.

But there was a lot of public pressure, and much of it was amplified by WIP. In addition to campaigning for Walker and encouraging their listeners to call the Eagles, the morning guys at WIP—Cataldi, Al Morganti and Tony Bruno—orchestrated a "Honk for Herschel" day on June 12. They encouraged people to drive by Veterans Stadium and lean on their car horns. "We had more than 200 people outside the Vet," Cataldi recalled. "Then we got Walker on the phone and we told him about the 'Honk for Herschel' campaign and we said, 'Herschel, you have to hear this.' Meanwhile, we took the sound of the car horns and amplified it about five times with sound effects. So we played it for Herschel on the air, and he was visibly moved by our horn-enhancement program. He said that day, on the air, that he wanted to play in Philadelphia. Did we have an effect? I don't know. But certainly there is the illusion that we had a great effect."

WIP also unwittingly got involved in the Keith Jackson story. Jackson was unsigned and locked in a protracted contract dispute when a man called WIP host Garry Cobb two nights before the September 6 season opener and pretended to be Jackson's agent, Gary Wichard. The imposter claimed that there was significant movement in the negotiations and that it was possible that Jackson would be signed for the season-opener against the Saints. The radio report led to a published report with the same sort of speculation, and that report was picked up by the Associated Press, put on the wire and picked up by ESPN.

The next night, Wichard sat in the living room of his Malibu home along with Brian Bosworth, the former Oklahoma linebacker who now was a movie actor. Jackson had just left the house to work out. On the television, ESPN reported progress in the Jackson negotiations. Wichard and Bosworth looked at each other. "Did we just black out or what?" Bosworth said.

For the Dallas game, WIP started its pregame show at 6 a.m., a full 15 hours before kickoff. All day the station broadcast from the tent across from the stadium. The crew encouraged the fans in attendance to shatter Cowboy helmets, tear up Cowboy posters, burn Cowboy pennants. "A 15-hour pep rally," Cataldi called it.

By 6 p.m., the air outside the stadium was charged with anticipation. Adding to the atmosphere were angry city workers, who gathered outside the gates of the stadium and handed out pamphlets emblazoned with the words "Sack Eddie." That was a reference to Mayor Ed Rendell, who was haggling with city workers over their union contracts. The workers were set to strike at midnight, leading to speculation that the stadium lights would go out at that time, leaving the Eagles and Cowboys and some 66,000 spectators in darkness.

The irony here was that Rendell was familiar with the wild atmosphere inside Veterans Stadium during Eagles-Cowboys games. Back on December 10, 1989, Rendell had made some news as the Eagles played the Cowboys two days after a massive snowstorm. The storm had hit Friday night, so the stadium was filled with snow on Sunday afternoon. Fans cascaded snowballs on the field, pounding the Cowboys and their first-year coach, Jimmy Johnson. It was a surrealistic scene. At one point, during a timeout, the public address system was broadcasting the song "Walking in a Winter Wonderland" as players and coaches dodged snowballs that were flying out of the 700 level of the stadium.

Eagles owner Norman Braman was livid after the game. He ripped the city of Philadelphia and, indirectly, then-mayor Wilson Goode for failing to clear the snow out of the stadium. Rendell got in the act. At the time, he was a former district attorney. According to a published report two days after the game, Rendell had bet a friend $20 that he couldn't hit the field with a snowball.

At first, Rendell denied the report. The next day, he called the *Philadelphia Inquirer* to fess up. Of a friend who had claimed that Rendell was innocent, the future mayor was quoted as saying, "Of course he lied. He's the best lawyer in town." Now, Rendell was the mayor and city workers were taking his name in vain as Johnson and the Cowboys arrived at Veterans Stadium by bus.

It was a clear, cool night. The temperature was 56 degrees at the kickoff of the Eagles' only Monday night game of the season. Most of the crowd of 66,572 went home early and happy. The Eagles jumped in front as defensive back John Booty intercepted Dallas quarterback Troy Aikman's first pass and returned it to the Cowboys' 14 yard line. That set up a 2-yard touchdown run by Randall Cunningham. The Cowboys rallied to even the score at 7-7, but it was all Eagles the rest of the way. Led by Reggie White and Seth Joyner, the Eagles' defense sacked Aikman four times and intercepted three of his passes. Safety Wes Hopkins had an important interception in the end zone and middle linebacker Byron Evans set up a touchdown with an interception midway in the third quarter. The Eagles also held Dallas running back Emmitt Smith, the 1991 NFL rushing champion, to just 67 yards, his season low.

Playing against his old team, Walker ran for 86 yards. He scored second-half touchdowns on runs of 9 and 16 yards. Keith Byars added a fourth-quarter touchdown run of 12 yards as the Eagles romped to a 31-7 victory. "The best team in the NFL," ABC-TV analyst Dan Dierdorf called the Eagles. A national television audience was listening.

Veterans Stadium was loud but peaceful that night. The few Cowboy fans in attendance slinked quietly out of sight. There were few disturbances and by the middle of the fourth quarter, with the Eagles firmly in command, much of the crowd started streaming for the exits. The lights stayed on past midnight.

The defining moment for the crowd came late in the second quarter. As part of their 60th anniversary celebration, the Eagles had a giant, inflated cake, a kind of parade float, brought in for the halftime ceremony. But workers brought the cake in through the tunnel behind the Eagles' end zone before the end of the first half. Dallas was driving, and the cake was blocking the view of several hundred fans in the lower section of the stadium, just to the right of the end zone. Suddenly, the cry went up, in the same cadence and with the same impassioned tone of the old "Block That Kick" cheer: "Move That Cake! Move That Cake! Move That Cake!" The cake was moved. The Cowboys' drive ended in an interception. Only in Philadelphia.

COACH IN CRISIS

Rich Kotite liked to walk. On late afternoons during the football season, Kotite liked to walk around the Veterans Stadium parking lot. He was a solitary figure, alone with his thoughts, circling the quiet, empty stadium. Kotite walked quickly, taking long, purposeful strides. This was his exercise. But sometimes his legs couldn't keep up with his mind. His thoughts raced ahead.

By the middle of October, as the afternoons grew a little colder and a little darker, Kotite was growing a little worried. His walks were filled with anxious moments. A lot of things were happening to his football team, and many of them were not good.

After a 4-0 start that stamped them as the best team in football, the Eagles had lost two in a row. They went to Kansas City on October 11, fell behind 24-3 and lost to the Chiefs by a 24-17 score in sold-out Arrowhead Stadium. They went to Washington on October 18, fell behind 16-3 and lost to the Redskins by a 16-12 score in sold-out RFK Stadium.

The Eagles were in second place in the NFC Eastern Division, tied with Washington, a game behind Dallas. Their confidence was shaken. They had lost their sharp edge, their swaggering air of self-assurance. "This is definitely a downer for us," Kotite admitted after his team's inelegant, uninspired performance against Washington. "There's no other way to cut it. We've lost two in a row and we've got to get our act together and correct what needs to be corrected."

Injuries were mounting along with losses. Strong safety Andre

Waters, whose hard-hitting and fierce game-day demeanor inspired the Eagles' defense, fractured his left fibula while making a tackle of Redskins running back Ricky Ervins in the third quarter in Washington. Waters would miss the rest of the regular season. Waters' partner, free safety Wes Hopkins, was hobbling with a sprained left knee. Hopkins could barely walk on the Monday after the Washington game, his knee swollen to the size of a large grapefruit.

Linebacker Seth Joyner also was nursing a sore left knee. He had sprained the knee in the first quarter of the October 5 game against Dallas when his best friend, defensive end Clyde Simmons, rolled into him while pursuing Cowboys running back Emmitt Smith. Joyner wore a knee brace in Kansas City and Washington and looked slow and tentative.

Both starting offensive tackles were limping, too. Left tackle Ron Heller sat out the Washington game with a sprained right arch. Heller, a mainstay of the offensive line, was spending most of his waking hours in the trainer's room, but his condition wasn't improving. Right tackle Antone Davis, a much-maligned, second-year player, sprained his right knee in the fourth quarter in Washington. Drafting Davis had been one of Kotite's first big moves as head coach. He had agreed to trade the Eagles' No. 1 picks in both 1991 and 1992 to Green Bay to move up in the selection order and grab Davis, a consensus All-America from the University of Tennessee.

That was back in April 1991, less than four months after Kotite had replaced Buddy Ryan as the Eagles' head coach. The team was desperate for a dominating offensive lineman, and Kotite made the bold move to select the 325-pound Davis. There was just one problem: Davis wasn't ready to make an impact. He was late reporting to training camp because of a contract dispute, he was overweight and he was a rookie. He started 15 games in 1991, but he surrendered 12 sacks, was charged with 12 penalties and generally looked like he was in over his head. Davis had been better in 1992. He started the first six games and played fairly well. He was avoiding penalties, and he wasn't getting beaten as often by defensive ends. Though Davis wasn't a star, he was improved. But now his right knee was badly sprained.

Another problem arose: outspoken, unhappy players. Like most football coaches, Kotite wasn't comfortable with criticism. He was sensitive to slights. And now he was getting the business from his own players. Following the loss in Kansas City, both Joyner and running back Keith Byars had been critical of Kotite. Both players said the game was lost late in the first half when Kotite's strategy backfired on the Eagles. "You've got to play smart," Byars said in the locker room after the game. "I was very disappointed with the way we handled things there at the end of the half. The thing that I didn't want to happen is just what happened." Joyner added: "There are certain times when you've got to play smart and we didn't do that. That was the whole game right there."

The situation: down 7-3, the Eagles took possession at their 18 yard line with 55 seconds left in the first half. Rather than attempt to run out the clock, Kotite called three pass plays, and the results were disastrous: a 2-yard sack of quarterback Randall Cunningham, an incompletion, an 11-yard sack of Cunningham.

It got worse. Jeff Feagles got off a wobbly 26-yard punt from his own end zone. The Chiefs took over at the Philadelphia 31 and got in the end zone in two plays, the second a 24-yard touchdown pass from Dave Krieg to J.J. Birden, who was left wide open by a busted coverage in the Eagles' secondary.

Eagles defensive coordinator Bud Carson had called a cornerback blitz, sending John Booty into the backfield after Krieg. That meant cornerback Eric Allen and safety Wes Hopkins had to adjust, with each one covering a Kansas City receiver. But Allen blew the coverage. He and Hopkins both covered Fred Jones and that left Birden alone in the end zone. "As soon as we both broke, I said, 'Oh, shit,' " Hopkins recalled in the locker room after the game. Allen took the blame: "It was my fault,' " Allen stated, "We didn't communicate all day. It was like we were talking Greek to each other."

The touchdown sent the 76,626 spectators in the stadium—most of whom seemed to be be wearing bright red outfits—into a frenzy. It also sent the Eagles into the locker room seeing red in more ways than one. "Next thing we know, we're down 14-3 and in the locker room saying, 'That was stupid,' " Byars said after the game.

Kotite defended his strategy. He noted that Cunningham is one of the best engineers of the hurry-up offense in football. But the criticism stung the coach. "They're players, I'm the coach," Kotite declared the next day at his weekly press conference. "They can say what they want. It doesn't bother me."

Keith Byars' criticism wasn't restricted to the sequence at the end of the first half, either. His outburst was kind of strange, too, since the Eagles' most visible problems against the Chiefs were in pass defense. Fooled by Krieg's play-action fakes, the Eagles surrendered 254 passing yards and three long touchdown receptions. On one memorable play, both cornerback Otis Smith and Andre Waters, the veteran strong safety, were caught flat-footed, looking in the backfield, as Krieg faked to running back Christian Okoye and lofted a 74-yard touchdown pass to a wide-open Willie Davis. "My fault," Waters said after the game. "I was so worried about the run that I didn't execute my assignment. I should know better. We just didn't play very smart and we got burned."

Byars' problem was with Kotite, not the pass defense. The veteran running back questioned Kotite's play-calling earlier in the first half, when

Herschel Walker was stopped three times on running plays on third down. "We were too predictable," Byars argued. "You can't run the ball 100 percent of the time on third-and-short. That's not the best way to play offense. That's not smart. We just got caught with our pants down."

Byars was one of Kotite's offensive captains, an athlete the coach called "the ultimate team player." But he wasn't happy. Three weeks earlier, Byars had complained about his role in the victory over Phoenix, calling himself a "tackle" and noting that he had touched the football just once that night in Sun Devil Stadium. "We can't win many games with that kind of game plan," he said of the offensive strategy in Phoenix, which featured a lot of three-tight-end formations and 28 rushing attempts for 115 yards by Walker. "We won't beat many teams that way." Three weeks later, Byars was upset again, and now he had a loss as hard evidence. Summing up the loss to Kansas City, he charged, "We've got to play smart, and we didn't play smart, from the top on down, from Richie to the last man on the roster."

The next week in Washington, Joyner lashed out. The Eagles, he said, were a sluggish, sloppy team and they were thoroughly beaten by the Redskins, the defending Super Bowl champions. The final score was deceiving, since the Eagles scored their only touchdown on a pass from Cunningham to wide receiver Calvin Williams with just 25 seconds left in the game.

The Redskins controlled the game. Like the Chiefs, they scored a touchdown on their first possession. They ripped off pass plays that gained 26, 32, 34 and 51 yards. They held Walker to eight rushing yards and they sacked Cunningham five times. They got a 32-yard punt return and a 47-yard kickoff return from Brian Mitchell.

The Redskins also beat up the Eagles. Andre Waters, a superstitious sort, had a premonition before the game. He found himself thinking about former Washington quarterback Joe Theismann, whose career was ended by a severe leg injury in 1985. "I don't know why I was thinking about Theismann," Waters recalled. "But I remember I kept thinking about whether that injury happened in RFK Stadium or on the road. Then I remembered seeing it on television and seeing the grass, so it was RFK. But it was weird because I usually don't think about stuff like that. This time I did and I ended up getting hurt."

Waters was hurt on a third-quarter run by Washington's Ricky Ervins. Waters raced up to make the tackle, but his left leg was caught under him. He fractured the fibula bone and tore ligaments in his left ankle. It was a devastating blow to the Eagles. Waters was one of the most physical run-supporters among defensive backs in the NFL. His tireless film study and mental preparation and his fierce game-day demeanor were key components of the Eagles' defensive makeup.

Without late defensive tackle Jerome Brown, without cornerback

Ben Smith (who would sit out the season with a knee injury), and now without Waters, the Eagles' defense was missing much of its grit and tenacity. "We're going to miss his toughness, his preparation and his spirit," Kotite would say about Waters.

To make matters worse, Wes Hopkins was limping badly. He would be in and out of the lineup for much of the rest of the season, and the Eagles would miss his experience and his physical style of play. It was one thing to lose a game. It was another to lose and limp away with a lengthy list of serious injuries.

Seth Joyner couldn't take it. An emotional athlete who takes losses to heart, Joyner tried to contain himself in the locker room after the game. It was no use. "I know you guys come to me for controversy," he told the small group of reporters around him. "I've really dedicated myself this year to trying to stay as positive as I can. We want to keep things within the team. I don't want to point fingers at my teammates. But . . ."

Joyner's message was short and not-so-sweet: the Eagles weren't as tough, as smart and as well-prepared as the Redskins. He didn't rip Kotite by name, but the implication was there. "Our special teams looked like garbage," Joyner charged. "Our defense gave up too many big plays. And our offense, just say the words 'Washington Redskins' and we fall to pieces."

Joyner said the Eagles got fat and satisfied after their 4-0 start. He said too many guys were bolting out of the locker room after practice instead of staying to watch films. He said the Eagles weren't working hard enough.

"I'm pointing fingers at the whole damn team," Joyner continued. "I really believe that we got some guys that got satisfied. All that talk about us being the best team in the league, I really believe it got in some people's heads. You don't see the people in there studying. Everybody's in a damn hurry to get out of the locker room. You've got to put the time in.

"You've got to realize that once you're labeled as the best team in the league, you have to work another 10 to 15 percent harder to stay where you are. You've got the whole nation watching, and you just dominate Dallas, and you got the top media people saying you're the best team in the league, so you know everybody is going to be gunning for you.

"I think a lot of guys just sat back and said, 'Hey, we're playing well. Things are going great. We're considered one of the best teams in the league. So we'll just put it on cruise control.' You can't put it on cruise control. There's 16 weeks to the season and you've got to put out every single week."

Again, Kotite downplayed the criticism during his weekly press conference. In fact, when a questioner noted that Joyner had said the Redskins "wanted it more than the Eagles," Kotite replied, "I would be inclined to agree with that. I just don't think we're playing with the same intensity that we played with in the first four games. I think we have to get that tenaciousness back."

Rough times were nothing new to Rich Kotite. He had been an NFL player from 1967 through 1972 and an NFL assistant coach from 1977 through 1990. Most of his teams lost more than they won. He knew the hard side of the business. He knew it was a fast, wild ride with more lows than highs.

Born and raised on Brooklyn, Kotite was a three-sport star at Poly Prep. He spent a year at the University of Miami—where he was the school's heavyweight boxing champ and once sparred against Muhammad Ali—before transferring to Wagner College on Staten Island. Kotite was a little All-America tight end at Wagner. Undrafted, he made the New York Giants' roster as a reserve tight end and special-teamer in 1967. He played for the Pittsburgh Steelers in 1968 and for the Giants again from 1969 to 1972. "I wasn't much of a player," Kotite once said. "I didn't have a lot of ability. I was one of those guys who had to give all he had on special teams just to stay in the league."

To Kotite, nothing mattered more than the team, the organization. He was a good soldier—loyal, stubborn, dedicated. He believed he was part of something special and that the fans (despite their good intentions) and the media around the team were outsiders, distractions. He was uncomfortable in the spotlight and was reluctant to make personal appearances, glad-hand strangers, play to the crowd. He wasn't that kind of player. He wasn't that kind of coach. He didn't want a radio show. His only concession to his new celebrity, his weekly television show, was filmed without a studio audience.

Kotite preferred that his players be the same way. "Keep it in this room," he often told them. "Keep it within the team." Kotite was grateful to Eagles owner Norman Braman and team president Harry Gamble for the opportunity to be a head coach. Just one year before he accepted the position, he was out of work. He didn't forget that.

Kotite was a team guy. Team first, that was his motto. The team was more important than fame, more important than money. He was among the NFL's lowest-paid coaches when he was hired, when he signed a three-year contract for an average of about $350,000 per year. But except for the television show, he didn't seek to supplement his income with outside interests. "That's not me," Kotite once said. "I don't feel comfortable doing all that. There's so much involved with this job, so many things that come across your desk, I just feel you have to concentrate on it." Kotite began his professional coaching career on Hank Stram's staff in New Orleans. He spent the next five years on Sam Rutigliano's staff in Cleveland, and it was there that Kotite went through one of the defining experiences of his life. In the summer of 1981, Kotite was having headaches. After a series of tests, doctors found a brain tumor. Surgery was his only viable option. "I remember I was in my hospital room the night before the operation," Kotite recalled. "The doctor came in and I told him, 'Just make sure you get a good night's sleep.' You can ask my wife. That's what I told him, 'Get a good night's sleep.' "

The operation took nine hours. Two weeks later, Kotite was back on the Browns' practice field, wearing a Cleveland Indians batting helmet. "It changed my perspective," he admitted. "I used to be more of a nit-picker. I think I take things a little easier now than I used to. I know what's important. It's family. It's your health."

Kotite spent seven years as an assistant coach on Joe Walton's staff with the New York Jets. He was a receivers coach for two years, then offensive coordinator for five. The end of Walton's stay in New York was ugly as the fans and the media buried the beleaguered coach. Walton and his entire staff were dismissed after the 1989 season.

Meanwhile, the Eagles were looking for an offensive coordinator. After they lost 21-7 to the Los Angeles Rams in a wild card playoff game on December 31, 1989, owner Norman Braman pressured Ryan to replace offensive coordinator Ted Plumb. Ryan offered Plumb, a close friend, a position in the personnel department of the Eagles front office. He also helped arrange an interview for Plumb with New York Jets president Dick Steinberg, who was looking for a head coach. Steinberg eventually hired Bruce Coslet. Plumb joined the Phoenix Cardinals as receivers coach. But first, he recommended his friend Rich Kotite to be his replacement in Philadelphia.

Kotite got off to a slow start with the Philadelphia-area media. At a press conference during a spring quarterbacks camp, a television reporter noted that Cunningham didn't seem to be giving Kotite's new offensive system "a ringing endorsement." Kotite flipped out. He interrupted Cunningham, and lashed out at the reporter, saying the question was "unfair" and a "cheap shot." It was a brief moment, but a telling one. Kotite never appeared very comfortable with the media. Some observers speculated that his mistrust of the media was a by-product of his background, the legacy of the hatchet job done on his good friend Joe Walton by the media in New York.

In 1991, Kotite became the first Eagles coach to close practices to the media. He said he wanted his team to "focus." He felt the presence of reporters on the sidelines during practices was a "distraction." Even so, Kotite could be warm and funny in interview sessions. When the Eagles traveled to London for an exhibition game in the summer of 1991, Kotite told reporters that his wife, Liz, "has a black belt in shopping."

But Kotite often was tense, defensive and brusque with reporters.

He sometimes made pointed references to critical comments in the newspapers. He got into loud, heated arguments with television cameramen over access to practice and with a radio reporter over a "dumb, f---ing question." In November, four days before the Eagles' game against San Francisco, Kotite instigated a profanity-laced confrontation with two beat reporters from suburban Philadelphia newspapers whom he accused of lacking professionalism and openly criticizing him in the press box during games.

On the other hand, Kotite was extremely quotable. He was accessible, meeting with reporters five times a week. He elaborated on his answers to questions far more than Ryan ever did. He could be expansive, especially when he started waving his arms, explaining his thinking, self-stoking himself to a near-fever pitch. "I understand that you guys have a job to do," Kotite told the beat writers during a wide-ranging session at the end of the 1992 training camp. "I understand that it's a big part of my job. I think I cooperate with you guys as much as any coach in the league."

Kotite did an impressive job as the Eagles' offensive coordinator in 1990. Under Kotite's guidance, Cunningham put together his best statistical season: 942 rushing yards, 30 touchdown passes, just 13 interceptions. The Eagles led the NFL in rushing and time of possession and scored a team-record 396 points. Kotite also impressed Braman and team president Harry Gamble with his professional manner as well as his offensive system. He was the antithesis of Ryan: polite, diplomatic, a company man.

Ryan was dismissed three days after a 20-6 wild card playoff loss to Washington. It was a wild day. Kotite said when he was summoned upstairs for an interview that he got on the elevator thinking he was going to be fired. Kotite and defensive coordinator Jeff Fisher, a Ryan protege, were interviewed by Braman and Gamble. Kotite was promoted to head coach later the same day. He called it, "One of the most amazing days of my life."

Kotite was given a mandate by Braman not just to win, but to win with class and dignity. He was not only to make the team better but to improve its image.

Braman was disgusted with the Eagles' bad-boy image under Ryan. He felt the Eagles were a rowdy, unruly, undisciplined team. He didn't like the black shoes worn by the players. He didn't like the cocky attitude. Kotite's job was to smooth out the rough edges. He was to mold a talented but immature team into a consistent, professional outfit. "I don't think you have to run around wearing capes," Kotite remarked during the summer of 1991 in a direct shot at the Ryan legacy. "I want us to play smart. I want us to use good judgment. I want us to be a four-quarter football team. I want us to play with discipline."

To Ryan's legion of supporters, Kotite was the "Anti-Buddy." Ryan was relaxed. Kotite was uptight. Ryan backed some players in contract disputes. Kotite always supported the front office. Ryan was loose around the media, especially the beat writers. Kotite was defensive and closed practices to the media. Ryan described himself as "short, fat and good-looking." Kotite was tall and thin and not prone to discuss his looks. Ryan was a shrewd judge of talent and an astute drafter. Kotite was unproven as a personnel man, and the early returns—especially his decision to sign 36-year-old retired former New York Jets quarterback Pat Ryan—were discouraging.

Ryan joined the Eagles after helping the Chicago Bears to the Super Bowl title following the 1985 season. He brought a crew of confident, swaggering assistants with him. Kotite spent most of his coaching career with losing teams. He had never been to a conference championship game, much less a Super Bowl, and most of his assistants, with the notable exception of defensive coordinator Bud Carson, fell into the same category.

Ryan's staffs were filled with young, ambitious assistants. Defensive coordinator Jeff Fisher, linebackers coach Ronnie Jones, offensive line coach Dan Neal and running backs coach Dave Atkins all were under 40 when Ryan hired them. Kotite hired older, more established assistants. Quarterbacks coach Zeke Bratkowski was 59 when Kotite hired him in 1991. Linebackers coach Jim Vechiarella was 54. Running backs coach Dick Wood was 55. Carson was 60.

The experience showed at times in Kotite's first season. He let the anti-Cunningham feeling among some of the quarterback's teammates run its course. He backed off those players who were fiercely loyal to Ryan and highly critical of management's decision to dismiss him. "Time heals," Kotite said at the time. "I know they are hurting. I know how they felt about Buddy. I understand. I want them to work through this and then dedicate themselves to playing their best football." Later, Kotite commented, "There was an uproar that was unbelievable. I'm just glad I got the job in January so there was time for things to settle down. I got broken in in a hurry with that situation."

Kotite's best move might have been hiring Carson as defensive co-ordinator. A 15-year veteran NFL coach, Carson quickly earned the respect and loyalty of Ryan's defensive players. Kotite also changed the team's training camp routine, backing off double sessions and heavy contact practices, emphasizing conditioning and mental preparation. "I think Richie's got the right idea," Byars said of Kotite's training camps. "Buddy worked us so hard it took us a few games to get our legs back from training camp. Maybe that's why we always seem to start slow."

"Camp Country Club, if that's what you want to call it, is the way to go," Kotite said. "We worked hard. We just weren't out on the field for seven hours a day. That's ridiculous. There's more than one way to do things. I want them fresh. I want them sharp. Believe me, if they didn't work hard, it wouldn't be this way. But this group works hard and plays hard."

Kotite's first season wasn't easy. Cunningham blew out his left knee in the second quarter of the season opener against Green Bay. He sat out the rest of the season. The Eagles started out with a 3-1 record but then reserve quarterback Jim McMahon went down. Kotite turned to rookie free agent Brad Goebel because the only other alternative was Pat Ryan, whom Kotite had plucked off a Nashville construction site when Cunningham went down.

The Eagles lost four in a row. They were 3-5 and in serious trouble. But McMahon's return to health, a big Monday night victory over the Giants and the play of the NFL's best defense led a second-half surge. Kotite and his staff kept the team together and focused. The Eagles won seven of their final eight to finish 10-6, just missing the playoffs.

"I learned a lot," Kotite said in the summer of 1992 of his first season. "I learned you have to be as consistent as possible, and you can't overreact to things. It's a long season. Things are going to happen to you and you have to work your way through them."

Kotite didn't trust prosperity. A career football man, he was most familiar with pulling down the brim of his baseball cap and fighting through adversity. It was a source of pride with him to battle through the bad times.

The 1991 season was marked by the loss of Cunningham. On June 25, 1992, the Eagles lost Pro Bowl defensive tackle Jerome Brown to a fatal car accident. Two months later, on the night of August 27, Kotite returned home from the Eagles' final exhibition game with his wife, Liz, and daughter, Alexandria, to find his mother-in-law, Stella Corkum, dead in the family's Mt. Laurel, New Jersey home.

"This is a very hard business," Kotite said a few days after returning from the funeral. "You can't stop. You have to keep working. You have to keep going. It's very tough, very difficult but this is the business that we chose. We know what it's like. You face adversity and you have to fight through it. That's the nature of this business."

Later in the season, Kotite had more to say: "I'm not a complainer. Believe it or not, I never complain. I never complain to the staff or talk about injuries or whatever. Someone's got to step in and do the job. Every week is another week and you just try to solve the problems that come up and just go on. That's all it is. Things come to your desk, across your desk, if you allow it to become a real distraction, you can lose your focus.

"That's the difference between being an assistant and a head coach.

I never realized all the different things that come up. Football-related and not football-related. The big thing is, we always try to get back on track. Whatever it is. And it hasn't been hard from that standpoint.

"They love to play football here and they work very hard. Some people have learned lessons, are learning them. I know I learn all the time. The minute you think you know everything and you've got all the answers, you're in trouble. If I do make a mistake, I try not to repeat the mistake. That's life. We're all like that."

The Eagles' current problems were no reason to panic. Kotite could walk through the parking lot late in the afternoon and consider his good fortune. This wasn't like last year, when Cunningham and McMahon went down, when the coach was forced to use five quarterbacks. Cunningham was slumping but he was healthy. The defense was in a little lull but still was ranked first in the NFL. The Phoenix Cardinals were next on the schedule, bringing a 1-5 record to Veterans Stadium.

"We're 4-2," Kotite considered. "We've lost two games. You're going to have periods like this. You're going to have little lulls in a season. That's the way this business is. You have to fight through them. You have to battle through the adversity. When we were 4-0, everyone was crowning us, and I felt that was very premature. I feel the same way about us losing two games in a row. You can't write this team off. You can't discount this team. You look at the light at the end of the tunnel, I don't think it's an oncoming train."

• 8 •

SCRAMBLED PLANS

By the first of November, Randall Cunningham needed a new hat.

Shortly after injuring his knee on September 1, 1991, Cunningham began wearing a black baseball hat with stitching on the front that read, "I'll Be Back Scrambling." By the summer of 1992, Cunningham had changed the tense and the pronoun and was wearing, marketing and promoting hats that read, "He's Back Scrambling."

Now it was November. The Eagles' regular season was half over. And neither of Cunningham's hats fit the bill. He was on the bench, watching Jim McMahon play quarterback for the Eagles. The only possible slogan for Cunningham's next lid was, "He's Coming Back from His Stunning Demotion with Renewed Confidence and Concentration." Something catchy like that.

"I'll never lose confidence in myself because once you do that, you might as well hang them up," Cunningham said in the locker room in Texas Stadium early on the evening of November 1, after a 20-10 loss to the Dallas Cowboys, after he was benched at halftime, after his promising Eagles season had careened out of control.

The Eagles were 5-3 after starting the season with four impressive victories. They were two games behind the haughty, hated Cowboys in the NFC Eastern Division race. Their defense had plummeted from No. 1 to No. 6 in the NFL rankings after Dallas rolled up 389 yards and 22 first downs in a dominating victory. Their offensive line was weakening.

But the most incredible development was the benching of Cunningham. The franchise quarterback, the superstar, the team's most popular, recognizable player had been demoted to second team. It was stunning. And it was all the more amazing considering the events of the first month of the season.

Cunningham had been the NFC's Offensive Player of the Month in September. He had completed 73.6 percent of his passes with eight touchdowns and no interceptions. He looked fully recovered from reconstructive knee surgery—those hats didn't lie.

His passing efficiency rating was an astronomical 141.2. He was light on his feet. His passes were precise. He was carrying himself with confidence. He was the old Randall, only better—smoother, smarter, more disciplined.

Somehow, it all got away from him. One week he was smooth and sure of himself, better than ever. The next week he was erratic, uncertain, playing the game like he was attached to a ball and chain. "He's pressing," Eagles coach Rich Kotite said after announcing that the 33-year-old McMahon would start the team's November 8 home game against the Los Angeles Raiders. "He just needs to step back. He needs a week off. He's working and trying too hard. He's pressing but that comes from not having success. I want to back him off a week. I want him to regather himself."

Cunningham was devastated by the news. It was the first time he had been benched for a full game for ineffective play since becoming a full-time starter in 1987. He had been through rough periods before—he struggled through much of November in 1989 and he was embarrassed by the one-series benching during the playoff loss two years before against Washington—but he always had been the man. Untouchable. Now he was being told to sit down, to turn over control of the team to McMahon, whose cocky air and status as a Super Bowl-winning quarterback always had threatened him. "It really hurt Randall to be benched," Keith Byars, one of Cunningham's closest friends on the team, said after the season. "That was his low point. He just couldn't understand why he was being singled out. He was saying, 'I know I'm not having a great year, but I'm still the second-ranked passer in the conference.' He was right, too. Randall took the blame but a lot of people weren't playing well at that time." Cunningham was confused and hurt. He lashed out at Kotite, saying, "If he thinks I need a week off, he doesn't know me very well."

It wasn't easy to get to know Cunningham. He moved in mysterious ways, both on the field and off it. He had been accused by some teammates of being arrogant and preoccupied with his own stardom, by others of being just plain weird. Still others saw Cunningham as a decent, honest but painfully self-conscious person, haunted by doubts despite his stunning success on the field, despite his financial standing, despite his status as a one-name superstar: Randall. No last name was necessary, not in Philadelphia, not around the NFL.

But for all his visibility, Cunningham felt misunderstood. "You guys have built up a negative image for me," he told reporters in training camp. "'He's a shy guy who is very sensitive. You can't do this to Randall because he's very sensitive . . . and he doesn't sign autographs. I'm just the opposite. I'm totally the opposite. People who know me know I'm a crazy guy. I do silly things. I crack jokes, people crack jokes on me.

"I get involved in a lot of charity that people don't know about because I don't care to publicize it, so I get dogged for that. People say I'm not involved in the black community. I'm heavily involved, but people don't know about it because I don't publicize it.

"The thing that most people don't know about me is that, like when they see me here talking to you guys with the cameras on, they don't see a lot of facial expressions and they think, 'Boy, he's really a mean guy.'

"But the way to get to know me better is to come to my TV show or at least watch it. I'm not just trying to promote my television show. It's just that I can go out and I don't have to think about what I'm saying, because on the show I know that if I say something wrong it can be taken out of there and I won't get crucified for it."

Sometimes during interview sessions it seemed as if Cunningham's consciousness was a giant, dusty attic filled with old impressions, new notions, half-baked theories, fears, insecurities and preconceived ideas totally unrelated to whatever questions he was asked. In the course of an interview, Cunningham would trip open a trap door and a bat of a thought would come flapping out. "He's Back Scrambling" could have referred to his conduct in interviews as well as his play on the field. He was known to change directions, double back, duck out of sight and generally perform the same improvisational acts in the public eye as he did on the football field. Both tacklers and reporters often were left baffled, exhausted and empty-handed.

Cunningham on his rebuilt left knee: "I don't think you're ever quite the same, but I'll be back to 100 percent."

Cunningham on his current relationship: "I don't have a girlfriend or anything. I'm not into that anymore. I do date a girl, a new girlfriend."

Cunningham on his part in the Eagles' offense: "I'll be doing the same things, but my role will change."

Soon after his dismissal as the Eagles' coach, Buddy Ryan was questioned on the role Cunningham might have played in his downfall. Cunningham had complained about Ryan's decision to yank him for one series in the January 5, 1991 playoff loss to Washington and had been quoted as being very supportive of offensive coordinator Rich Kotite, who replaced Ryan three days later. "Whatever Randall said, he didn't mean it," Ryan said, a phrase that some believed would later belong on Cunningham's tombstone. "Being confused has a lot to do with my personality," Cunningham once admitted.

Cunningham's problem might have been that he talked too much. He was greatly appreciated by the media around the team because of his accessibility and cooperation. Cunningham took seriously his role as a team spokesman. He was one of the most accessible, quotable superstars in sports. The problem was that all that talking tended to lead to a lot of contradictions. It also tended to lead to a lot of self-examination, a lot of quotes about "me" and "my" and "I," some of which tended to bother his teammates.

That was the problem for Cunningham soon after Ryan's dismissal. A bitter, frustrated team—stung by three consecutive playoff losses, disappointed in Ryan's dismissal—turned its anger on Cunningham. He was roundly criticized by many teammates—most of whom spoke on the condition of anonymity—for being self-centered, egotistical and preoccupied with his own stardom. Reggie White was among the few who permitted their names to be placed behind their quotes. "Randall has to realize there's a lot of other guys out there on the field with him," White said. "It's not just him. He has a lot to learn."

The criticism came at a difficult time for Cunningham. In truth, he wasn't that disappointed by the dismissal of Ryan, since he felt the coach paid too little attention to the offense. He suspected, along with a lot of others, that a change might be best for the team.

But now Cunningham was under fire from his teammates. He also was under fire from the media and a lot of fans because of his play in the post-season. He was a three-time Pro Bowl selection for his play during the regular season. But in the playoffs, Cunningham was sporting an 0-3 record, and he had thrown five interceptions and zero touchdown passes.

Cunningham was so hurt by the criticism from his teammates that he pondered retirement. "I thought about it," he later recalled. "I said, 'Maybe I should just not play anymore.' It was hard. Man, it was hard. It was like I was in a coffin or something but I had to keep pushing back up on the lid."

Cunningham wasn't the most popular player on the team. He tried to get along with everyone, to be a regular guy, but he was preoccupied with his status and with the trappings of his fame—his local television show; his mansion in Moorestown; his fleet of automobiles, including a white limousine that he used for personal appearances; his acquaintanceship with celebrities such as singer Whitney Houston and talk-show host Arsenio Hall.

Cunningham also was surrounded by an entourage of business managers, consultants, appointment secretaries and assorted hangers-on who were related, in some way, to Scrambler, Inc., his endorsement and promotion business. He designed and marketed T-shirts and hats all bearing his name or likeness. He dabbled in children's television programs. He decided that 1992 was a good year to come out with his own candy bar and to write his autobiography.

Much of this tended to rub his teammates the wrong way. He was probably the only star on the team who never haggled with management over his contract. Cunningham could come across as aloof, stranded on an island of wealth. He was the only player on the team who refused to give his home phone number to the team's public relations staff. He offered the office number for Scrambler, Inc., instead. "Randall sometimes forgets that he's part of a team," Reggie White said back in February 1991, when frustration over the team's third consecutive playoff loss, anger over the dismissal of Ryan and resentment of Cunningham came bubbling to the surface like molten rock. "He's one of 47 guys. He's not out there by himself. He can't do it all himself."

A players-only team meeting was set for April 1, 1991, the first day of the Eagles' first minicamp under Kotite. Three days before that meeting, Cunningham sat in the kitchen of his 26-room, $1.4 million mansion in Moorestown, New Jersey. It's a big white house surrounded by a black iron fence—part of a small complex of similar homes, an enclave of wealth and status just off Interstate 295, about 20 miles from Veterans Stadium.

Cunningham sat in the kitchen and looked out over a vacant lot next to his house. He had purchased the lot for $250,000 with the idea of building a field where his teammates and friends could work out, a field of dreams.

Upstairs, the house had a series of guest rooms. One wing had an apartment—including a kitchen, living room, bathroom and bedroom—with a sign on the double-doors that read, "Guest Quarters." Another bedroom was set aside for Indianapolis Colts running back Eric Dickerson, a close friend. From the shelf in the closet of that room, Cunningham pulled out a door plate that read, "Eric's Domain."

Off his own bedroom, Cunningham had a walk-in closet lined with suits and shoes. On one wall was a bank of tiny televisions that display the pictures taken by security cameras around the outside of the house. He showed a visitor how he could manipulate the cameras, even zoom in on the entrance to the complex. If angry teammates were coming, brandishing torches and pitchforks, he would spot their approach.

"Man," Cunningham said, "this will work out. I know it will. I've been through worse situations than this. I'm not going to quit. I'm going to be myself and everything will work out. Guys are mad. Guys are frustrated because Buddy got fired, but they're not really upset with me. It will work out. I know it will.

"Know what this is all about? Know what the problem is?"

With that, Cunningham rubbed his fingers together in the sign of money. In September 1989, he had signed a five-year contract extension that would pay him an average of close to $3 million per season. He had been approached by management, an unprecedented move by a front office that tended to be conservative in such matters. "Money has a lot to do with this," he continued. "But it will pass. I'm really not that worried about it."

Cunningham often compared the traumas he faced in his professional life with the pain of losing both his parents only a year apart. Born and raised in Santa Barbara, California, he was the youngest of four boys, and he spent his youth in the shadow of his famous older brother, Sam "The Bam" Cunningham, a star running back at the University of Southern California and later with the New England Patriots of the NFL.

Randall Cunningham was a star quarterback at Santa Barbara High School and USC, his brother's alma mater, tried to recruit him as a defensive back. But another brother, Bruce, had played at the University of Nevada-Las Vegas, so Randall went there. Both his parents died during his first two years away at college. He once said the death of his mother and father made him feel alone in the world because his brothers were older and a little distant from him.

Moody and introspective, Cunningham often walked through his mansion at night, alone with his thoughts. He once admitted hearing voices in his head. "There's an evil spirit and a good spirit," he contended. "I lean toward the good spirit all the time because that's where my heart is, and I know I can be tricked."

Cunningham flourished on the football field at UNLV. He set every school and Pacific Coast Conference passing record. He was an All-America selection as a punter. The Eagles picked him in the second round of the 1985 draft. His progress as an NFL player was astounding. He was starting by his second professional game, although he was benched a month later. By the end of the 1986 season, though, Cunningham was in the starting lineup to stay. He started every Eagles game from the beginning of the 1987 season through his injury in the 1991 opener. He made the Pro Bowl after the 1988, 1989 and 1990 seasons.

Cunningham had a strong arm, but the signature element of his game was his running ability. He led the Eagles in rushing from 1987 through 1990, becoming the first NFL quarterback in the modern era to lead his team in rushing four years in a row. He revolutionized the position, running unlike any other NFL quarterback. In 1992, he would set the all-time NFL record for rushing yards by a quarterback, passing Fran Tarkenton's total of 3,674.

Tarkenton set the record in 18 seasons. By the end of 1992, after just seven NFL seasons, Cunningham had 4,223 rushing yards. "The Halley's Comet of quarterbacks," NFL Films president Steve Sabol once called Cunningham. "He's a talent that will come along once in a generation." Sighed Washington coach Joe Gibbs: "I just wish he'd break a sweat. He's out there running around, driving us crazy, and he comes over to our sideline and he's not even sweating."

Cunningham put together his best statistical season in 1990, when Kotite was the team's offensive coordinator. Cunningham passed for 30 touchdowns with just 13 interceptions. He ran for 942 yards, just 26 yards shy of Bobby Douglass' 1972 record for single-season rushing yards by a quarterback.

Late in the first half of a 30-23 loss to Buffalo in Rich Stadium, Cunningham somehow avoided Bills All-Pro defensive end Bruce Smith in the end zone, spun around, ran to his left and threw a 95-yard touchdown pass to Fred Barnett. "Sometimes I amaze myself," Cunningham boasted, a comment that rankled a lot of his teammates both for its content and its timing—after all, the Eagles had lost the game.

The missing item in Cunningham's resume was a playoff victory. He was linked with the Eagles' playoff failures because of his own subpar statistics in those games, because of the one-series benching by Ryan in the loss to the Redskins, and because of Ryan's subsequent dismissal.

Cunningham entered 1992 determined to lead the Eagles deep into the playoffs. He said he gained some perspective from sitting out most of 1991, from watching McMahon and other quarterbacks. He felt the injury changed him for the better. Cunningham was hurt on the first play of the second quarter in the 1991 season opener. He was throwing a pass when he planted his left leg and took a direct hit on the knee from Green Bay linebacker Bryce Paup. The medial collateral and posterior cruciate ligaments were completely torn. Three days later, Cunningham underwent reconstructive surgery in Los Angeles. Dr. Clarence Shields, the same surgeon who had operated on Cunningham's right knee when he was a senior in high school, fused together the medial collateral ligament and replaced the posterior cruciate with an Achilles tendon from a cadaver. "Hope it was Jesse Owens," Cunningham said of the donor.

Cunningham rehabilitated the knee for 11 months before putting on his uniform again for an August 8, 1992 exhibition game in Pittsburgh. "It was hard but I never lost faith," Cunningham commented about his rehabilitation. "I was prepared for it. I worked hard. When I traveled in the off-season, I made sure I stayed in a hotel with a gym. Or I went to a gym. I worked six days a week. I worked at it. I think people found out that Randall's a guy who is going to go out and work hard. When times are down, he goes out and does what it takes. I think that's how you show your leadership."

Cunningham's comeback was incredible—for a month. He completed 72, 77.2, 72 and 57.8 percent of his passes in the first four games. He threw two touchdown passes against New Orleans, three against Phoenix and three against Denver. He ran for the first touchdown in the big Monday night victory over Dallas. "I gained a lot of maturity from watching last year," Cunningham stated. "I feel so comfortable. I used to come out and hurry and try to make things happen. It's not about that. It's about dropping back like you normally do in practice."

Cunningham lost his way in a steady, mysterious decline. The loss in Kansas City on October 11 was laid at the feet of the Eagles' defense, but Cunningham wasn't sharp that day. He finished with 168 passing yards and two touchdowns, but 91 of those yards and both scores came in a desperate fourth quarter. He was sacked six times, lost a fumble and threw two interceptions.

It got worse the next week in Washington. The Redskins' defense, with its changing coverages, frequent blitzes and disciplined pass rush, always spelled trouble for Cunningham. He was sacked five times and didn't complete a pass for more than 20 yards. "They know how to defense me," Cunningham said after an unsightly 16-12 loss to the Redskins in RFK Stadium.

It got even worse the next week at home against Phoenix. The Eagles won 7-3 thanks to a heroic goal-line stand by the defense, but the offense was in serious decline. Cunningham's statistics in the second half: 2-for-9 passing for 11 yards. He was sacked five more times.

Cunningham was fortunate the Eagles' defense rose up with one of the most remarkable performances in recent NFL history. Ahead 7-0, the Eagles stopped the Cardinals from scoring on seven goal-line plays late in the first half. "That's something I'll remember the rest of my life," said Eagles reserve linebacker Britt Hager, a key member of the team's goal-line defense. "It showed the heart of this defense and caliber of this defense. You could just feel it. You could just sense it on the field. Everybody's eyes were glassing over. You just knew they weren't getting in." Linebacker Seth Joyner added: "By the end, it was like, 'OK, let the refs call what they want, let them run whatever play they want. They're not getting in.'"

The Cardinals didn't get in the Eagles' end zone late in the first half despite running seven plays after taking possession on an interception return at the Philadelphia 3 yard line. "Magnificent," declared Kotite after his team improved its record to 5-2 heading into the following Sunday's showdown with the NFC Eastern Division-leading Dallas Cowboys in Texas Stadium. "It was the greatest I've ever seen."

Most goal-line stands are pretty remarkable. This one was all the more special because of the circumstances. For one thing, the Eagles got charged with three penalties, giving the Cardinals three extra tries at the end zone. For another, the Eagles had little else going for them on a cool, sunny day besides their defense. Playing against the NFL's 26th-ranked defense, the Eagles' offense managed just 247 yards and 11 first downs. The seven points were their lowest total in a victory since 1957. "Sometimes you play good and lose," Eagles center David Alexander noted. "Sometimes you play like spit and win. We played like spit, at least on offense, but we still got the win." Cunningham threw a 40-yard touchdown pass to Calvin Williams in the second quarter but struggled for most of the game. He finished 9-for-20 passing for 121 yards, including 2-for-9 for 11 yards in the second half. "It's alarming, it's frustrating," Eagles guard Mike Schad admitted. "Things just haven't been going the way they should." Kotite was worried, too, saying, "I'm not happy at all [with the offense]. We had opportunities. We had problems but we overcame them and won and that's what good teams do."

Playing without three injured players, running back Keith Byars and tackles Ron Heller and Antone Davis, the Eagles' offense had seven possessions that lasted four plays or less. They had second-half drives that netted 3, minus 7, 12, minus 3, minus 11 and minus 13 yards.

But they were saved by the incredible goal-line stand. The situation was that the Cardinals took over at the 3-yard line after Aeneas Williams returned a Cunningham interception 23 yards.

On first down, running back Johnny Bailey gained two yards to the 1. Then came a remarkable sequence of four plays and three penalties. First, the Cardinals' Chris Chandler tried a quarterback sneak and lost a fumble that was recovered by the Eagles' Mike Pitts. But there was a penalty: Joyner off-sides, half the distance to the goal. Next, Bailey ran off-tackle to the left and was hit by Mike Golic and Byron Evans. No gain. Next, Bailey ran off-tackle to the left again. No gain again. Penalty: Tommy Jeter off-sides. Half the distance. Then, Chandler tried a second quarterback sneak. No gain again and again a penalty: William Thomas off-sides. Half the distance. Then, Bailey ran off-tackle left again, but was hit by Joyner. No gain. Finally, Bailey ran off-tackle right, and was hit by White. No gain. It was the Eagles' football. "After the second off-sides penalty, we didn't even care," Hager remarked. "It was like, 'Go ahead, give them 12, 15 chances. They're not getting in.' "

The goal-line stand deflected some of the heat from Cunningham, but he was in a funk. After the game, he searched for reasons for his steady slide. "I think the credit goes to not having Keith Jackson," Cunningham said, referring to the former Pro Bowl tight end who had signed with Miami as a free agent on September 29. Jackson was Cunningham's favorite receiver: they had hooked up on 194 passes from 1988 through 1990.

Cunningham was brilliant in September, but he was devastated when Jackson took off for Miami. In the days before Jackson's departure, Cunningham was telling reporters that the tight end was going to remain with the Eagles. But Jackson was gone, leaving Pat Beach and Maurice Johnson as the Eagles' tight ends, and neither of them compared to Jackson as a receiver.

"That really bothered Randall," Reggie White stated shortly after Jackson's departure. "It bothered a lot of us, but especially Randall. He was waiting for Keith to return. In Randall's mind, Keith was coming back. I think when Keith left, Randall took it very personally and he's fighting to get over it." Rich Kotite had his own theory: retroactive rust from the season of injury rehabilitation. "A year off is a year off," Kotite said. "He just needs to play. He needs work. This man will come roaring back."

There was another theory: Cunningham wasn't working hard enough, wasn't studying. Teammates who spoke under the condition of anonymity said Cunningham was having trouble interpreting the signals from the sidelines, that he was miscalling plays, that he seemed to have a loose grip on the weekly game plans. "His confidence was way down," Kotite commented late in the season, "and it was affecting him in a lot of different ways."

It got even worse the next week in Dallas. This was a huge game, a battle for supremacy in the NFC Eastern Division. With a victory, the Eagles would improve their record to 6-2, the same mark as Dallas. But Philadelphia would have both the tie-breaker and the psychological edge based on a series sweep of two games against Dallas.

But Cunningham was atrocious. He was 3-for-8 passing in the first half for 13 yards. He looked tentative, confused, indecisive. He bounced one pass to an open Maurice Johnson and bounced another one to an open Fred Barnett. He threw one of the worst interceptions of his career: a lazy pass straight at stunned Dallas cornerback Larry Brown.

Kotite made the switch at halftime. He called both quarterbacks into a side room off the main dressing area and told them the news: McMahon was in, Cunningham was out. McMahon led the Eagles on a touchdown drive on the first series of the second half, but the Cowboys took control of the game behind running back Emmitt Smith who finished with 163 yards.

Smith ran for 115 yards in the second half. He broke off a 51-yard run late in the third quarter. He wore down the Eagles' vaunted defense, gaining 35 yards on five carries on a memorable fourth-quarter drive that ended with a 14-yard touchdown pass from quarterback Troy Aikman to fullback Daryl Johnston.

Smith, the NFL rushing champion in 1990, had never gained 100 yards against the Eagles in five previous games. On this day, he became the first player to run for 100 yards against the Eagles in the regular season since Washington's Gerald Riggs on September 17, 1989, a span of 54 games. "They were running the ball against us at will," said Eagles safety Wes Hopkins. "I think it was pretty evident that as a defense, we were fatigued. We spent an awful lot of time [20:08 of a possible 30:00] on the field in the first half. We got tired and they took advantage."

It was an ominous loss for the Eagles. Their record dropped to 5-3 and they fell two games behind the 7-1 Cowboys in the NFC East race. Dallas was gathering strength and momentum. The Cowboys had won two out of three from the Eagles after losing nine in a row in non-strike games. They were starting to break the psychological hold the Eagles had on them for all those years. But in the moments after the game, the long-term prospects of both teams seemed of little concern in the Eagles locker room. The dominant issue was the quarterback situation.

In a brief, post-game press conference, Kotite said that he planned to start Cunningham against the Raiders. The next day, Kotite changed his mind on the plane flight back to Philadelphia after the game. His new plan: McMahon would start Sunday, Cunningham would step back and watch for a week. "I just have a feeling that a week off is going to help him," Kotite stated. "This is just for a week, OK. This isn't a week-to-week thing. He [Cunningham] is still the guy. That has not changed."

Cunningham wasn't so sure. He was devastated by the development. He wasn't just another player, he was The Franchise. The star was stung by Kotite's decision. He knew that McMahon would grab for the starting job with both hands. This was his worst nightmare. What if McMahon played well and led the Eagles to an impressive victory over the Raiders? What then?

"It's started, man," Cunningham noted. "The quarterback controversy has started, so let's get it going."

──── ■ 9 ■ ────

BEHIND THE MASK

New quarterback, new hat.

At the age of 33, in his eleventh National Football League season, Jim McMahon had a weary, worldly air about him. He was a man with a past. Once he was the original punk quarterback, the outrageous leader of an outrageous band of Chicago Bears. He showed up for his first professional practice with a beer can in his hand, wore headbands in defiance of NFL officials, feuded with his coach, butted helmets with offensive linemen, mooned a helicopter, and led the Bears to the Super Bowl title following the 1985 season.

McMahon was a legendary figure. He was a record-setting quarterback at Brigham Young University, a hard-edged, foul-mouthed Irish Catholic in a sea of Mormon morality. He was the rebellious field general of those loose, intimidating Bears. He was hip and irreverent, a cool counterpoint to uptight, overheated head coach Mike Ditka.

But that was a long time ago. In 1992, McMahon was an older veteran, a seen-it-all, done-most-of-it source of humor and wisdom in the locker room. Many of his teammates revered him. "I used to hate the guy," said Eagles offensive tackle Ron Heller, who played for the Tampa Bay Buccaneers during McMahon's heyday in Chicago in the mid 1980s. "I just thought he was this arrogant jerk that won all the time. We couldn't beat them. I couldn't stand him. Now, I think he's the greatest. He just had this air of greatness around him. You get around him and you just think, 'This guy is something special.' "

McMahon had been with the Eagles since the summer of 1990, and his stay was marked by two extremes: either he was the center of attention, or he was nearly invisible. McMahon rarely talked with the media, a stance that earned him a lot of points with his friends along the much-maligned offensive line, so he would disappear from public view if he wasn't playing. But when he was playing, McMahon found a way to generate excitement. That was his style. He was either replacing Cunningham for one series in the last Eagles game ever coached by Buddy Ryan, or he was getting hurt, or he was overcoming an ailment to lead a miraculous comeback.

For the Eagles, McMahon's emergence from the shadows usually meant there was a crisis. It's that way with a lot of backup quarterbacks in the NFL, but McMahon was such a powerful personality that his presence tended to turn up the voltage on supercharged situations. "He's a winner," said Eagles coach Rich Kotite, who tabbed McMahon to start the team's November 8 home game against the Los Angeles Raiders in place of slumping superstar Randall Cunningham. "I'm glad we have him. I can make a move like this, allow Randall to step back and collect himself, because we have a guy like Jim McMahon."

McMahon was born in Jersey City, New Jersey, moved to California as a youngster and then to Roy, Utah, where he was a three-sport star in high school. A tremendous natural athlete, McMahon played every baseball position except catcher and was offered a basketball scholarship to Utah State.

McMahon might have been the best all-around athlete in the Eagles locker room, which was another source of his status. He was a scratch golfer whose booming drives approached 300 yards. He was the MVP of the Eagles' Monday night bowling league in 1990. He was a tremendous racquetball player. McMahon often would be seen throwing a football around the field a couple of hours before the kickoff of Eagles games. He was a great punter, driving the football 60 yards in the air. He sometimes threw 40-yard spirals with his left hand.

At Brigham Young University, McMahon furthered the tradition of great passing quarterbacks at the Provo, Utah, school. He set 71 NCAA records in passing and total offense. He passed for 9,563 yards and 84 touchdowns and led the Cougars to a 22-3 record in his final two seasons. The Bears selected McMahon in the first round of the 1982 draft with the fifth overall selection. He was a full-time starter by the end of the 1983 season and the unquestioned leader of an NFL power by 1984.

McMahon made his first and only appearance in the Pro Bowl after leading the Bears to a dream season in 1985. He passed for a career-best 2,392 yards and 15 touchdowns as the Bears—with a ferocious defense directed by soon-to-be Eagles coach Buddy Ryan—won 18 of 19 games as one of the most dominating teams in modern NFL history.

McMahon's statistics never were gaudy, but he was regarded as a natural leader who inspired his teammates. Eagles player personnel director Joe Woolley loved to retell an anecdote that underscored McMahon's instincts, intelligence, and feel for the sport and his position. The Bears were playing the Redskins, and their tight end, Emory Morehead, had been alerted to run a slant pattern in the event of a safety blitz. Morehead would get the signal on an audible from McMahon at the line of scrimmage. The Bears came to the line and McMahon audibled for a tight end slant. Morehead thought it was strange, since the safety was back at his normal position, but he ran it anyway. The safety blitzed, and McMahon hit Morehead for a long gain. In the huddle, Morehead asked McMahon how he knew the safety was going to blitz. "He didn't look at me," McMahon replied. "Every other time, he looked at me when I came out of the huddle. This time, he was looking away."

McMahon's only shortcoming as a quarterback was his tendency to get hurt. He missed seven games in 1984 with hand, back and kidney problems. He missed three games in 1985 with shoulder and neck ailments and 10 games in 1986 with a bum shoulder. He missed nine games in 1987 with lingering shoulder problems and a pulled hamstring, and seven games in 1988 with a sprained knee.

Ditka and the Bears lost patience with McMahon and traded him to the San Diego Chargers in the summer of 1989. McMahon started 11 games that season for the Chargers, including a dramatic 20-17 victory over the Eagles, but he was replaced late in the year by rookie Billy Joe Tolliver, who was regarded as the team's quarterback of the future.

The Chargers released McMahon in April 1990, and he signed with the Eagles in July. It was a reunion for McMahon and Ryan, who had shared the same swaggering confidence and disdain for Ditka and others in authority during their brief but memorable time together in Chicago. "He could start for more than half the teams in the NFL," said Ryan, who wanted McMahon to serve as a backup to Cunningham.

McMahon stayed on the bench for most of the 1990 season. Cunningham was brilliant, passing for 30 touchdowns and running for 942 yards en route to his third consecutive Pro Bowl berth. McMahon made mop-up appearances in five games, throwing just nine passes. But midway in the third quarter of the Eagles' first playoff game, Ryan sent McMahon into the game to replace Cunningham. It was a stunning move—the Eagles were trailing the Washington Redskins by just 13-6 and Cunningham never had been benched since becoming a full-time starter. McMahon played just one series. He threw three incomplete passes and Cunningham returned to play the rest of the Eagles' 20-6 loss.

The move set off a storm of controversy—"We're down a touchdown and he embarrasses Randall on national television," team owner Norman Braman was quoted as saying after the game—and took on added significance when Ryan was fired three days later. "We were logjammed," Ryan said at the time. "I was just trying to get something started. What was I going to wait for?"

McMahon had a clause in his contract that called for him to be unprotected during the Plan B free agency period in the spring. But no other team was seriously interested, and he re-signed with the Eagles before the 1991 season, figuring on another quiet year as Cunningham's caddy.

That changed September 1, 1991, on the first play of the second quarter of the season opener in Green Bay. Cunningham went down with a season-ending knee injury, and McMahon was thrust into the spotlight. McMahon led the Eagles to a 20-3 victory over the Packers that day, earning NFC Offensive Player of the Week honors. He would start 11 games for the Eagles in 1991, and the team would win eight of them.

McMahon led the Eagles with his deft passing touch, charisma and high pain threshold. They were 9-2 in games in which he played more than a quarter. He was a mesmerizing presence, fighting off knee and elbow injuries to lead the Eagles back from a 3-5 start to playoff contention. "Jim's biggest asset may be his uncanny ability to raise the level of play of those around him," Kotite contended. "He does the little things well. He doesn't have a real powerful arm, but he's bright, anticipatory and reads and reacts so well. He's got a photographic memory. His mind is like a computer."

That was one of the ironies of Jim McMahon. He was this loose, irreverent character, with a ponytail, earring and trademark dark sun-glasses. But there was nothing loose or unconventional about his play. He was an old-fashioned quarterback, relying on his intelligence, instincts and understanding of defenses. He played the odds and the angles. "It's just football," McMahon once said. "They've got 11 and we've got 11. It's not like it's brain surgery or anything."

Most of McMahon's teammates loved his attitude, his image, his intelligence and his style both on the field and in the locker room. He was a natural leader. "What you see isn't what you get with Jim," Kotite observed. "You see the ponytail, the earring and the other stuff, but what you don't see is this guy is extremely bright. He has a complete knowledge of the offenses and defenses and a tremendous amount of savvy. He has such leadership qualities and charisma. When Jim walks into the room or onto the field, people gravitate toward him." Commented Eagles center David Alexander: "Number 9, there's something special about him. When he steps in the huddle, you can just feel it." And guard Mike Schad added: "Jim has a lot of confidence in himself. He enjoys his job and he knows he's good at it. That attitude rubs off on people."

McMahon led the Eagles to a 3-1 start in 1991. But he went down with a sprained knee in the first quarter of an ugly 23-0 Monday night loss in Washington and missed the next two games, both losses. He was back in the starting lineup for the San Francisco game—throwing a 19-yard scoring pass to Keith Byars that represented the Eagles' first touchdown in 14 quarters—but he aggravated the knee and limped away from another loss.

McMahon would start the next six games, all victories. His most memorable performance came in Cleveland when he rallied the Eagles from a 23-0 deficit to a 32-30 victory.

McMahon had taken an injection of pain-killing medicine in his aching right elbow on Saturday morning, before the Eagles' flight to Cleveland. He had an allergic reaction to the drug. He was nauseous and his elbow swelled to twice its normal size. "No way I thought he was going to be able to play," said Ron Heller, McMahon's roommate on the road. "He couldn't even tie his ponytail. I had to tie it for him."

McMahon arrived at Cleveland Stadium at 7 o'clock Sunday morning, five hours before kickoff. He received massages and heat treatment, and finally his elbow was drained of fluid. He then went out and passed for 341 yards and three touchdowns. He threw touchdown passes of 16 yards to Keith Jackson, 70 yards to Fred Barnett and 5 yards to Calvin Williams. The last scoring throw capped the Eagles' greatest comeback since 1959. "It was one of the most incredible performances I've ever seen," Kotite marveled after the game. "This man couldn't even lift his arm yesterday, and he went out and played about as well as I've ever seen a quarterback play."

McMahon's elbow never really healed. He led the Eagles to victories over Cincinnati and Phoenix, but needed relief help from Jeff Kemp in the big Monday night victory over Houston on December 2 in the Astrodome. The next Sunday, McMahon's season ended when 319-pound New York Giants nose tackle Lorenzo "Big Foot" Freeman landed on him, fracturing four of his ribs.

Randall Cunningham watched McMahon's exploits from an awkward distance. Cunningham was around the team, often rehabilitating in the trainer's room. But he wasn't part of the team. It was an odd, uncomfortable situation for the sensitive quarterback. When Cunningham reported to training camp in 1992, he vowed to be more like McMahon, more outspoken, more of a leader. He said he learned a lot watching McMahon in 1991.

McMahon was unprotected again during the Plan B free agency period in the spring of 1992. But he couldn't work out for other teams because he was recuperating from elbow surgery. The Minnesota Vikings expressed some interest in him, but the Eagles didn't want to trade him. "Book it—he's coming back here," Kotite promised in June.

McMahon had hoped to compete for the starting job in training camp, but he haggled with Eagles management over a new contract and didn't sign until August 17. By then, Cunningham was showing few signs of his knee injury and was firmly entrenched as the No. 1 quarterback. "McMahon is No. 2, put that in granite," Kotite said when McMahon reported to training camp in West Chester.

McMahon arrived in a bad mood. He felt he had been "misled" by the team in 1991. He said he was told that he would have a chance to compete for the starting job in 1992 and that he would receive a substantial raise. He said none of that happened. "Last year, when I was playing hurt, they told me that I would have a chance to be a starter, that I would get a bonus, that I would get a nice contract, this and this," McMahon claimed after reporting to training camp. "None of that seems to be coming true and that's what irritates me."

McMahon had made $525,000 in base salary in 1991, although he earned almost that much in incentive bonuses because he had started 11 games. He had sought a $1.6 million contract for 1992, but the Eagles never budged from their $800,000 offer and he ended up accepting that. "They told me things to keep me playing last year, and none of it happened," McMahon said. "I finally had to make a decision." He made no secret of his desire for the starting job. He wasn't content to be a backup, especially not to an inconsistent player such as Cunningham.

They were an odd couple, Cunningham and McMahon. But they had one thing in common: they both loved the locker room. For Cunningham, it was his home. He had that big 26-room mansion over in South Jersey, but there was no family there. That was his residence—clean, spacious, filled with televisions and a huge white pool table and a suit of armor that stood on the landing between the first and second floors—but it wasn't really his home. Cunningham felt at home in the locker room. He enjoyed the company of his teammates, the attention of reporters, the structure of his routine. It was harder for him to float off on a tangent because he was serious about his profession. He was grounded there.

In the off-seasons following the 1986 and 1987 seasons, Cunningham was in the locker room almost every day. He lifted weights and rode the exercise bikes and jogged and watched film across the hall in the meeting rooms and was a willing, active participant in the team's off-season program. "Bubble 101," Buddy Ryan used to call it, after the nickname of the team's indoor practice facility, and the coach said Cunningham was a straight-A student.

Although Cunningham has the image of an effortlessly gifted player, a natural athlete, he had worked hard to make himself into a Pro Bowl star. His insight into the demands of his position and his understanding of the NFL game grew out of those countless off-season hours at Veterans

Stadium. "Randall is a workaholic," Eagles offensive star Keith Byars once said. "That's one thing that people don't understand about him. He's not afraid to work. He always wants to work. He's self-made."

In 1992, though, there were whispers about Cunningham's work habits. Some teammates suggested that Cunningham fell into the slump that led to his benching because he wasn't studying the game plan, wasn't watching extra film, wasn't applying himself the way he did before he was an established superstar.

McMahon loved the locker room, too. He loved the camaraderie, the sanctity of it, the way it was a private place where he could joke and curse. Kind of a men's club. He cherished the bonding that came from playing together on a team. McMahon also loved golf, but sometimes he was criticized for his boorish behavior on the course. In fact, several members of the exclusive Laurel Creek Country Club in Laurel Springs, New Jersey, had complained in the fall of 1992 about McMahon's off-color language. That wasn't a problem in the locker room. "He's the only guy I've ever been around that loves training camp," Kotite once said of McMahon. "He loves it. Most guys complain about the two-a-days, the routine, whatever. McMahon loves hanging around." After he reported to training camp in the summer of 1992, McMahon admitted, "I enjoy training camp. I've missed it. The rookies get dumber and dumber every year. It's getting too easy to play jokes on them."

Mostly, though, Cunningham and McMahon were different. And in the debate that raged on the radio call-in shows, in the newspapers and in the locker room, there was no avoiding the racial issue. It was subtle but it was there: the stereotyping of both players along racial lines in the discussions of their styles, personalities, strengths and weaknesses. Cunningham was a great athlete. He relied on his natural ability, on his speed and moves, his arm strength and improvisational skills. McMahon relied on his brains and cunning. He wasn't that big or fast, but he was smart and tough, and he was a leader. Cunningham was arrogant and aloof. McMahon was fiery, down-to-earth, a regular guy. Cunningham was having problems with the game plan, with the signals from the sideline, with reading defenses. McMahon was a master at that stuff.

Adding fuel to the fire were the published comments of two NFL coaches whose teams had recently played the Eagles. "Cunningham is a great player and a great athlete," Phoenix Cardinals defensive coordinator Fritz Shurmur was quoted as saying. "He scares you half to death every time he touches the ball. But there are some things that give him trouble. He has difficulty playing against a zone defense. If you give him a lot of different looks on defense, he becomes hesitant with the ball. The more you change things, the tougher time he has."

It was Shurmur, then the defensive coordinator of the Los Angeles Rams, who devised the myriad of zone coverages that baffled Cunningham and the Eagles' offense in a 1989 playoff game in Veterans Stadium. Eagles coach Buddy Ryan called it a "junior-high defense," but Cunningham and the rest of the Philadelphia offense could manage just one touchdown in a 21-7 loss. Dallas coach Jimmy Johnson seconded the theory on Cunningham. "It seems like he has a tough time reading zone defenses and doesn't unload the ball that quickly," Johnson was quoted as saying.

In 1992, Cunningham was one of just three black quarterbacks who were starters in the NFL. The others were Warren Moon of Houston and Rodney Peete of Detroit. It was an old issue for Cunningham, the paucity of black quarterbacks in the NFL. He had talked about it since entering the league in 1985. "I feel like guys like Doug Williams and James Harris were trailblazers," Cunningham once said, referring to a pair of black former NFL quarterbacks. "They were the first ones out there, and it was difficult for them. I've talked a lot with Doug about how difficult it was for him. I try not to make an issue out of it. People are always trying to stir things up, but I just look at myself as a quarterback. Period. I don't look at colors and I don't think other people should either."

Cunningham was close friends with Williams, the former Washington Redskins quarterback. Williams felt that his race was the reason he was out of the league just two years after leading the Redskins to the Super Bowl title in January 1988.

Williams, who bitterly charged the NFL with racist bias in his ironically entitled autobiography, *Quarterblack,* was one of the people who called Cunningham after his benching. "He told me to hang in there," Cunningham recalled. "He said to remember what he went through. He told me to be myself and things will work out."

In the locker room, many of the offensive linemen, most of whom happened to be white, seemed to prefer McMahon as the starter. They raved about his leadership, his charisma, his ability to raise the level of play of those around him. Guard Mike Schad, while not openly critical of Cunningham, noted that his scrambling style and unwillingness to throw the ball away often led to sacks. McMahon was a master at quickly releasing the football, avoiding the coverage sacks that infuriate offensive linemen. "They've made it pretty clear they want Jim in there," linebacker Seth Joyner remarked.

McMahon, as was his wont, was taking his own sly slant on things. For some time, many of the Eagles' black players had been wearing the popular "X" caps, inspired by the promotion of Spike Lee's forthcoming movie epic about Malcolm X. McMahon took to wearing a cap with an "O" on the front. He wore his "O" cap and a futuristic pair of wrap-around sunglasses during pre-game national television interviews before the Raiders came to town. " 'O' caps are for white guys," McMahon joked.

But this wasn't so much a black-white issue in the locker room as a football issue. Time was wasting. This team was struggling. Most of the players cared a lot more about winning than they did about the identity or the color of the starting quarterback. "If we win with Jim, then I think we have to stick with Jim," Joyner said before the Raiders game. Defensive tackle Mike Golic contended: "I really don't care who the quarterback is. I still have to do my job. If a quarterback is struggling, then sometimes a change is what's needed. Just like any other position."

For many of the players on defense, a more pressing concern than the identity of the quarterback was their own performance. The loss in Dallas marked the fourth time in five games the Eagles had surrendered more than 300 yards. They allowed more than 300 just once in 1991.

On Monday, November 2, injured safety Andre Waters asked for a few minutes after film review to speak to the defense. Waters was aggravated not only because of the team's slip to No. 6 in the NFL rankings in overall defense, but also because of a noticeable decline in intensity and aggressiveness. Waters was concerned that the team was losing its focus, that players were forgetting the importance of dedicating the season to Jerome Brown. "Where has all the emotion from the first game gone?" Waters asked his teammates. "You know how much Jerome meant to us. It's time to start playing like it. We're wearing the 99 patch, but we might as well be wearing the 60th anniversary patch if we're not going to play like Jerome would want us."

McMahon made his first start for the Eagles since Week 14 of the 1991 season on a sunny, cool afternoon in Veterans Stadium. The Eagles were playing the 3-6 Raiders, who had been off for two weeks because of the bye in the schedule. It wasn't much of a game. The Eagles won 31-10 to improve their record to 6-3, including a 5-0 mark at home. McMahon's play was solid but unspectacular. He completed 12 of 24 passes for 157 yards and one touchdown with one interception.

The stars of the game were running back Heath Sherman and the Eagles defense. In his first significant action since the season opener, Sherman gained 81 yards on just nine carries and scored on a 30-yard run. He would emerge as an offensive force for the Eagles in the second half of the season.

The defense flustered Raiders quarterbacks Todd Marinovich and Jay Schroeder, coming up with three sacks and four interceptions. Cornerback Eric Allen had two interceptions and safeties Wes Hopkins and John Booty each had one. Defensive end Reggie White had two sacks as the Eagles held the mistake-prone Raiders to just 215 total yards.

McMahon wasn't terrific but his one touchdown throw was something special. The play called for wide receiver Fred Barnett to run an "in" pattern, crossing the middle after about 15 yards. But in the huddle, McMahon told Barnett to fake the "in" route, break off his pattern and go deep. "Give me time, guys, and we'll get a touchdown," McMahon told the offensive linemen in the huddle.

He was right. Barnett's fake froze cornerback Terry McDaniel and safety Eddie Anderson. Barnett broke free and McMahon hit him with a 42-yard touchdown pass that gave the Eagles a 17-3 lead late in the second quarter. "He called it," Mike Schad remembered. "It was like, 'Eight ball in the corner pocket.' " Added Joyner in admiration: "It was a sandlot play. When you've got a quarterback who can make decisions on the run like that, who is not afraid of the ramifications, good things are going to happen."

Kotite walked into his post-game press conference and announced: "I'm going to say this one time: Cunningham is starting this week." Publicly, McMahon was a good soldier after the game. He accepted his demotion back to the bench without a fuss. "All I wanted to do was go out and get us a win," McMahon insisted. "I don't worry about whether I won a job or not. I'm part of this team and I don't worry about things I don't control. If we start complaining about who's playing and who's not, it's going to divide the team. That's what we don't want."

Cunningham was in an odd mood after the game, even by his standards. He was relaxed and candid and strangely cheerful. He had been critical of Kotite's earlier decision to bench him, but not in a bitter, pouting way. He talked about feeling restricted in the offense. He said he was glad to be back in the lineup.

The next day, November 9, Cunningham stood in front of his locker, wearing a San Francisco 49ers cap, and vowed to be more vocal, more assertive and less understanding. "I don't plan on looking over my shoulder," Cunningham stated. "If they want to put Jim in, that's their decision. But I'll have another decision I'll make later on, after that."

At the other end of the locker room, Joyner sat with his elbows on his knees. He was wearing jeans and a sweatshirt. He was trying to make sense of the quarterback switch—from Cunningham to McMahon and back to Cunningham. "He kind of opened up a can of worms for himself," Joyner said of Kotite. "I said that if Jim went in and had a good game and we won, then what? Where do you go from there? Well, now what? I guess we'll have to wait and see. It will be a long time before you see the full effects of this week."

· 10 ·

THE TRIANGLE

They wouldn't look. They couldn't look. On the day of Jerome Brown's funeral, Seth Joyner and Clyde Simmons stood in the parking lot of the First Baptist Church of Brooksville. Inside the building, hundreds of people filed past the open casket of their friend.

Joyner and Simmons stood under a tall shade tree to avoid the glaring Florida sun. They wore dark suits and sunglasses. They talked quietly with some teammates and exchanged handshakes and hugs, but they stayed far away from the door to the church.

Only after the public viewing and private memorial service were finished, only after Brown's casket was closed, only then did Joyner and Simmons venture inside for the funeral ceremony. "I just couldn't see him like that," Joyner said later. "I didn't want to see him like that. When I think about him, when I dream about him, I want it to be the way he was when he was alive."

Joyner, Simmons and Brown. They were just about inseparable, a triangle formed by an intense, serious-minded linebacker; a quiet, imposing defensive end; and a boisterous, irrepressible defensive tackle. They were a fascinating trio. They were close friends who were so different in background and personality and playing style. Each one complemented the other two, each one brought something different to the mix. "You couldn't separate them," Eagles safety Andre Waters said. "They were like brothers." Defensive tackle Mike Golic agreed: "When Jerome died, we all took it hard. But nobody took it as hard as Seth and Clyde. They had something special together. They couldn't have been any closer."

For Joyner and Simmons, there was only one theme to the 1992 season, only one overriding reason for the Eagles to make the most of their opportunity, to finally realize their potential: to honor Brown's memory. Nothing else really mattered. They talked about it early in training camp. They talked about it before a capacity crowd at the Eagles' annual United Way Kickoff Dinner on August 26 at the Bellevue Hotel in Philadelphia. They talked about it during the season—during midweek interviews and following games, after victories and after losses.

Joyner spent the season with Brown's old jersey number, 99, shaved into the hair on the back of his head. The quieter, more reserved Simmons simply dedicated himself to playing his best season. "Jerome was a winner, and we have to win for him," Simmons said. "That's why we can't stop this year. We can't be stopped. We can't allow ourselves to be stopped until we reach our ultimate goal, which is to win the Super Bowl. That's what Jerome would have wanted."

Ten games into the season, the Eagles didn't look like Super Bowl contenders. They were a confused, disappointed team, uncertain of themselves, uncertain of their coaches. Their special season was spinning out of control. Late on the afternoon of November 15, in a musty old locker room on the second floor of Milwaukee County Stadium, Joyner and Simmons sat in a state close to shock. Just a few minutes earlier, Chris Jacke had kicked a 41-yard field goal on the final play of the game to lift the Green Bay Packers to a stunning 27-24 victory over the Eagles.

Everything was coming apart. The Eagles record was 6-4, with four losses in their last six games. They had been beaten by a Green Bay team that was considered among the weakest clubs in the NFL, a team that had gone 4-12 in 1991 and entered play on that cold afternoon with a 3-6 record in 1992. The Packers had generated 410 yards of offense against the Eagles' defense. They did it behind a second-year quarterback, Brett Favre, who played the final three quarters with a separated left shoulder. The Packers also recovered two fumbles by Philadelphia running backs in the final five minutes of the game.

Joyner and Simmons were devastated. This was a special season? This was a tribute to their fallen friend? Simmons refused to talk after the game, shaking his head sadly and telling a reporter, "Not now." Joyner took a different approach. He stood before his locker and bared his emotions. He talked about his disappointment in the overall defense, in his own play, in the loss and most of all, in the play-calling strategy of coach Rich Kotite. "You've got to have some guts about you and some nuts about you," Joyner warned. "You can't play scared. You can't play not to lose. When you do that, that's what usually happens."

This was nothing new for Joyner. The Eagles' Angry Young Man, Joyner was known to erupt in anger after losses, chastising teammates for not working hard enough, for making mistakes, for failing to bring enough burning intensity to their profession.

Joyner was a brooding, serious-minded man. He had come so far, overcome so many obstacles, to become a star in the NFL that he was unable to take anything for granted. It just wasn't his nature. He grew up in Spring Valley, New York, raised by his mother, Pattie, who had separated from his father when Joyner was a small boy. Joyner was a star running back and linebacker at Spring Valley High School, but he was lightly recruited and accepted a scholarship to the University of Texas-El Paso. Joyner was a four-year starter for UTEP, but he never made any All-America teams, never received any recognition. He wasn't even invited to the scouting combine meetings, a gathering of more than 300 draft-eligible players, held in Indianapolis in February 1986.

Joyner was a good college player, not a great one. He played his first three years at outside linebacker and his senior year at inside linebacker, a position for which he wasn't really suited, according to Eagles player personnel director Joe Woolley. "I think that's what threw a lot of people on him," said Woolley, who scouted Joyner for the Eagles. "You had to go back and look at the tapes of him playing outside [linebacker]. That was where he belonged."

The Eagles selected Joyner in the eighth round of the 1986 draft. He was the 208th player picked. He was so unimpressive that the Eagles cut him at the end of training camp, although they told him to stay in shape. "That really opened my eyes," Joyner recalled. "It was just, like, rejection. It hits you. It makes you realize how quickly something you hope for and dream for can be taken away from you. It made me work harder. I went back to school, thinking I would work toward my degree, but I wanted another chance."

The Eagles called him back on September 17. They released veteran running back Earnest Jackson after trying unsuccessfully for weeks to trade him. They signed Joyner to take Jackson's spot on the roster. Four days later, they lost 33-7 to the Denver Broncos in Veterans Stadium to fall to 0-3 under first-year coach Buddy Ryan. Joyner thought the world of Ryan. He was the coach who drafted him, who cut him, who brought him back, who taught him about the NFL. He was earthy and tough, and he gave the Eagles an identity, and Joyner wanted to be part of that.

Joyner made his first NFL start on October 19 against the New York Giants in place of another rookie, injured outside linebacker Alonzo Johnson. Joyner made 10 tackles that day, and took over the left linebacker spot for good. "The best left linebacker in football," Ryan was calling Joyner by the 1988 season. Hardly anybody believed him. Joyner was a solid, unspectacular player early in his career. He rarely made mistakes, but he rarely made big plays either. He averaged four quarterback sacks, two interceptions, two forced fumbles and one fumble recovery in his first four seasons.

At 6-foot-2, 235 pounds, Joyner was a strong defender against the run from the start of his career. He wasn't much of a pass rusher in his early days, but he was regarded as one of the better man-to-man pass coverage players among linebackers in the NFL. Mostly, Joyner was renowned for his studious approach to the game. He devoured film of opposing teams, coming in to Veterans Stadium on Tuesdays, the players' day off, to watch for tendencies, to pick up clues. On regular practice days, Joyner would stay late at night, long after many of his teammates left the building. Joyner believed in Ryan's gospel: that it wasn't enough to be tough—a player had to be tough and smart. He had to study. It wasn't enough to have the will to win, Ryan often said. A player had to have the will to prepare to win.

That was Joyner. That was Simmons. That was Andre Waters and Wes Hopkins, and Eric Allen, guys who spent hours in darkened film rooms, looking for the smallest of clues—a slight step here, an angle in the stance there. "You see so many of them leaving at night, three or four hours after the others have gone," Kotite said in training camp. "They are in there, studying, studying, studying. What happens with this team, especially with the defense, is that people get caught up as spectators, 'Oh, look at these aggressive guys flying all over the field.' You never think about their mental preparation. They know what it takes to prepare themselves to play in the NFL. You have these overachievers—Andre, Wes, Seth. Seth's not the biggest linebacker in the league. But there's not a better outside linebacker than Seth Joyner. He's self-made. It's because of his determination and his hunger to be the best. That hunger has to do with taking the time, the hours to prepare. A lot of people aren't prepared to do that."

By 1990, Joyner had made himself into a terrific NFL player. He led the Eagles in tackles that season with 132. He set career-bests in sacks with 7.5 and quarterback pressures with 37 and forced fumbles with 3. He was named the Eagles' Defensive MVP by his teammates. Still, it was a season noted mostly for its disappointments. For all his brilliance, Joyner was snubbed in the Pro Bowl voting by his peers around the league, who preferred pass-rushing outside linebackers such as the New York Giants' Lawrence Taylor, New Orleans' Pat Swilling and the Los Angeles Rams' Kevin Greene to all-around players like Joyner. Worse yet, the Eagles lost their first playoff game for the third year in a row, and Ryan was dismissed three days later. "I'll never understand," Joyner said after Ryan was dismissed and replaced by Kotite. "He had built something here and now they're just tearing it apart. You work hard and you sweat and bleed and they just take it all away. They're tearing us apart, limb by limb."

Joyner, Simmons and Brown all needed new contracts to play in 1991. Under NFL rules, players could not report to training camp until they were under contract. The three of them missed all of training camp, taking turns traveling together to Brown's home in Florida, to Simmons' in North Carolina, to Joyner's in Texas. Most players describe their contract holdouts as lonely, difficult ordeals, but Joyner, Simmons and Brown were together, strengthened by their numbers, comforted by their common condition. "That made it easier," Joyner noted. "We supported each other. We weren't alone. We were together. Just about everything we do, we do together."

It wasn't a smooth negotiation for Joyner and Simmons, both of whom were represented by agent Jim Solano. On more than one occasion, according to Solano, Joyner told him to demand a trade from the Eagles. Simmons followed suit. "I'm telling you, Seth wanted out," Solano said when the negotiation finally was over. "He was so angry. He didn't feel the Eagles showed him the respect that he deserves."

Once, the Eagles offered to pay Joyner the same amount that the Atlanta Falcons were going to pay linebacker Jesse Tuggle. Eagles president Harry Gamble told Solano that Joyner and Tuggle were similar players that should have similar contracts. "Tell them to call the Falcons right now and offer to trade me for Jesse Tuggle," Joyner told Solano. "They'll trade him for me in a minute." Solano told Gamble about Joyner's offer. Gamble declined.

Joyner and Simmons finally signed identical, three-year, $3 million contracts on August 28, four days before the season opener in Green Bay. Brown signed a three-year, $3.3 million deal the next day. Angered by Ryan's dismissal, hardened by their contract disputes, the trio went out and put together their best seasons. They helped the Eagles become the first team in 16 years to rank first in the NFL in total defense, pass defense and run defense. All three made the Pro Bowl.

Joyner finally burst into national prominence. He made 110 tackles and 6.5 quarterback sacks. He had three interceptions, six forced fumbles and four fumble recoveries. In a memorable Monday night victory over the Houston Oilers in the Astrodome, Joyner had eight tackles, two sacks, two forced fumbles and two fumble recoveries. He was anointed a star that night by the ABC-TV national broadcast crew. By the end of the season, Joyner was underrated no more: he was named the NFL's Player of the Year by *Sports Illustrated* magazine. "Before I came here, I heard the name Seth Joyner, but I really didn't know who he was," said Eagles defensive coordinator Bud Carson, who joined the team in 1991. "Now everybody is saying they knew how good he was all along. But I had to see him first and when I saw him in the flesh I wondered, 'How come I haven't heard about this guy?' "

Success made Joyner even more outspoken in his criticism of himself, and of others. After the Eagles' 20-6 loss to Washington in the playoff game following the 1990 season, Joyner unleashed a withering attack in the direction of quarterback Randall Cunningham.

Joyner didn't mention Cunningham by name. But he clearly was upset with the quarterback, who had been unable to move the offense and was benched for one series by Ryan. "You have to commit yourself to something," Joyner stormed. "You have to commit yourself to winning. You don't half-ass commit. You put everything you've got into it. If you don't want to do it, fine, then find something else to do. If you want to be selfish, if you want to think about yourself, go be a damn ice skater, run track, play golf or something."

At halftime of the Eagles' final game in 1991, a largely meaningless affair since the Eagles already were eliminated from the playoffs and the Washington Redskins already had clinched the NFC Eastern Division title, Joyner jumped on the team's offensive linemen. The Eagles were behind 13-7. Their offense was pathetic. Their only points were courtesy of an interception return for touchdown. "Block somebody!" Joyner screamed at the offensive linemen in the locker room. "Grab them, hold them, do something! Dammit, do something!"

It was an unbelievable scene. Joyner named names. He pointed fingers. Some of his teammates yelled back. "You don't make it personal, and 59 [Joyner] made it personal," center David Alexander said that day. "He went too far."

"I thought they needed somebody to light a fire under their butts," Joyner returned. "They weren't blocking anybody. They're very upset with me. But I'll be honest with you. I could care less."

Simmons was Joyner's opposite in many ways. Where Joyner was outspoken, Simmons was taciturn. Where Joyner was demanding and often critical of others, Simmons was easy-going and gracious. But they were close friends, bonded by similar circumstances. They had entered the NFL on the same day, in the same way—Joyner an eighth-round pick, Simmons a ninth-round pick. Both were unknown players from smaller college programs. Both made themselves into Pro Bowl players.

Clyde Simmons was born in Lane, South Carolina, and grew up in Wilmington, North Carolina. He was a Babe Ruth League baseball teammate of future basketball superstar Michael Jordan. Simmons became a three-sport star at New Hanover High School in Wilmington, but he was a reluctant athlete. "I started playing football as a way of keeping afternoons from getting too boring," Simmons recalled. "When I got to high school, it was just a way of getting an education. I had no ambition to be a professional football player. I wasn't raised that way. I was raised with the idea of trying to better yourself with education. I thank my mother for that. She showed me about hard work. Growing up without a lot of things can make you work harder for other things."

Simmons said he never thought about playing in the NFL as a youngster. Even when he received a scholarship to Western Carolina University, his first priority was his schooling, not a ticket to the big leagues. "I went to college to get an education," Simmons stressed. "I never dreamed about being a professional football player. When I was young, playing sandlot football, you always pretend you're somebody running with the ball. But I never thought about professional ball, not even when I went to college. Before my senior year I started thinking about it. I knew I had to have a good year to get a look from the scouts."

Simmons was a 235-pound standup defensive end in college. He was a first-team, Division 1-A All-America as a senior, but he was 40 pounds lighter than most top professional prospects at his position. The Eagles made him the 234th pick in the draft. He was an afterthought, a longshot with little chance to make the roster. "I just wanted to make the team," Simmons said. "I wasn't thinking about the Pro Bowl or anything like that. I was a low-round pick and a lot of them don't make it. I just wanted to make the team and try to stick around for a little while."

Simmons became a starter at right defensive end in 1987, his second season, after veteran Greg Brown was traded to Atlanta for defensive tackle Mike Pitts. Simmons had added weight and strength—he was carrying around 260 pounds on his 6-foot-6 frame by his second season— without losing speed and agility. Simmons was a natural pass rusher, with smooth upfield moves and a knack for reaching the quarterback. He had six quarterback sacks in 1987, eight in 1988 and 15.5 in 1989. Like Joyner's, Simmons' progress was gradual—he just seemed to get a little better every year.

But Simmons got better faster than Joyner. He made more big plays. In 1988, he returned a blocked field goal for a touchdown in a dramatic overtime victory over the New York Giants. He also sealed a 1-point victory over Pittsburgh by blocking a late field-goal attempt. In 1989, Simmons returned an interception 60 yards for a touchdown in a victory over the Giants. His 15.5 sacks ranked him fourth in the NFL, but Simmons didn't receive enough votes from his peers around the NFC to make the Pro Bowl.

"Clyde's as good as any defensive end in the league," Eagles defensive end Reggie White commented after Simmons was passed over for the Pro Bowl. "He doesn't get enough recognition. I guess it's because he's quiet. The guys that play with him know how good he is." Simmons had other thoughts: "I'm disappointed but the guys that were chosen deserved to go. I can't say anything against them. I'm just going to have to work harder and maybe my day will come." Simmons was slowed in 1990 by a nagging Achilles tendon that required surgery following the season. He played in all 16 games but managed just eight sacks.

Like Joyner, Simmons broke through in 1991. He set a team record with 4.5 sacks of Dallas quarterback Troy Aikman as the Eagles set a team record with 11 sacks in a 24-0 victory. He had two sacks against Pittsburgh, Cincinnati and the New York Giants. He scored his fourth career touchdown when he recovered a fumble, which was caused by Joyner, in the end zone in Phoenix.

Like Joyner, Simmons finally received some national recognition. In his sixth season, Simmons was voted to the Pro Bowl. He would join Brown, White, Joyner and Allen as five Eagles defenders in the NFL's annual all-star game in Hawaii. "You should have seen Jerome's face when we found out Seth and Clyde made the Pro Bowl," Andre Waters recalled. "He was so happy, so excited. He punched a hole in the meeting-room wall he was so excited." Joyner added: "It's just so special for me and Clyde because of how far we've come. When we go out there, we know there's not going to be a lot of eighth- and ninth-round picks in the Pro Bowl. But we'll be two of them. That's something that only we can understand."

In Hawaii, Brown played in his last football game. Typically, he got into a fight with some American Football Conference offensive linemen and found Joyner and Simmons at his side. The trio also pursued their new passion—golf. "Me and Clyde had been playing for a while, but we decided we had to get Jerome involved," Joyner reminisced. "A lot of times we would be places and we would golf and Jerome wouldn't play. So we got him started. Jerome, he was a good athlete. He was better at it than a lot of people would think. If you knew Jerome, you wouldn't think he would have the temperament to play golf. When we first started, he didn't have the patience to play 18 holes. We would play nine. But Jerome was changing quite a bit. He was growing up. He had come such a long way."

Brown was the loud, mischievous one in the inseparable trio. The other two had worked hard from such humble NFL beginnings. Brown was a former No. 1 draft pick, a tremendously gifted athlete, a player for whom so much came easy. He was always joking, laughing, yelling at Joyner and Simmons. Each personality highlighted the others. Brown lightened up Joyner, loosened up Simmons. They toned him down a bit, taught him the importance of hard work and dedication to their profession.

"I think that's what it was—we just seemed to get along so well," Joyner said. "Me and Clyde, we had worked so hard. We used to tell

Jerome about working out in the weight room, staying in shape, watching his weight. I know it was starting to show with him. That's why he was playing so well. But he had such a great effect on us, too. He could just light you up." Simmons commented: "From Day One, when Buddy drafted him, we just seemed to hit it off. Over the years, the friendship grew into more than just teammates and working companionship. We developed a true concern for one another. It stemmed from the football field, but it grew into something more off the field."

Joyner said his first impressions of Brown were not positive ones. "I don't pull many people close to me," he admitted . "To be honest, I didn't think we'd ever be friends. I knew a guy like that when I first went to college—a good player but real loud. I really didn't like him. Jerome was the same way. He would say things. He had a tendency to step on people's feelings. I just never thought we would get along. Jerome was intimidating to a lot of people. They wouldn't say anything back to him. I was the kind of person who would tell him if he said or did something I didn't like. He liked that. We started to get along and I saw him grow.

"There was a side of Jerome that most people never saw. They just saw Jerome the football player or Jerome the loud-mouth, so to speak. But there was another side to him that showed itself to me and Clyde and some other people, especially in his last couple of years."

Joyner said he was "in shock" when he heard about Brown's death. Joyner was in Los Angeles at the time, filming an appearance on the "American Gladiators," a made-for-television competition. "I guess it didn't really hit me until I got home," he added. "I have this picture on the wall of the three of us—me, Jerome and Clyde. I was looking at it, and I just couldn't believe it."

Joyner was near tears in the locker room following the Eagles' 1992 exhibition season opener in the Hall of Fame Game on August 1 in Canton, Ohio. "It really just hit me again," Joyner said that day. "When I was running on the field, I kept waiting to hear Jerome's voice. When they introduced us, I kept looking for him at the end of the line. He was always waiting for me at the end of the line, always yelling, clapping. He was always there and this time he wasn't there."

Joyner also took the occasion to rip the Eagles organization for starting voluntary camp on July 6, just four days after Brown's funeral; for failing to make any donations to Brown's Youth Foundation; for designing a No. 99 patch for the players' game jerseys that was, in his opinion, too plain. "It just goes to show," he remarked. "You're just a piece of meat to them."

Joyner and Simmons were at midfield, along with White, for the pre-game tribute to Brown before the regular season opener against New Orleans on September 6. Joyner told the capacity crowd in Veterans

Stadium of his love for Brown, of his friend's "charisma." Simmons stood to the side, a silent sentinel. "There's not a day that goes by that I don't think about him," Simmons said later that day. "Some days more than others but he's never out of my mind. You see different things that are going on and it reminds you of things he used to do. I see things that come up, driving down the street or something, and I'll think of him and things we did together."

Simmons was credited with nine quarterback pressures that day. He forced hurried passes by Saints quarterback Bobby Hebert that led to both of the Eagles' interceptions. Joyner had the Eagles' only sack and a forced fumble in a 15-13 victory. "I know he was up there watching," Joyner said after the game.

The Eagles got off to a 4-0 start and it looked like the dream might come true—they might win the Super Bowl for Brown. But things were starting to unravel. Joyner was hobbling with a sore knee. His production was down. Simmons was putting together a big season in terms of sacks— he had 11 entering the Green Bay game—but he was missing Brown, who lined up on his left shoulder for five seasons. The defense was starting to sink in the rankings. The death of Brown and the injuries to Andre Waters, Wes Hopkins and Ben Smith were beginning to take their toll.

Everything came loose against Green Bay. Eric Allen, the Eagles' fifth-year cornerback, later said he looked in his defensive teammates' eyes that day and saw the strangest thing: nothing. "It was like we didn't answer the bell," Allen recalled. "It was the first time I ever remember that happening. It was like, nothing. I was looking at guys and there was nothing. For some series, it was like we were helpless."

The Packers play three home games every season in Milwaukee, along with five in Green Bay. A crowd of 52,689 spectators, many of whom made the two-hour trip down from Green Bay, filled Milwaukee County Stadium on a clear, 28-degree afternoon. The Packers took a 14-3 halftime lead behind Brett Favre, who completed 11 of 11 passes despite the pain and discomfort from a separated shoulder, which he suffered on the second series of the game.

The Eagles got within 14-10 after three quarters, then the game got wild: there were four turnovers and 27 points scored in the final 15 minutes. The Packers scored on a 3-yard pass from Favre to Darrell Thompson. But the Eagles answered with a 75-yard scoring pass from Randall Cunningham to Heath Sherman—a short screen pass followed by a long, winding run by Sherman. "I didn't think I'd have to run that far," Sherman said later. "I almost ran out of gas."

The Eagles then embarked on their oddest drive of the season: 89 yards, 83 of which were generated by two pass-interference penalties. When Herschel Walker crashed into the end zone from 2 yards away, and

Roger Ruzek added the extra point, the Eagles were in front 24-21. Things looked even better for the Eagles when Byron Evans intercepted a Favre pass and returned it to the Green Bay 20 yard line. Evans did a little dance in front of the Packers' bench. The time seemed right to celebrate: with just 5:17 to play, the Eagles looked in control.

But no. On the next play, Sherman burst through the left side for nine yards but hit the ground hard. The football popped loose. The Eagles screamed that Sherman had hit the ground with possession of the football, that the fumble should have been disallowed. But instant replay, which likely would have overturned the call on the field, had been eliminated by the NFL during the owners' meetings in March 1992. Eagles owner Norman Braman was among those who voted for its elimination.

Green Bay's LeRoy Butler had recovered Sherman's fumble and returned it to the 27 yard line. The Packers drove the Eagles' 10, thanks in large part to a 34-yard pass from Favre to Sterling Sharpe, and tied the game when Jacke made a 31-yard field goal with 1:34 left on the clock.

Vai Sikahema returned the ensuing kickoff to the 11 yard line. The Eagles' offense trotted on the field with 1:25 left to play. Kotite said he wanted to get the football out beyond the 20 yard line before switching to the hurry-up offense.

On first down, Walker gained nine yards over the left side. On second down, the Eagles tried the same play to the right side, but Walker was hit by Don Davey, a defensive lineman who had been signed by the Packers just four days earlier, and the football came loose. Green Bay linebacker Johnny Holland recovered at the 23 yard line with 0:43 to play.

The Packers ran one play for no gain, then let the clock run down before calling time out with 0:03 left. Jacke trotted on the field. The crowd rose to its feet. The snap, the hold and the kick were perfect: 27-24, Green Bay, on the final play of the game.

"Disbelief" was the way Allen described the feeling among his teammates as Jacke's sure, solid kick cut through the uprights. "There's no way we should have lost this game." Center David Alexander agreed: "Right now, I think everybody's kind of in shock. It's kind of hard to believe."

The Eagles' only source of solace that day was from the scoreboard of games around the league. Dallas lost to the Los Angeles Rams. Washington lost to Kansas City. The New York Giants lost to Denver. Minnesota lost to Houston.

The Eagles still were tied for second place in the NFC Eastern Division, still just two games behind the Cowboys. But something was wrong and Joyner knew it. "We've got to get our act together, from the coaches on down," he said. "I don't understand the way we do some things. I don't understand the thinking. You can't play scared in this league. You have to play to win. You have to play with confidence, not like you're afraid to lose."

At issue was Kotite's play-calling when the Eagles took possession at their own 11 yard line with 1:25 left in the game. Joyner and some other players thought the Eagles should have gone immediately to their hurry-up offense and attacked the Packers. "You've got to be all-out," Joyner insisted. "You've got to have some guts, you've got to play to win and go for it. Pass the ball. They're sitting up there in an eight-man line, waiting for you to run. What do you think you're going to accomplish?"

Byron Evans went a step further. He invoked the name of former coach Buddy Ryan, wistfully remembering the Eagles' approach under their old boss. "The Philadelphia Eagles have always played to win," Evans argued. "Now we're playing not to lose. We always played to win under Buddy Ryan. We're not doing that anymore. We're playing not to lose and when you do that, you're asking to lose."

Joyner was disgusted. Simmons was disgusted. The season that seemed so special in the summer was dissolving in disappointment. This wasn't the plan. This wasn't the idea. This wasn't a tribute to Jerome Brown.

"Maybe it's me," Joyner wondered. He was angry and exasperated. He looked around the emptying locker room, his eyes smoldering like fires inside two caves. "Somebody explain it to me," he pleaded. "I just don't see the logic. I don't understand. If you play the game that way, bad things are going to happen and that's just what happened."

· 11 ·

UNLIKELY HEROES

Like every NFL team, the Eagles were a wild bunch of oddballs and eccentrics, a loose union of iconoclasts, a repository of rebels and regular guys. Only more so.

This team had more than talent. It had personality. The Eagles had more than All-Pros and established veterans and rising stars. They also had a cast of unforgettable characters. "I've played on a few teams," said reserve linebacker Ken Rose, who had played for the Saskatchewan Rough Riders in the Canadian Football League, the Tampa Bay Bandits in the United States Football League and the New York Jets and Cleveland Browns in the NFL before hooking up with the Eagles. "But I've never been around a team like this. It's different. It's loose. There's just a lot of togetherness and a lot of craziness in this locker room."

This was a team whose most ferocious defensive player was a licensed minister, a large, powerful man who often told opponents, "Jesus is coming," before unleashing an otherworldly amount of controlled violence. Reggie White was a man of peace, love, understanding and quarterback sacks.

This was a team whose star quarterback's stylish grace on the field stood in direct contrast to his awkward self-consciousness off the field. Randall Cunningham was a mystery man to more people than just opposing defenders.

This was a team whose strong safety taped motivational slogans to his head and described himself as a "beast, an animal." Andre Waters was regarded by many outsiders as the dirtiest man in the NFL. But he also was tireless in his charity work, zealous in his religious faith, remarkable in his devotion to underprivileged children.

This was a team whose menacing middle linebacker, Byron Evans, was a muscular, hard-hitting athlete who shaved his head and scowled and downplayed his lack of recognition because "I don't want to be on the cover of *TV Guide*." This was a team whose star running back, Herschel Walker, was an Olympic bobsledder, martial arts expert, exercise fanatic and former ballet performer. This was a team whose backup quarterback, Jim McMahon, was a former Super Bowl hero who had cut off his ponytail but still strutted through the locker room wearing colorful tights, an earring, sunglasses and a Joe Cool smirk.

"This team is not just a bunch of professionals who work together," offensive star Keith Byars observed, looking back after the 1992 season was over. "We really do have a very close, very tight team. We see each other a lot all year around. There's a real feeling of togetherness on this team. I remember, right before Jerome's death, we were all sitting around at Keith Jackson's charity benefit in Little Rock, Arkansas. Who would have thought it would have been the last time we were all together, just hanging out like we did all the time in the locker room, just being ourselves?"

The NFL season is a war of attrition. It's a long, difficult campaign, and a team needs every one of its 47 active players. It's not enough to have a few stars, a couple of characters. By late November, NFL teams often rise and fall on the quality of their reserves, on the ability of their lesser-known players to step into crucial situations and make the difference between winning and losing.

The Eagles' record was 6-4. They had lost four of their last six games. It was getting cold. It was getting late. The Eagles would need all their weapons for a pivotal November 22 game against the New York Giants in Giants Stadium in East Rutherford, New Jersey.

They would need Vai Sikahema, the 30-year-old kick returner who had been signed by the team during the Plan B free agency period the previous spring. Sikahema had been left "unprotected" by the Green Bay Packers, which meant he was free to sign with any team. Sikahema was living the American Dream. He was the hero of a classic immigrant tale, with a slight twist.

Sikahema came East, not West. He crossed the Pacific Ocean, not the Atlantic. He landed not in New York harbor, hard by the Statue of Liberty, but in Phoenix, just south of the Grand Canyon. But it was the same old story, the one told and retold of immigrants who fled the poverty of their homeland in search of something better in America.

"My parents wanted a better life for their children," Sikahema said of the long, difficult trip that took him, his parents and his brother and sister from their tiny village in the South Pacific island of Tonga to the land of opportunity.

Now, Sikahema was a key member of the Eagles. He was an established NFL player, the league leader among active players in punt-return yardage, a wealthy man who had made well over $1 million in his professional career. But 21 years earlier, Sikahema was a stranger in a strange land, a small, frightened foreigner living with his family in a garage apartment in oppressive heat.

"Our first summer in Phoenix was the summer of '71," Sikahema recalled. "It was 115 [degrees] at times and it probably averaged about 110. We had two fans blowing the hot air around." His father, Loni, worked in a Mexican-food cannery, stirring vats of refried beans. He made $1.79 an hour. "To a child, everything is magnified," Vai Sikahema noted. "All I'd known my whole life was ocean water, coconut palms and 80-degree weather. It was horrible."

Sikahema had been born in the Tongan village of Nuka'Alofa. He was raised on a coconut plantation. His first job was gathering wood. Later, he helped remove coconut meat from shells and prepare it for drying. "That's how we made our living," Sikahema said. "My family had done that for generations. But there wasn't much of a future there for us. Fortunately, my parents had the foresight to know that if we were going to make anything of ourselves, our opportunities were here in the states and not drying coconut meat in the South Pacific."

Loni and Ruby Sikahema, who had met at a Mormon school in Tonga, placed their three children with grandparents and left the island to prepare the way for Vai and his brother and sister. They went first to Hawaii and then to Phoenix, where Loni's brother was living. "I had a dream," Loni Sikahema remembered, looking back on his decision to come to America. "Even though Tonga is one of the most beautiful islands in the world, I wanted to come to the mainland, to the place where people come to fulfill their dreams."

Loni had done some boxing in Tonga. He took his son to a gym in the Phoenix area three or four times a week, to learn to box, to learn to defend himself. A natural athlete with strength and speed and toughness, Vai Sikahema became a good boxer. At the age of 13, he was the Arizona state Golden Gloves champion at 147 pounds. "I wanted my son to be the champion of the world," Loni Sikahema stated. "But one time we were driving home from a fight and he said he didn't want to box anymore. He said I was always telling him when he made mistakes. I was his manager. I was supposed to tell him. I didn't want the other boy to hit him in the face. But he wanted to play football. He said I wouldn't know when he was making mistakes."

Reggie White, Clyde Simmons, Seth Joyner

Vai Sikahema

Cunningham against Minnesota

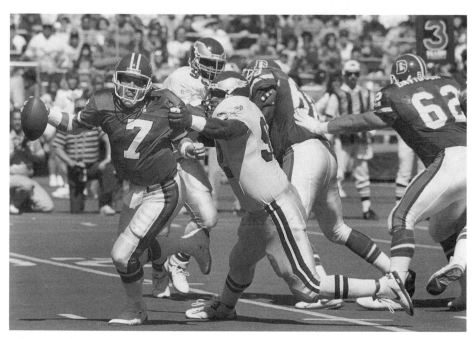

White sacks Denver's John Elway

Williams against Denver

Fred Barnett scores against Denver

Reggie White hits New York Giants' Jeff
Hostetler

Jeff Hostetler injured after hit by Eagles' Mike Golic

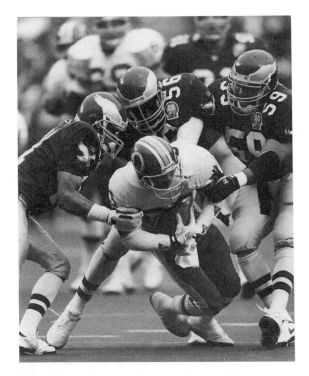

Eric Allen, Byron Evans, Joyner hit
Rickey Sanders

Ken Rose after scoring TD against Giants

Herschel Walker

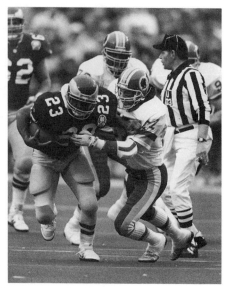

Heath Sherman

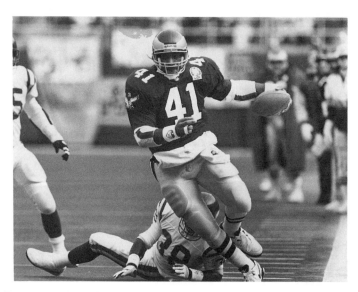

Byars against Minnesota

Barnett leaps against Giants

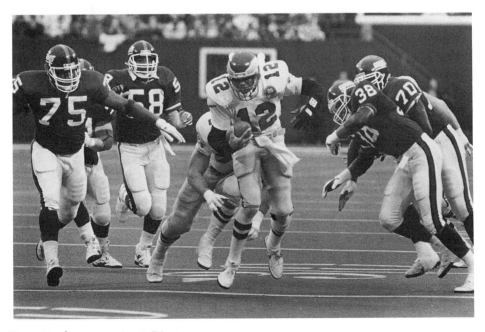

Cunningham against Giants

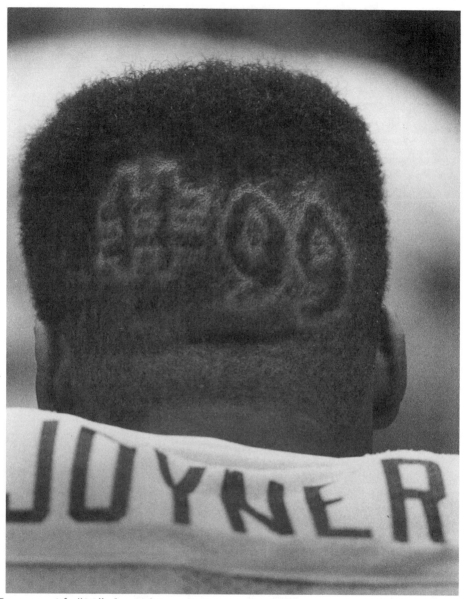

Joyner with "99" shaved into hair

Vai Sikahema had seen some football games on television. He had heard his friends talk about it. But he really didn't understand it. "Baseball and football were really popular with the kids I was friends with," Vai Sikahema remembered. "I remember collecting cards and watching games on TV and not really knowing what was going on. By the time I got to high school, one of the coaches pulled me aside and asked me if I wanted to go out for the team. I said no. One, because I didn't know the rules and two, because I couldn't afford the equipment. He said you don't have to pay for the equipment. You just have to pay for the shoes. I told him I couldn't afford the shoes. The next day he bought me a pair of Puma football shoes and told me I didn't have any more excuses."

Still, there was the sticky matter of his father's feelings on the subject. Loni Sikahema didn't want his son to play football. "He didn't like it because it took me away from the gym," Vai said. "But my father is a man of principle. He understood that the primary reason for bringing us here was our education. Knowing that, I told him that football was part of the education program at school. I sort of lied."

Vai Sikahema became a great high school football player, and his father became his greatest fan. Vai was a two-time all-state quarterback at Mesa High School, and his father was a fixture at his games, a sideline regular who danced alongside the cheerleaders. "The first game I went to, he made three touchdowns," Loni Sikahema reminisced. "I was so happy, I danced around the end zone. They know me all over here. I would dance and steal their hearts."

Vai Sikahema went to Brigham Young University on a football scholarship and then on to the St. Louis Cardinals of the NFL. He was twice named to the Pro Bowl as a return man, and he set virtually every Cardinals punt-return record. The Cardinals let him go after the 1990 season, and he signed with Green Bay. He played just one season for the Packers and now, at age 30, he was finishing his career with the Eagles. "This is my last stop," Sikahema declared. "I want a chance to play for a Super Bowl team before I retire."

Ken Rose was 30 and near the end of his career, too. At 6-foot-1, 215 pounds, Rose was the smallest linebacker on the team, but he was a devoted weight-lifter who was known for his strength, his intensity and his intelligence. He was the captain of the Eagles special teams. Born and raised in Sacramento, California, Rose had played with Eagles quarterback Randall Cunningham at the University of Nevada-Las Vegas. Rose wasn't drafted by any NFL team and he played two seasons for the Saskatchewan Rough Riders of the Canadian Football League. He also spent a season with the Tampa Bay Bandits of the United States Football League.

Rose was nothing if not persistent. He was determined to play in the

NFL. He tried out for the NFL's Tampa Bay Buccaneers in 1984, the NFL's Los Angeles Raiders in 1985 and the NFL's New York Jets in 1987. He was cut in training camp by each team. "I was determined to play in the NFL," Rose once said. "It was just a matter of keep knocking, keep knocking, keep knocking on the door." He finally caught on with the Jets when the union players went on strike two games into the 1987 season. Rose played all three games with the Jets replacement team and stuck on the roster when the regular players returned to work.

Rose played for the Jets through 1989. He played in Cleveland for seven games in 1990. But when the Browns fired Bud Carson—the veteran coach who had been the defensive coordinator in New York during Rose's time with the Jets and would meet up with him again in Philadelphia—Rose was released "five minutes later," he said. Rose signed with the Eagles a week later. He played just eight games for that 1990 Philadelphia team, which would finish 10-6, lose to Washington in the first round and see its coach, Buddy Ryan, fired three days later. But Rose was named special-teams Most Valuable Player in a vote of his teammates.

With a long black ponytail, Rose was one of the most distinctive-looking players in the Eagles locker room. He also had some creative interests away from the game: he had been a regular on the Home Box Office cable television series "First and Ten," had appeared in commercials for Pepsi and Gatorade and in a Bruce Willis movie entitled *The Last Boy Scout*

Rookie cornerback Mark McMillian was slated to see his first extended amount of NFL playing time that week against the Giants. The 5-foot-7, 162-pound McMillian was the lightest player on the Eagles roster and one of the lightest in the NFL. McMillian hadn't played organized football until his senior year at John F. Kennedy High School in south central Los Angeles, an area that would be devastated by riots in the spring of 1992. He was 130 pounds when his mother, Gloria, told him to go out for the team. "She said that was the only way I was going to go to college," he later recalled. "She wasn't going to be able to come out of pocket to pay for me to go to school."

McMillian went to nearby Glendale Community College and then to the University of Alabama, where he started 21 games as a junior and senior. The Eagles selected him in the tenth round of the 1992 draft, with the 272nd overall pick. He made the team with his impressive man-to-man coverage skills. "The best coverage cornerback I've seen enter the NFL in a long, long time," Carson said of McMillian in training camp.

Mark McMillian was one half of the Eagles' dynamic, diminutive duo of draft choices. The other was kick returner Jeff Sydner, a 5-foot-6, 170-pounder whom the Eagles had selected in the sixth round of the draft from the University of Hawaii. With their small stature and boyish looks, McMillian and Sydner had been nicknamed "Kris Kross" by their teammates, after the popular rap-music group that was led by two preteens. In fact, quarterback Jim McMahon had hung up a poster of the group on the wall next to his locker and pasted cut-out pictures of the faces of McMillian and Sydner over the faces of the two rap stars. "They're like two eighth-graders," Eagles coach Rich Kotite once commented. "When we go to a hotel the night before a game, they come running up to me and asking, 'Can we go to Red Lobster for dinner?' "

Wide receiver Fred Barnett's start in football was exactly the opposite of McMillian's. Barnett was a great athlete at Rosedale High School in Gunnison, Mississippi. He was a two-time Most Valuable Player for the basketball team and set the state record in the high jump with a leap of 6 feet, 11 inches. But Barnett wasn't allowed to play football until his senior year because his mother, Earlean, a devout Jehovah's Witness, thought the sport was too dangerous. "I didn't want him to get hurt," Earlean Barnett recalled. "Finally, I got tired of listening to him and I said, 'OK.' But the first time I went to see him play I couldn't believe it. He got the ball, and I said, 'All those boys are trying to hurt Fred.' "

The other starting wide receiver, Calvin Williams, had played basketball as well as football at famed Dunbar High School in his hometown of Baltimore. Williams had a hotel and restaurant management degree from Purdue University, loved to cook and dreamed of opening his own restaurant.

Reserve wide receiver Roy Green was the team's oldest player at age 36. Green was in his fourteenth NFL season but had played in just one playoff game. That was back during the strike-shortened 1982 season, when the expanded playoff field consisted 16 teams, including his own St. Louis Cardinals. "That's all I'm playing for now," Green had said in training camp. "I've done all I can as an individual. I want to feel what it's like to get into the playoffs with a chance to get to the Super Bowl."

Left tackle Ron Heller's career had been resurrected when he was traded to the Eagles a week before the start of the 1988 season. Heller had played four seasons with Tampa Bay, was traded to Seattle in the 1988 off-season, then traded again to the Eagles. In his four seasons in Tampa, Heller played for teams that won a total of 14 games. In his first four seasons in Philadelphia, Heller played for teams that won a total of 41 games. "It's an honor just to play on this team," the 30-year-old Heller once said.

A native of upstate New York and a graduate of Penn State with a degree in administration of justice, Heller was one of the more insightful athletes on the team. He had received the "Good Guy" award from the Philadelphia Sports Writers Association in 1989. "See," Heller had told his family and friends in the audience at the association's banquet that night. "That's why I'm always late coming out of the locker room."

Center David Alexander was among the team's most durable players.

Alexander had grown up in Broken Arrow, Oklahoma and attended the University of Tulsa. He was the Eagles' fifth-round draft choice in 1987, and he had been a starter since the middle of the 1988 season. Against the Giants, Alexander would make his 71st consecutive start, the longest streak among the team's offensive linemen.

Left guard Mike Schad was one of the few native Canadians in the NFL. Born in Trenton, Ontario, Schad had starred at Queen's University in Kingston, Ontario. The Los Angeles Rams picked him in the first round of the 1986 draft, making him the highest-ranked Canadian ever selected in the NFL draft.

Injuries slowed Schad's development with the Rams. He was left unprotected in the Plan B free agency period in 1989 and signed by the Eagles, who made him a starter. Schad started for the Eagles in 1989 and 1990 but missed all of the 1991 season with a back injury. "That was the darkest road I've ever been down," Schad admitted. "I'll never forget the feeling of isolation. It was the worst feeling in the world."

In 1992, Schad would return to the starting lineup, thanks in part to an extensive rehabilitation program that included learning karate. "I didn't know what I was getting into at first," Schad said of his karate classes. "But I have nothing but good feelings after a year of depression. It's given me the eye of the tiger again."

Right guard Eric Floyd had been signed by the Eagles in the Plan B free agency period in the spring of 1992. Floyd had played two seasons for San Diego, but the Chargers left him "unprotected" and the Eagles paid him a signing bonus of $50,000 to come to Philadelphia. Actually, the Eagles thought they were getting a different starting right guard in Plan B. They spent $110,000 to outbid the New England Patriots for John Bruhin, who had played four seasons for Tampa Bay. But Bruhin was a bust in training camp, and Floyd emerged as a starter.

Floyd was a big, laid-back athlete who had been raised in Rome, Georgia. He played at Auburn University but wasn't drafted by an NFL team. He was cut twice by the Chargers before finally sticking on their development squad for rookies and first-year players in 1989.

At 6-foot-5, 310 pounds, Floyd was the biggest starting guard in Eagles history. He combined with 325-pound tackle Antone Davis to give the Eagles 635 pounds of push on the right side of the offensive line. "That's a lot of man," line coach Bill Muir said of the combination.

Antone Davis was something of an enigma. The Eagles had traded two No. 1 draft picks in 1991 to move into position to select Davis, who was generally regarded as the best offensive lineman in college football during his senior season at the University of Tennessee. Because the team had invested so much in him, Davis was under tremendous pressure as a rookie. He had trouble adjusting to the NFL, allowing 12 sacks and committing 12 penalties. He was criticized for being overweight and out of shape. "I just took the approach that the people criticizing me didn't know what they were talking about," Davis remarked. "I knew I was getting better. I could feel myself improving, even if nobody else could."

Davis was the youngest of seven children. He had been born and raised in Fort Valley, Georgia. He was a quiet, sensitive athlete who felt he had been unfairly criticized by the media during the 1991 season. Davis was a much improved player in 1992. He cut down on his sacks allowed and penalties, although he still wasn't a dominant player. His progress was gradual, and his lapses would create anew concerns that the Eagles had made a major mistake by spending two No. 1 draft picks for him.

On Wednesday, November 18, four days before the game against the Giants, running back Keith Byars approached coach Rich Kotite with a proposal: Byars would be willing to play tight end on a full-time basis. The move would clear a spot in the starting lineup for running back Heath Sherman, who had been the team's most productive offensive player the last two games.

Sherman was nicknamed "Teen Wolf" by his teammates because of his prominent widow's peak. "Feed the Wolf," his teammates would yell, demanding that Sherman get the football.

Sherman was a pool aficionado, and the 1992 season was his best-ever bank shot. He was a serious student of the game made famous in movies such as *The Hustler* and *The Color of Money*. Sherman had a pool table in his home, and he said he racked 'em up nearly every day. "It's a great game because every time you play, it's going to be a little different game than the last time," Sherman noted.

But no three-cushion carom shot could have been as improbable as Sherman's reemergence as a prominent member of the Eagles' offensive backfield. He would bounce back in a big way. Regarded as a longshot to make the team before training camp, Sherman would become a key player in the offense as the Eagles headed into the stretch run of the season. Sherman, a sixth-round draft choice out of tiny Texas A&I in 1989, was a featured runner for the Eagles in 1990. He ran for 685 yards and put together back-to-back, 100-yard games, including a 124-yard performance in a Monday night victory over the Washington Redskins.

By his own admission, Sherman rested a little on his laurels during the off-season following his breakthrough in 1990. He didn't work out as much as he should have. He added some weight, lost some quickness and found himself in serious trouble when he reported to training camp in 1991 after missing three exhibition games in a contract dispute.

"It was my own fault," Sherman admitted. "It was a long season, and I guess I just didn't do much during the off-season. I stayed at home, mostly. I didn't work out that much. I did a little but not that much. When I got to training camp I wasn't quick or in tune. I was out of shape. I was a little overweight also. You think to yourself, 'I should have done this, I should have done that.' But it was too late at that time. It's kind of hard to try to get in shape during the season."

Sherman's statistics tumbled in 1991. He ran for just 279 yards. His 2.6-yard average was dead last among the 76 NFL rushers with 200 or more yards. He gained just 85 yards in the final 10 games. "It was just something that I went through and hopefully I learned something from it," Sherman recalled. "It should have never happened. But I think I learned a lot from that. It will never happen like that again."

Sherman's career with the Eagles looked over when the team used two of its first three draft choices to select running backs—Alabama's Siran Stacy in the second round, and Notre Dame's Tony Brooks in the fourth round—and signed Herschel Walker as a free agent. Sherman said the possibility of playing for another team crossed his mind. But his first priority was to get in shape and make the most of whatever chance he got in a crowded rotation in training camp.

With Walker slowed by sore ribs, second-year man James Joseph slowed by a sore knee and Stacy and Brooks struggling to adjust to the NFL, Sherman was by far the Eagles' best runner in exhibition games. He led the team with 131 yards on 35 carries and scored two touchdowns. "He's like a bowling ball, and those pins scatter when he hits people," Eagles coach Rich Kotite said of Sherman in training camp.

Sherman ran eight times for 50 yards, including a 34-yard scamper, in the season-opening victory over New Orleans. Then he virtually disappeared: he had a total of two carries in the next five games and a total of seven carries in the next seven games. But as the Eagles prepared for the November 22 game against the Giants, Sherman was beginning to emerge as a featured member of their offense. He had gained 81 yards on just nine carries in the 31-10 victory over the Los Angeles Raiders on November 8. His 30-yard touchdown run that day was the longest by an Eagles running back since Herman Hunter went 74 yards against Dallas on November 24, 1985.

Sherman continued his big-play ways the next week against Green Bay in Milwaukee. He ran six times for 31 yards, including a 17-yard touchdown, and he took a screen pass from Randall Cunningham 75 yards for a touchdown. It was just another bank shot for Sherman. He learned to play pool as a youngster in a club called "The Squeeze Inn" that was managed by his mother in Spanish Camp, Texas. He would play after school. The bus driver would drop him off at the club, and he would play pool while waiting for his mother to get off work. "Sometimes there wouldn't be hardly anybody in the club at that time of the day so I would be in there shooting pool," Sherman remembered. "That was back when I was 8 or 9. Ever since then, I've been playing pool all the time."

Defensive tackle Mike Golic was the product of a football family. His father, Louis, played seven seasons in the Canadian Football League. His brother, Bob, was a former Pro Bowler who, at the age of 35, was still playing for the Los Angeles Raiders.

Golic was a self-deprecating guy who once chalked up a batted pass to his "two-inch vertical leap." In the week before the Raiders played the Eagles in Veterans Stadium on November 8, Golic noted that neither he nor his brother had a quarterback sack yet in the season. "We always have a race," Golic said. "Usually, when one of us gets one, it's an insurmountable lead."

Defensive tackle Andy Harmon was a young player on the rise. The Eagles' sixth-round pick out of Kent State in Ohio in 1991, Harmon had become an active, productive player. He would finish 1992 with eight quarterback sacks, an especially high total for an inside pass rusher.

Harmon was born in Dayton, Ohio, and raised in nearby Centerville. He was a three-year starter at Kent State, a school not known for turning out NFL players, and admitted to feeling slightly in awe of his current situation. "When you think about the odds of making a professional team, especially when you go to a small school—I just never gave it much thought," Harmon once said. "You watch Reggie White on TV every Sunday after you watch game films in college, and you just say, 'Wow, what a stud.' And now here you are playing with him. It's a weird experience."

Veteran defensive tackle Mike Pitts, who would rotate with Golic and Harmon, was in the twilight of a good career. Pitts had been a No. 1 draft pick by the Atlanta Falcons back in 1983. The Eagles acquired him in a trade for defensive end Greg Brown just before the start of the 1987 season. Born in Pell City, Alabama, Pitts had moved to Baltimore with his family and attended Polytechnic High School in that city. He returned to his home state to play for legendary coach Bear Bryant at the University of Alabama, where he was a two-time All-America selection.

Right linebacker William Thomas had started seven games as a rookie in 1991 for the NFL's top-ranked defense. Thomas was the Eagles' fourth-round draft pick in 1991 out of Texas A&M. Born and raised in Amarillo, Texas, Thomas was considered undersized by NFL standards. He stood 6-foot-2, but weighed just 218 pounds. He had been a free safety early in his college career before converting to linebacker. "I eat and eat and eat, but I just don't gain weight," Thomas once said.

Rich Miano was starting at strong safety in place of the injured Andre Waters. Miano had been born in Newton, Massachusetts, but moved with his family to Hawaii as a teenager. Miano attended the University of Hawaii on a diving scholarship. He made the football team as a walk-on, and he was a sixth-round draft pick by the New York Jets in 1985.

Miano's professional career looked over in 1989. He underwent major reconstructive knee surgery and sat out that season and all of 1990. The Jets released him, and he was selling real estate when the Eagles called in the spring of 1991.

Miano decided to try a comeback. He made the team as a backup to starting safeties Waters and Wes Hopkins. When Waters went down with a fractured fibula October 18, 1992, Miano moved into the starting lineup. "There's not a safety in the league that plays the run as well as Andre," Miano claimed. "I know I'm not going to be as aggressive as he was or the same kind of run player that he was. I have to play my own game. That's the best thing I can do to replace him, just be myself and play my all-around game. Andre is a great player. But injuries happen in this league, and you have to be prepared to move on. He knows that. The best thing I can do for him is to play as well as I can in his absence."

The Eagles' punter was Jeff Feagles, who excelled at kicking the football inside the opponents' 20 yard line. Feagles had led the NFL with 29 punts inside the 20 in 1991. He was third in the league and first in the conference, in the same category with 26 in 1992.

Born in Anaheim, California, and raised in Scottsdale, Arizona, Feagles was an avid golfer who compared trying to punt the football inside the 20 to trying to land a golfball on the green. "The 5 yard line is the green," Feagles once said. "The end zone is a trap."

Roger Ruzek was the Eagles' place kicker. A native of San Francisco, Ruzek played at Weber State in Utah and started his professional career with the New Jersey Generals of the United States Football League. Ruzek spent little more than two years with the Dallas Cowboys but was released by them on November 6, 1989. The Eagles signed him on November 22 of that year, and the next day he was kicking for Philadelphia in a Thanksgiving Day victory over Dallas in Texas Stadium. He made both of his field-goal attempts and recovered a fumble.

In 1991, Ruzek made a remarkable 28 of 33 field-goal attempts for the Eagles. He also made a 38-yard field goal with 0:17 to play to lift the team to a 24-22 victory over the soon-to-be Super Bowl champion Washington Redskins in the regular-season finale. "I wouldn't trade him for any other kicker," Kotite said of Ruzek during training camp.

This loose, talented team was in serious trouble in the week before the Giants game. Kotite was trying desperately to pull the team together, but it wasn't going to be easy. The Eagles were shocked by the loss to Green Bay, which dropped their record to 6-4 and created all kinds of concerns about the defense; about the benching of Cunningham; about the discipline, dedication and focus of the team under Kotite's leadership.

The season of great expectations, the special season that was dedicated to the memory of Jerome Brown, was careening out of control.

The controversial comments by linebackers Seth Joyner and Byron Evans in the locker room in Milwaukee County Stadium in the bitter aftermath of the loss to the Packers had turned up the heat on Kotite. This was the most direct, defiant challenge to his authority. He needed to do something.

On the day after the game, Kotite fired back. In a meeting with the team before they reviewed the game films, Kotite told the players to be certain their own performance was above reproach before they started pointing fingers at him. It was the old "glass-houses" speech, but Kotite had a point: the players who had been most critical of him were part of a defense that was burned for 410 yards and 27 points by the Packers. "Check your own performance," Kotite told the players. "Look in your own yard before you look in somebody else's. We've all got a job to do here. You better be sure you've done yours as well as you can before you start talking about how somebody else did theirs."

The Giants had problems of their own. They were grumbling about head coach Ray Handley, who would be fired after the season, and defensive coordinator Rod Rust. Without legendary linebacker Lawrence Taylor, whose season was ended when he tore his Achilles tendon two weeks earlier, the Giants were just a shadow of the team that had won the Super Bowl after the 1990 season.

Four days before the game against the Eagles, Giants linebacker Pepper Johnson created a stir when he ripped Handley and Rust and suggested that maybe the defensive players ought to take matters into their own hands rather than follow the game plan. "Mutiny," screamed the headline in the next day's *New York Post*.

Johnson was Keith Byars' best friend. He had been best man at Byars' wedding. In 1990, the Giants were 10-0 when they visited Veterans Stadium. The Eagles blew them away 31-13. The most memorable moment: Byars' bone-jarring, blind-side block of Johnson, who was chasing a scrambling Randall Cunningham. When the replay was shown on the Phan-O-Vision screen near the top of the stadium, the players in the Eagles' huddle were so preoccupied with watching it that they needed to call a timeout to avoid a delay of game penalty. "I'll be telling him about that one when we're both old and gray," Byars had remarked after the game.

The Eagles had plenty of good memories of playing the Giants. Since 1988, they were 7-1 against the Giants, who had won two NFC Eastern Division titles and a Super Bowl crown in that span. This time, the Eagles went into Giants Stadium and promptly fell behind by a 20-6 score. The Giants got a pair of field goals from Matt Bahr and a pair of touchdowns from scatback Dave Meggett—the first on a 14-yard pass from quarter-back Jeff Hostetler, the second on a 92-yard kickoff return.

The Eagles' only points came on a 21-yard touchdown pass from Cunningham to Walker, who slid out of the backfield into the left flat, caught the football and raced untouched into the end zone. But it was a sign of the Eagles' problems that kicker Roger Ruzek would miss the extra point.

Ahead 20-6, the Giants had possession of the football at their own 40 yard line when they lost control of the game. On a second-and-three, the Giants tried a pass, but Hostetler threw the football away and was nailed by Golic. Hostetler was obviously shaken up on the play, but the Giants tried another pass on third down. This time, Hostetler was chased out of the pocket by blitzing safety Wes Hopkins. Hostetler tried to throw the football across his body and across the field to Meggett.

Joyner read the play, reached out and intercepted the pass and raced 43 yards into the end zone. Meggett gave desperate chase but never closed ground on the Eagles' linebacker. After crossing the goal line, Joyner fired the football against the blue wall behind the end zone. It ricocheted back to Hopkins, who did the same thing. "That was the play that got us started," Kotite said after the game. Joyner, who had sworn off interviews for the rest of the season earlier in the week, said nothing.

The Eagles dominated the rest of the game. They would score 40 points in the second and third quarters. After Joyner's touchdown made it 20-13, Walker ran 11 yards for a score to tie it at 20-20 at halftime.

The third quarter was remarkable. In one stretch, the Giants snapped the football 22 times in a row. They didn't score a point in that period, while the Eagles scored 14. The Eagles took a 27-20 lead when Cunningham escaped a pass rush and shoveled a short pass to Byars, who caught the football at his shoe tops, turned and raced into the end zone. The 38-yard touchdown gave the Eagles their first lead and set the stage for the most remarkable sequence of the season. It was all special teams. First, Ken Rose broke through the middle of the line and blocked a punt by Sean Landeta. Rose picked up the football and staggered three yards into the end zone for the first touchdown of his NFL career. "We needed that," Rose said after the game. "After we let them get a touchdown on that kickoff return, we wanted to make amends. You make a play like that, it just gets your heart thumping."

Next, Sikahema took a long Landeta punt, skirted to the right, cut back and raced 87 yards for a touchdown. It was the longest punt return in Eagles history. After racing through the end zone, Sikahema stopped at the goal-post support and began working the padding like a heavy bag. He threw left hooks, right crosses, even an uppercut. "I worked the body," Sikahema recalled later in the Eagles' locker room. "Not like some of these younger fighters who go for the head. I know better. I know you have to work the body. I had gone to the Art Museum in Philadelphia last week, and it reminded me of Rocky Balboa, so that was for him." Sikahema's touchdown gave the Eagles a 40-20 lead. They would add another score on a 30-yard touchdown by Sherman in the fourth quarter. The Giants added two meaningless touchdowns to make the final score 47-34.

It was a typically wild and weird victory for the Eagles in Giants Stadium. The place wasn't an opposing stadium to the Eagles as much as a Fun House. "We were telling the young guys all about the stuff that happens up here," Eagles cornerback Eric Allen said after another mind-bending romp through the Meadowlands. "They hadn't been through it, so they had to see it for themselves. Now they believe." Safety Wes Hopkins added: "I was telling guys, 'No matter what happens, we're going to make big plays and beat the Giants.' It's just something we have over them. It's just past experience."

The Eagles' victory would have been even more bizarre if it wasn't so typical. The sight of Joyner, Rose and Sikahema racing into the Giants' end zone might have been even more startling if they weren't preceded there over the years by Herm Edwards, Rich Kraynak, Clyde Simmons and Andre Waters. The Eagles had occasionally scored touchdowns in Giants Stadium by conventional means. They had run for some, passed for some. But they always seemed to beat the Giants, again and again, by the most unusual methods. This game's trio of return touchdowns wasn't so much a shocking development as the continuation of a remarkable trend. "Bizarre things always happen when we come up here," Byars claimed. "It's just something that we believe is going to happen. It just carries over from year to year."

The craziness started back in 1978 with the "Miracle of the Meadowlands," cornerback Herman Edwards' unforgettable fumble return for a touchdown. The games got pretty quiet after that. There was Kraynak's return of a blocked punt for a touchdown in 1984, but mostly there was a series of routine affairs—three victories in a row by the Eagles from 1979 through 1981, five victories in six games for the Giants from 1982 through 1987. Then the Eagles became a good team. The Giants already were a good team. And the games started to get really important, really wild and really weird. In 1988, the Eagles won when Simmons scooped up a blocked field goal and rumbled 15 yards into the end zone in overtime. A lasting impression from that game was Giants coach Bill Parcells racing from the sideline to the end zone, screaming at the referee, to no avail. In 1989, the Eagles won when Waters scored a touchdown on a lateral of a fumble return from William Frizzell, when Simmons scored a touchdown on an interception return and when quarterback Randall Cunningham unleashed a 91-yard punt.

That was about as weird as it got until the November 22 game. The Eagles were able to rally in large part because their veteran leaders were well aware of the history of this series. They were in Giants Stadium. They believed. "Buddy Ryan started it," said Byars, who became still another veteran to invoke the name of the Eagles ex-coach at this time. "He always used to say that we were going to beat them, we just didn't know how and they didn't know how. But we were going to beat them. That was the feeling we had, even when we were down. That feeling carries over when we play them. We were going to win the game. We knew that. We just didn't know how." Eric Allen commented: "That's the way it is when we come up here. We always score like that. It's always something. We always find a way to do things like that against the Giants."

After a week of soul-searching, wagon-circling and media-bashing in the wake of a stunning loss to the Packers, the Eagles had found sweet solace in the Meadowlands. The three-hour, 42-minute game featured 81 points, 710 yards, 40 first downs, 12 quarterback sacks, and four returns for touchdowns. The 47 points were the most ever scored against the Giants in Giants Stadium. The 81 points were the second-most ever scored in an Eagles game. The game also had 20 penalties for 169 lost yards, eight turnovers, 378 yards in kick returns and two missed extra points. "Man, that was the most fun I've ever had playing football," said Cunningham, who passed for 209 yards and two touchdowns with three interceptions. "That was one crazy game," Mike Golic added. "How long did it last? Six hours? I told Mike [Pitts] after the game that it was time to go get the Christmas tree."

The Eagles scored three touchdowns on returns, including two on special teams. Their defense generated eight sacks and came up with two interceptions and two fumble recoveries. Reggie White and Clyde Simmons each had three sacks. Golic knocked out Jeff Hostetler with a clean but jarring tackle in the third quarter. Hostetler was carted off the field. He would miss the next three games. The Philadelphia offense produced 184 rushing yards, two rushing touchdowns and two receiving touchdowns. Heath Sherman ran for 109 yards in his first start of the season.

"You had your heart in your mouth half the game," Rich Kotite remembered. "But the thing that signifies what kind of team we have is the way we came back when we were down 20-6. There's a lot of character on this team and that was very gratifying. You can't buy that. That means a lot. This was a must game. This was our playoff. They [the Giants] were doing the same math we were doing. We had to win. And when this team, this group of guys, gets in that kind of situation, they respond."

___ ▪ 12 ▪ ___

SO CLOSE, SO FAR

The Eagles traveled 5,856 miles in the course of a late November road trip to San Francisco. They came up short by an inch and a half.

The Eagles' long journey to northern California and back for a November 29 game against the San Francisco 49ers wasn't quite long enough. They generated plenty of excitement and 280 yards on a cool, clear afternoon in Candlestick Park, but they fell shy of success by the narrowest of margins. "I can't believe it," cornerback Eric Allen was saying in the locker room after the game. "We come all this way, play this well against a team like that and we end up losing because of, what? an inch?"

Actually, it was an inch and a half, according to referee Howard Roe, who got down on his hands and knees on the soft grass and determined that, no, the Eagles had not managed a first down on their 61st and final offensive play of the game. The Eagles' comeback from a 10-0 halftime deficit, and their dramatic drive toward the potential game-winning touchdown late in the fourth quarter, ended when wide receiver Calvin Williams landed just short of the San Francisco 10 yard line after catching Randall Cunningham's fourth-down pass.

The loss left the Eagles with a 7-5 record. It left them three games behind Dallas in the race for the NFC Eastern Division title with just four games to play. It left them with five losses in their last eight games, all on the road. "At that point, we were in trouble," tight end Keith Byars conceded, looking back after the end of the season. "For some reason, the

123

league always manages to give us three road games in a row. When I first saw them—Green Bay, the Giants, San Francisco—I was thinking we would go 2-1 at worst and maybe 3-0. But when we went 1-2 and lost that game in San Francisco, that was when things started to get away from us."

The Eagles needed only to look across the field that day to add to their sense of frustration. The 49ers were the envy of most other NFL teams, especially talented but unfulfilled ones such as the Eagles. San Francisco's victory that day improved the 49ers' record to 10-2. It clinched a playoff berth and marked the tenth season in a row that the 49ers had managed 10 or more victories.

It also added further evidence that the 49ers were the NFL's premier franchise, a team that set the standard for commitment to winning. The Eagles, for all their accomplishments, tended to shrink in comparison.

One way to measure the San Francisco 49ers against other NFL teams was to check out their record over the last 12 years: 132 regular-season victories, 14 playoff victories, 4 Super Bowl titles. Another way was to check out their Santa Clara training facility: two natural grass fields, an artificial turf field, a 52,000-square-foot building that housed administrative and coaches' offices, meeting rooms, a spacious locker room, state-of-the-art training and weight rooms, racquetball courts, a players-only lounge and an indoor swimming pool.

Still another way was to check out their personnel: this was a team with 15 assistant coaches, four of whom are African Americans, and eight full-time scouts. The 49ers had former players in their front office (Dwight Clark), on their coaching staff (Dwaine Board and Eric Wright) and in their scouting department (Tommy Hart). "That's an organization with a consistent commitment to winning," Eagles defensive end Reggie White said on the Wednesday before the game. "It starts at the top and it goes all the way down through the coaches to the players. I'm not comparing them with any other team, but I just think they have the commitment to winning."

White didn't need to add, "especially compared to the Eagles," but that was how he felt. He had made that clear for four years. It was the primary reason he was thinking about signing with another team as a free agent after the season.

The Eagles had 10 assistant coaches, which was about the league average. Their only African American assistant coach, Dave Atkins, had been shifted from running backs coach under Buddy Ryan to special teams coach in his first season under Rich Kotite to tight ends coach in his second season with Kotite. Atkins would resign at the end of the season, taking a job as a running backs coach with the New England Patriots. The Eagles also had the NFL's smallest scouting staff with just two full-time scouts. There wasn't a former player working in the organization. The Eagles looked bad next to the 49ers, but that didn't make them unique. Most of the rest of the NFL looked bad next to the 49ers, too.

San Francisco was regarded around the league as a first-class organization. Along with the Dallas Cowboys and Washington Redskins—two other teams with whom the Eagles annually vied for NFC supremacy— the 49ers had invested in a modern training complex. The Marie P. DeBartolo Sports Centre was the model for Cowboys Center and the brand-new Redskins Park, state-of-the-art facilities that reflect the Dallas and Washington organizations' commitment to excellence.

The 49ers believed you got what you paid for. Their equipment manager didn't hassle players over socks, jocks and sweatpants. This was a team that made sure that each player had two seats on the airplane and his own hotel room for road trips. The 49ers held investment classes for their players during the off-season. They had a team chef who prepared meals at home, on the road, and for the airplane trips. The 49ers didn't cut corners—not in scouting, not in facilities or equipment, not in staffing and certainly not in terms of player payroll—and that kind of philosophy tended to seep into their locker room.

According to league documents released during the antitrust trial in Minneapolis the previous summer, the 49ers lost $16 million during the 1989 season. They spent a league-high $27.5 million on salaries. Owner Edward DeBartolo Jr. flew every player and his family to Hawaii for a week to celebrate the Super Bowl victory over Denver. In 1992, the 49ers again led the league with a $35 million payroll, according to figures released by the NFL Players Association.

"I've got some friends that play out there," Reggie White remarked. "They love playing there. It's just the atmosphere. It's just the attitude of the entire organization. That's why they've been able to be one of the most successful teams in the league for such a long period of time."

The 49ers won the NFC West title eight times between 1981 and 1990. They would win it again in 1992. They were the only team since the 1979 Pittsburgh Steelers to win back-to-back Super Bowl titles, capturing the crown after the 1988 and 1989 seasons. It was all attitude and atmosphere with the 49ers. This was a franchise that was in the business of winning football games, and championships. They spent the money. They paid the price. Their bottom line was their win-loss record, not their operating profits.

The Eagles team that arrived in the Bay Area on Saturday, November 28 was nearly the match of the 49ers during recent regular seasons. The Eagles would finish 1992 with 52 victories in their last five seasons, more than any other NFL team except San Francisco, which would have 60, and Buffalo, which would have 57.

But while the 49ers had won two Super Bowls and seven playoff games since 1988, the Eagles were winless in post-season play during the same period. And there was a nagging, persistent sense among many players in the Eagles organization that the team's problem was a lack of complete commitment from the front office. "It's not something that you think about consciously when you're on the field," Allen had said two days after tight end Keith Jackson skipped off to Miami as a free agent back in late September. "But subconsciously, it affects you. It's something guys talk about in this locker room. It's just a general feeling that guys have, especially defensive guys, that maybe there isn't the commitment there that some other teams have." On the day after the end of the season, White would say, "If you're asking me if this team is as committed as Washington and Dallas, I would have to say no."

Norman Braman's image took a beating in the summer before the 1992 season. Braman had insisted since buying the Eagles in April 1985 that he didn't expect to make money on the franchise. He had called his purchase of the team from beleaguered former owner Leonard Tose "a solid business deal deeply immersed in sentimentality." But according to testimony during the antitrust trial the previous summer in Minneapolis, the Eagles were the most profitable team in the NFL. The Eagles' own financial records, which were disclosed during the trial, showed that the team made an operating profit of $34.3 million from 1985 through 1989— by far the largest return of any of the NFL's 28 franchises.

The league's records showed that the Eagles made the highest operating profit in 1986, 1987 and 1988. The Eagles' operating profits were second-highest in the league in 1989 and 1985, Braman's first year with the team. In addition, the records revealed that the Eagles made an additional $6.7 million in operating profit in 1990, not including the $7.5 million in salary that Braman took from the team that year.

Operating profits are those before taxes and interest expenses are factored in. The Eagles, according to lawyers for the NFL, had higher-than-average interest costs because of the large debt Braman incurred when he bought the team for $65 million in 1985. In addition, NFL commissioner Paul Tagliabue testified that Braman's $7.5 million salary in 1990 was partial repayment of an $18 million loan Braman made the club to save it from bankruptcy when he bought it. But that statement was disputed during the trial by Stanford University economics professor Roger Noll, who analyzed NFL financial figures for the players. "The club [the Eagles] never faced bankruptcy," Noll testified. "The only one was [former owner] Leonard Tose's personal bankruptcy. The Eagles have been profitable since 1980."

Trial testimony also revealed that in 1990, when Braman was paying himself $7.5 million, Buddy Ryan was the NFL's lowest-paid head coach at $297,789. Also that year, the combined salary for the Eagles' coaching staff was the lowest in the NFL and 10 New York Giants assistant coaches made more than the $99,000 earned by Ryan's highest-paid assistant, offensive coordinator Rich Kotite. "Norman can make the money, that's fine," White had said after reporting to voluntary camp in July. "But he's got a football team he's got to be concerned about also. The guys playing on the field are giving their bodies to try to win for this organization. They just want to feel a total commitment to winning."

While the Eagles had ranked among the top 10 teams in recent seasons in player payroll—their $21.4 million in player salaries in 1989 placed them tenth in the NFL—they tended to rank near the bottom in other spending areas. In 1990, for example, the Eagles reported spending $4.7 million on team expenses, which included travel, equipment, the cost of training camp and coaching and scouting staffs. That year, the average NFL team spent $6.5 million on the same items.

Players in the Eagles organization had long complained about the facilities at Veterans Stadium, including an undersized weight room, cramped meeting rooms and the absence of a players-only lounge. The Eagles were tenants at Veterans Stadium, which was owned by the city of Philadelphia, so the organization was limited in its ability to improve the dank atmosphere in the aging, poorly maintained facility. But the players also felt the team was tight-fisted with equipment and clothing. That was one reason safety Andre Waters used to wear his jockstrap on the outside of his sweatpants. "I look at it like this," Waters once said. "When I'm done with this, they're going to give it to somebody else. So that means somebody else wore it before me. So I'm not letting it touch me."

Under Braman, the Eagles usually ended up paying their top players top salaries. When Reggie White signed a four-year, $6.1 million contract in 1989, he was the highest-paid defensive player in NFL history. When quarterback Randall Cunningham signed a five-year, $18 million contract extension in 1989, he was among the five highest-paid players in the NFL. When Seth Joyner and Clyde Simmons signed identical three-year, $3 million deals in 1991, they became the first non-Pro Bowl players in NFL history to sign for $1 million per season, excluding quarterbacks and No. 1 draft picks. But there had long been an acrimonious air between the Eagles players and the front office since Braman took over for the free-spending Tose and vowed to bring "fiscal sanity" to the team. According to figures compiled by *Pro Football Weekly* magazine, from 1987 through 1992, the Eagles had players miss 1,727 days of training camp in contract disputes, the second-highest total in the NFL. "The Eagles pay their players fairly," argued Jim Solano, a local agent who had represented more than 50 Eagles players. "But they make you jump through hoops to get the deal."

The team's failure to sign three-time Pro Bowl tight end Keith Jackson, who took advantage of a window of opportunity to flee to Miami as a free agent in late September, only added to the perception among many players that the Eagles lacked a total, complete commitment to winning. "Keith Jackson is the best tight end in the NFL," safety Andre Waters said after Jackson signed with Miami. "If some other team was willing to pay him that kind of money, why weren't we?" Complained linebacker Seth Joyner: "It's frustrating as hell. You just can't allow a great player like that to walk away. You need all the players you can get to win in this league."

Braman had purchased the team from Leonard Tose, a former trucking magnate whose extravagant lifestyle and free-spending ways endeared him to his players and coaches—and to the media, which got spoiled on lavish pre-game meals that sometimes included filet mignon and Lobster Newburg. But Tose's lifestyle eventually cost him control of the franchise.

Tose, who had purchased the Eagles for $16.1 million in 1969, was a big spender who arrived at training camp in a helicopter and chartered a private jet to transport himself and hundreds of friends and family members to New Orleans to watch the team play in the Super Bowl following the 1980 season. He also was a heavy drinker and a bad gambler, at least according to his own contention in a lawsuit that was filed while the 1992 Eagles were driving for the playoffs.

It might be said that Tose lost the Eagles on the green-felt gambling tables in Atlantic City. According to court records that were filed in December 1992, Tose lost $14.67 million at the Sands Hotel Casino in Atlantic City between 1981 and 1986. And that was just one of the casinos he frequented.

In January 1991, the Sands had filed suit against Tose seeking $1.35 million in unpaid gambling debts. Tose filed a countersuit in December 1992, claiming that he gambled because his hosts at the casino kept him drunk. According to a memorandum filed in U.S. District Court in Camden, New Jersey, Tose claimed that he was treated as a "high roller" at the casino, escorted to a private table in the baccarat pit and assigned a personal cocktail waitress whose job was to keep his glass of Dewars scotch filled.

Tose often played all seven hands at the blackjack table simultaneously, sometimes for $5,000 per hand, according to the memorandum. The more Tose drank, it was alleged, the worse he played and the more he tipped the waitresses, dealers and pit bosses. Tose has said that his gambling losses eventually cost him the Eagles. He considered selling the team in 1983 to a group headed by harness race horse syndicator Lou Guida, but backed out of the deal. In 1984, Tose seriously considered moving the Eagles to Phoenix to solve his financial troubles.

For a week in December 1984, the Eagles' proposed flight to Phoenix was front-page news in Philadelphia. It was revealed that with Tose's daughter, Eagles vice president Susan Fletcher, leading the way, the team had secured office space in the Phoenix area and negotiated a lease to play their home games in Arizona State University's Sun Devil Stadium. Tose's plan was to sell part of the team to Arizona businessman James Monaghan, using that money to solve his personal financial troubles and still remain in control of the franchise.

But after extensive negotiations with city officials, Tose agreed to keep the team in Philadelphia in exchange for a new lease with the city, which agreed to defer the team's $800,000 rent for 10 years, to spend $2 million on new practice fields for the team and to build 89 luxury suites around the top of Veterans Stadium. Those penthouse suites would earn the Eagles $4.4 million in 1990, more than any other NFL team generated from luxury boxes.

Another part of the complicated deal was the promise of cooperative action from other NFL owners, who formed a committee to study the Eagles' financial problems. Tose still was hoping to sell partial interest in the team and retain control. But because he was $42 million in debt, and because he was due to pay off a $12 million note to Crocker National Bank in California on March 31—and because the bank was threatening foreclosure—Tose was forced to seek a buyer for 100 percent of the Eagles.

Enter Norman Braman, a native Philadelphian from south Florida who was the owner of one of the largest automobile sales and leasing organizations in the world. Braman was born in West Chester, Pennsylvania, and raised in Philadelphia. His father, Harry, had emigrated from Poland and his mother, Katie, from Romania. As a youth, Braman had served as a water boy for the Eagles during their training camp and sneaked into Shibe Park to watch games. "I didn't have the money to buy a ticket," Braman once admitted.

Braman earned a marketing degree from Temple University in 1955. He soon made his mark in the business world, opening a small discount department store in Lebanon, Pennsylvania, and then organizing Philadelphia Pharmaceuticals and Cosmetics. In 1968, at the age of 36, Braman sold that business and retired to Florida as a millionaire. By 1972, he was back in business, selling cars. When he purchased the Eagles, Braman's automobile empire included a string of dealerships across the state of Florida.

Braman paid about $65 million for the Eagles. As part of the deal, he agreed to pay off Tose's bank loans, including the $30 million that was owed to Crocker National Bank. Braman also paid Tose $10 million in cash, plus $1.5 million to pay taxes; he agreed to pay Tose $1.5 million annually for 10 years and agreed to pay $5 million to Tose's heirs upon his death.

At a press conference in March 1985, Braman held up a green T-shirt with the words "Super Bowl 1986" printed on it. Braman wanted to win. He also wanted to bring the Eagles' finances into line after the excesses of the Tose era. He created a lot of animosity among the players during the summer of 1985, when he pledged to bring "fiscal sanity" to the team. The team opened training camp that summer without 12 veteran players who were involved in various contract disputes, including the team's all-time leading rusher, Wilbert Montgomery, who eventually was traded to Detroit.

Braman inherited coach Marion Campbell, who had been hired by Tose to replace Dick Vermeil after the 1982 season. Braman said he decided to replace Campbell after watching the Eagles blow a 23-0 lead in a 28-23 loss to Minnesota on December 1, 1985 in Veterans Stadium. That morning, Braman had read a *New York Times* article about Chicago Bears defensive coordinator Buddy Ryan. In eight weeks, Braman would hire Ryan as the Eagles' head coach.

Ryan's brazen attitude toward management helped create distance between Braman and the players, most of whom became fiercely loyal to their outspoken coach. But Braman became an enemy to many of the players during the 1987 players strike. He was an outspoken critic of the players who walked off the job two games into the 1987 season. He was supportive of the NFL management council's plan to break the strike by staging replacement games. "We all talk about the poor football players, the poor union players, all of whom are making an average of $300,000," he said at the time.

At an emotional press conference on the day after the strike was called, Braman said there was "no justification" for the players' actions and noted that the average player makes $1.35 million in his career. "That's equivalent to 44 years for a teacher in Philadelphia," he noted. "For a policeman, it's 50 years. It's more than 43 years for a registered nurse."

Braman was outraged by the lawless atmosphere during the replacement game played on October 4, 1987 in Philadelphia, when striking veterans and hundreds of teamsters and other supporters of the union harassed many of the 4,074 spectators who filed into Veterans Stadium to watch the bogus Chicago Bears beat the ersatz Eagles by a 35-3 score. It was an ugly scene outside the stadium: people were shoved into iron gates, spit upon and verbally abused with the most offensive language.

"It was the worst situation, frankly, that I've ever seen in my life," Braman declared after the game. "There's a court order [to control picketing outside the stadium]. We live on the basis of what the courts say.

Otherwise, we're animals." Braman also said that Philadelphia police "didn't seem to care," and that if the team was forced to host another replacement game, he would call the governor and request the presence of the "state militia."

In recent years, Braman had distanced himself a little from the team. He had vowed not to be an "absentee owner" when he bought the team, but he never relocated in Philadelphia. Instead, he spent most of his time in his home in Miami. He spent his summers in a villa in the south of France, a villa he once said that he bought "on a whim." A collector of art and fine wine, Braman was seen by many of the Eagles players as aloof, condescending and out of touch with them. He made only occasional contact with the players, usually after games. During the summer months, when contract problems arose, Braman usually was on the French Riviera.

The Eagles were run on a day-to-day basis by team president Harry Gamble, a man who joined the organization as an unpaid voluntary assistant coach in 1981. Gamble's rise through the organization had been meteoric: from special teams coach to administrative assistant to director of football operations to general manager to vice president to president-chief operating officer in the span of five years. "I wish I had a Harry Gamble for every one of my business entities," Braman once said. "I'm more a shooter from the hip. He's a calm, analytical, solid football man."

Gamble chafed at the perception that his job was to keep expenses under control and maximize Braman's bottom line. He would point with pride to the team's player payroll and its string of winning seasons as evidence of the Eagles' commitment to winning. Braman had brought stability to the franchise. The Eagles were making money, and they were winning games: they were about to fashion their fifth consecutive season of double-digit wins in 1992. There was no longer the crisis atmosphere around the team that had marked the last years of the Tose era.

"When you get into any kind of business, you want to be as successful as possible," said Eagles coach Rich Kotite, a man whose public praise of his superiors was in marked contrast to the approach taken by his predecessor, Buddy Ryan. "I think the thing that hasn't been mentioned in this is that when he [Braman] bought this team, the franchise was in shambles and they brought it back and they have done an outstanding job."

But Kotite's opinion wasn't shared by the majority of his players. There was a feeling among many in the Eagles locker room that the team paled in comparison to an organization like the 49ers. In 1990, when the Eagles led the NFL with a combined operating profit and owners' salary of $14.2 million, the 49ers were at the other end of the spectrum, reporting a league-high loss of $8.3 million.

None of this was immediately important as the Eagles took the field for their game against the 49ers. San Francisco was 9-2 and one victory away from clinching a playoff berth. The Eagles were 7-4 and desperate to reestablish themselves as one of the NFL's elite teams. "It's about respect," Reggie White stated a few days before the game. "We're not regarded as one of the elite teams anymore. We were, back when we were 4-0. But we're not now. We have to beat a team like this to proof that we're one of the best teams in the league, that we can beat anybody."

The Eagles were no match for the 49ers in the first half. Behind quarterback Steve Young, who was on his way to winning the NFL's Player of the Year award, the 49ers generated 270 yards and 12 first downs in the first half and took a 10-0 lead. The Eagles also took a blow in the first half when free safety Wes Hopkins, who had been in and out of the lineup for much of the season, aggravated his sprained left knee. Hopkins had been nursing the injury since the Washington game back on October 18, but this was serious.

A respected veteran who had been with the Eagles since 1983, longer than any other player, Hopkins brought experience and a strong physical presence to the deep secondary. He was regarded as one of the hardest-hitting free safeties in the NFL. But now Hopkins' left knee was badly sprained. It was the same knee that he had injured back in 1986, when he needed reconstructive surgery and sat out most of two seasons. This injury wasn't that severe, but Hopkins wouldn't play again in 1992. In all, Hopkins and Waters, the tenacious tandem who made the Eagles' secondary such a dangerous place for opposing receivers and running backs, would play together in just five games during the 1992 season. After that October 18 game in Washington, Hopkins would miss seven games, including the final six, and Waters would miss 11 games, playing only in the final one. "That's something that will always bother me," Waters would say after the season. "I just would have liked to have seen what would have happened if we could have stayed healthy."

The 49ers' first score that November 29 day came on a 22-yard touchdown pass from Young to Jerry Rice, the eighth-year player regarded by many as the greatest wide receiver in NFL history. The touchdown catch was the 100th of Rice's career, tying him with former Seattle Seahawks' star Steve Largent for first place on the NFL's all-time list. The 49ers added a 22-yard Mike Cofer field goal in the second quarter. But the Eagles caught a break when Cofer missed a 28-yard field-goal attempt with just 0:08 left in the second quarter. "That really gave us a boost," Kotite said after the game.

The Eagles' offense had done little in the first half, generating just 86 yards and five first downs. The running game had produced just 11 yards on eight carries. But rookie Jeff Sydner, a sixth-round draft pick from Hawaii, returned the second-half kickoff 45 yards to give the Eagles good field position. Cunningham completed a pair of 11-yard passes to Heath Sherman and Calvin Williams, respectively, then lofted a perfect 23-yard scoring pass to Fred Barnett, who was a step behind cornerback Don Griffin in the end zone. Suddenly, the Eagles were within 10-7.

The 49ers added a 28-yard Cofer field goal later in the third quarter, then increased their lead to 20-7 when Young lofted a 43-yard scoring pass to Dexter Carter on the fourth play of the fourth quarter. But by now the Eagles' offense was in gear. For the first time since returning from his one game on the bench, Randall Cunningham looked sharp. He was throwing in rhythm, using tight end Keith Byars as an outlet, playing with confidence and decisiveness. "There was something in his eyes," Eagles guard Mike Schad said of Cunningham. "He was confident. He was in control in the huddle. You could just tell looking at him."

It was an interesting time for Cunningham. Three days earlier, on Thanksgiving, he had been engaged to marry Felicity de Jager, a 25-year-old from South Africa who was a member of the Harlem Dance Theater. Cunningham had met de Jager three years earlier at a "Night of the 100 Stars" television production in New York. "I'm happy because I have somebody to share my life with," Cunningham remarked.

Whatever the reason, Cunningham was back at the top of his game for the final 30 minutes in San Francisco. Forced to play from behind, the Eagles abandoned their running game and turned to their quarterback. He completed 19 of 26 passes for 174 yards and two touchdowns in the second half. "I got in a rhythm again," Cunningham observed. "It wasn't run-run-pass. It was pass-pass-pass. That enabled me to get back in the flow of things."

Byars, who was still groping to become comfortable as a tight end after six-plus seasons as a running back, caught five passes for 47 yards in the second half. His 11-yard touchdown reception pulled the Eagles to within 20-14 with 10:54 left in the game. "He was working the patterns like Keith Jackson used to," Cunningham said of Byars.

The Eagles' defense, which had been pushed around for much of the day, rose up and stopped the 49ers on their next two possessions. Both times, San Francisco's vaunted offense went three-plays-and-punt. With 4:13 to play, the Eagles took possession at their own 47 yard line. They had plenty of time to drive 53 yards for a touchdown that would vault them into the lead.

Cunningham was confident. On first down, he scrambled 11 yards. Two short completions and a 3-yard Sherman run produced another first down. Another scramble by Cunningham and a 7-yard pass to Herschel Walker gave the Eagles a first down at the San Francisco 20 with 1:40 to play. The Eagles took their first time out. "We were going in," Byars said after the game. "There was no doubt in my mind."

After an incompletion, Cunningham completed a 3-yard pass to

Walker. But on third down, San Francisco defensive end Tim Harris swooped inside and sacked Cunningham for an 8-yard loss back to the 25. The Eagles took their second time out with 0:53 left, facing a fourth-and-15.

Cunningham dropped back and looked for Barnett, who was double-covered by San Francisco defensive backs. Cunningham saw Williams cutting across the middle and fired a hard, accurate pass. Williams collided with 49ers defensive back Merton Hanks just as the pass arrived, but the third-year wide receiver held the football as he tumbled to the ground just shy of the 10 yard line. The spot was crucial. No official was close when Williams hit the ground, but back judge Ken Baker ran quickly to the scene and put his foot down just behind the 10 yard line, marking the spot.

The Eagles were sure it was a first down. Cunningham and others were pointing in that direction when the chain crew brought out the down markers. Referee Howard Roe got on his hands and knees as the crew stretched the marker and brought it down right next to the nose of the football. "It was a first down, no doubt about it," Byars stated after the game. "You could tell from the 49ers' reaction. They knew it."

But no. Roe saw a gap between the marker and the football. He stood up and pointed toward the Philadelphia goal line. First down, 49ers. The Eagles were outraged. Cunningham threw his helmet, as did Keith Byars and guard Eric Floyd. The Philadelphia defensive players ran on the field and berated the officials. "Reggie almost cussed," said San Francisco guard Roy Foster of Philadelphia defensive end Reggie White, a Baptist minister. "His lips started moving, but he caught himself just in time." Young twice took the snap and knelt down, running out the clock and securing the 49ers' tenth victory in 12 games. The Eagles were left with another loss, but some of them took sweet solace in their stirring comeback against a team considered by many to be the best in the NFL.

"We're back," Kotite bellowed in the locker room after the game. Later in the season, Kotite said he sensed that the Eagles had "recaptured something, a rhythm, a confidence" in the second half against the 49ers. "This is a confidence-builder," Cunningham agreed after the game. "We can take this negative and make a positive out of it. We know we're back playing the same style we were playing in 1990." Center David Alexander concurred: "There's a positive to take out of this. This team showed a lot of character."

The loss left the Eagles three games behind the first-place Dallas Cowboys with four to play. The 10-2 Cowboys needed only to win two of their last four games to clinch the division title. Philadelphia also stood as the No. 3 team in the race for three NFC wild card berths. The Eagles were two games behind 9-3 New Orleans and rated behind 7-5 Washington based on the Redskins' victory over them earlier in the season. At 6-6, with three consecutive victories, the Green Bay Packers were just a game behind the Eagles and Redskins. Green Bay also held the tie-breaker advantage over Philadelphia based on their November 15 victory over the Eagles.

But the Eagles' locker room was an oddly upbeat place after the game. Down the hall, in the 49ers' locker room, Roy Foster seemed to explain why the Eagles were feeling so good. "Philadelphia," he predicted, "is going to be hell in the playoffs."

· 13 ·

SHADOW OF THE PAST

It was a weekend in the way-back machine. Nostalgia was in the air. The Eagles' past was present during their December 6 game against the Minnesota Vikings in Veterans Stadium.

The mood was set Friday night, December 4, at the first celebrity auction to benefit the Jerome Brown Foundation. Game jerseys, warm-up jackets, autographed footballs and posters were among the items up for bid, with all proceeds set to benefit underprivileged youth in the Delaware Valley.

Nearly every player on the Eagles' roster as well as all the coaches and most of the front-office staff were in attendance at the Sporting Club Atop the Bellevue, an upscale health club on the top floors of a swank Center City hotel. But on a night dedicated to the memory of a former player, the center of attention was a former coach.

"Buddy!" Reggie White bellowed when he saw the short, stout man with the ruddy complexion in the center of the room. Buddy Ryan, who had acquired most of the players on the Eagles' roster, who had coached the team from 1986 through 1990, who had brought the franchise from mediocrity to national prominence, was back in town at the team-related function for the first time since he was dismissed by owner Norman Braman on January 8, 1991.

Ryan wore a gray sports jacket and tie and a wide smile as he greeted player after player. "Jimmy Mac," he said in greeting to reserve quarterback Jim McMahon, who approached with his wife, Nancy. It was Ryan who signed McMahon as a free agent in July 1990 and installed him as the backup to starting quarterback Randall Cunningham. When Cunningham was injured in the 1991 season opener, McMahon led the Eagles to a 10-6 record in their first season after Ryan's dismissal.

"Big Ron," Ryan called to Ron Heller, the veteran offensive tackle whom Ryan acquired in a trade just two weeks before the 1988 season opener. Heller never played for a winning team in his first four seasons in the NFL; he never played for a losing one after Ryan brought him to Philadelphia.

"Hey, 46, how come you don't play no more?" Ryan asked Izel Jenkins, a defensive back who wore No. 46. Ryan drafted Jenkins in 1988 and made him a starter in 1989 and 1990. But now Jenkins was a reserve, playing mostly on special teams.

Limping on his injured left ankle, safety Andre Waters' face lit up when he approached Ryan. "Coach Ryan," Waters began, embracing the man who made him into a prominent NFL player. Waters was a reserve defensive back and special-teams player when Ryan arrived in Philadelphia. Ryan made Waters a starter, citing his speed, toughness and tenacity. "It's great to see you," Waters added.

In Ryan's mind, the Eagles were still very much his team. He had acquired the team's nucleus—drafting Keith Byars, Seth Joyner, Clyde Simmons, Byron Evans, David Alexander, Eric Allen, Fred Barnett and Calvin Williams, trading for Ron Heller and Mike Pitts, grabbing Jeff Feagles, Roger Ruzek, Mike Golic and Mike Schad as free agents. He had made stars of Randall Cunningham and Reggie White. He had given the team its identity: the Eagles were brash, bold, black-shoed villains to much of the rest of the NFL.

"That was the first time I had seen most of them since I left," Ryan said after the season. "I had heard from a lot of them on the telephone, and Reggie had stopped down the farm one time to see me. But it was the first time I was back with all of them together and it brought back a lot of memories.

"We had a cause there in Philadelphia. We had a lot of camaraderie on that team. Hell, they would go bowling together every Monday night, and how many teams you ever heard of that did that? That's what you have to have first, that togetherness. Then the winning will come.

"That's what I tried to build when I got there. I had them open up the pool table in the center of the locker room, just to try to get guys to hang around, to spend time together. You need that closeness, with everybody focused on that same thing. If you don't have that, it doesn't matter how much talent you have.

"I brought in a lot of talent. Hell, I made all the picks and all the trades. But the thing that team had also was that togetherness."

Ryan never doubted his ability as an evaluator of talent, never wavered in his belief that his team was destined to win the Super Bowl. Even after he was fired, Ryan remained convinced that he had assembled a group of athletes that were certain to dominate the NFL. "The thing that bothers me most," Ryan commented soon after he was fired, "is that the people that built this team won't be around to enjoy the celebration when they win it all. Somebody else is going to get to take all the bows."

Seeing Ryan only served to remind the players that time was passing. When he was around, they were a young, confident team on the rise. But he had been gone for nearly two years now, and the Eagles were an older, more mature team, running out of time to realize their vast potential.

Ryan's five seasons in Philadelphia had been remarkable. The Eagles weren't so much a football team as a carnival, a collection of characters who followed the lead of their outspoken, uncompromising coach. "We had a lot of talent, but we also had a great attitude when Buddy was around," said tight end Keith Jackson, Ryan's top pick in the 1988 draft. "Buddy was a great coach and a great judge of talent but he also created a great atmosphere around that team. He knew how to get talented players ready to play and to play aggressively. Not a lot of coaches can do that."

Ryan fascinated many of his players because he was so straightforward in his dealings with his own superiors in the Eagles organization. Ryan squabbled with the big boss, team owner Norman Braman. He took shots at his immediate boss, team president Harry Gamble. Ryan once stood in front of a ballroom full of people at a luncheon and referred to Gamble as "the illegitimate son of the owner, Braman." He openly complained about the Eagles' decision to ban beer on post-game flights, calling it an "Ivy League rule," in reference to Gamble's time as head coach at the University of Pennsylvania. Ryan also feuded with legendary NFL coaches Tom Landry of Dallas and Don Shula of Miami. He drew their ire, he once said, "because I won't kiss their rings."

The Eagles reflected Ryan's personality. They were loud and brash and aggressive. They led the league in finger-pointing and trash-talking. In each of Ryan's five seasons, they were hit with more penalty yardage than in any other season in franchise history. They switched to black shoes in 1990 to reinforce their renegade image. "That bothered some people," Ryan admitted. "But they were just looking to manufacture reasons to make a change. We played hard but we played smart. We weren't an undisciplined team. You can't be undisciplined and win as many games as we won."

The Eagles were a dull, mediocre team when Ryan arrived in January 1986. They had put together four consecutive losing seasons, the last three under soft-spoken coach Marion Campbell, who deflected all controversial questions by drawling in his South Carolinian accent, "Guys, I can't get into that." Campbell also refused to criticize his players. Asked specifically about the mistakes that marred many of the games during his tenure, Campbell would say, "I'm not going to assassinate anybody's character."

Ryan was different. He had earned his reputation as a defensive coach during his time as an assistant with the New York Jets, Minnesota Vikings and Chicago Bears. Ryan had been to the Super Bowl with each of those teams. He wasn't lacking in confidence. Ryan's defense with the Bears had led the team to the Super Bowl after the 1985 season. The Bears led the NFL in nine defensive categories and were regarded as one of the most intimidating units in NFL history. After a 46-10 victory over New England in the Super Bowl, several Chicago defensive players carried Ryan off the field on their shoulders.

Ryan was 51 when the Eagles hired him. He had been an assistant coach in the NFL for 16 years. He had waited a long time to become a head coach, and he had his own ideas about how to run a team. At the press conference where Ryan was introduced a week later, Braman compared him to the legendary Vince Lombardi, another tough taskmaster who had made his mark in the NFL late in life. "He's the next Vince Lombardi," Braman declared. "He has a lot of the same qualities and characteristics that Vince Lombardi had. There are a lot of similarities."

Interest in the Eagles had waned under Campbell. During the 1979, 1980 and 1981 seasons—the team's best years under former coach Dick Vermeil—the Eagles had drawn 550,611; 557,275 and 547,642 spectators, respectively, to their eight regular-season home games. During Campbell's three seasons, the Eagles drew 445,682; 458,997 and 486,019 spectators, respectively. The Eagles' only star in those days was wide receiver Mike Quick, who would make the Pro Bowl five times in a row starting with the 1983 season. Quarterback Ron Jaworski, who had led the Eagles to the Super Bowl following the 1980 season, was near the end of his career. Cunningham and White joined the team in 1985, but both were young, unestablished players when Ryan arrived.

Ryan was unlike any coach the Eagles had seen. On the eve of his first minicamp in Tampa in March 1986, Ryan said starting fullback Michael Haddix, the team's No. 1 draft pick in 1983, was so out of shape he looked like a "reject guard from the USFL." Ryan's acerbic wit was the soundtrack for his flurry of personnel moves. He traded veteran linebackers Joel Williams, Anthony Griggs and Reggie Wilkes. He cut running back Earnest Jackson, who had gained 1,028 yards for the Eagles in 1985. First, Ryan tried to trade Jackson, saying he would take "two beers—and they don't have to be cold."

"They blamed me for not being able to trade him," Ryan said after the 1992 season. "But people look at film. They knew what the situation was with the guy. I tried to trade ĥim and then I wanted to cut him and

Harry [Gamble] told me to keep him around for a couple of weeks. After we got rid of him, Harry called his agent and said, 'That wasn't the Eagles organization saying that stuff. That was Buddy Ryan.' So you had people being pansies instead of being men and working to make things happen. I stood up. I took the heat. People see that. They respect that. That's why I'm a leader of men."

Ryan's first draft pick was Keith Byars, an All-America running back two years earlier at Ohio State. Byars had sat out most of his senior season with a broken foot. The night before the draft, Ryan had gone on a radio program and called Byars "a medical reject." The next day, he grabbed Byars with the tenth overall selection in the draft. "People ran a gut check on the Philadelphia Eagles and we stepped up," Ryan quipped.

Ryan also used a second-round pick in 1986 on Florida linebacker Alonzo Johnson, whose stock had fallen because he had tested positive for drugs during a scouting combine gathering of the top prospects in February. "This ain't Russia," Ryan remarked. "I believe in giving people a second chance."

Johnson would run into trouble with drugs again during his brief time with the Eagles. He never developed into a front-line player, and he was released after two mediocre seasons. But most of Ryan's early personnel decisions were solid: Byars would develop into one of the Eagles' most valuable offensive players, and the coach found two future Pro Bowl defensive players in linebacker Seth Joyner and defensive end Clyde Simmons at the bottom of the 1986 draft.

The Eagles went 5-10-1 in Ryan's first season. He set the tone during his first game, when he ordered Cunningham—who was playing in relief of Jaworski on third-down-and-long situations—to attempt a fake punt from deep in Eagles territory. Cunningham's hurried punt banged off the rear end of guard Ron Baker, a play that summed up the Eagles' 41-14 loss to the Washington Redskins in their first game under Ryan. "Buddy . . . Buddy . . . Buddy," serenaded the sarcastic sellout crowd that day in RFK Stadium.

A lot of good things happened for the Eagles in 1986. White established himself as a dominant defensive end. He would make the Pro Bowl for the first time. Byars, Joyner and Simmons got experience as rookies. Cunningham got experience as a third-down quarterback early in the season and started five games in place of the injured Jaworski late in the season.

The pivotal period in Ryan's tenure might have been during the 1987 season. Two games into the season, with the Eagles sporting a 1-1 record, the NFL players went on strike. The strike lasted 24 days. It finally was broken by the NFL owners' brilliant, ruthless strategy of staging games with replacement players who crossed the picket line. On many teams, those replacement players were joined by veterans who returned to work. The Eagles were one of the few teams that didn't have a single healthy veteran cross the picket line. Ryan infuriated Braman by supporting the veteran players, urging them to "stick together" on the picket line and maintain their solidarity.

Ryan expressed disdain for the replacement team of Eagles. He called them a "bunch of dumb jerks." Not surprisingly, the ersatz Eagles went 0-3, including a 40-22 loss to a Dallas Cowboys team that included picket line-crossing veterans Danny White and Tony Dorsett. "It still burns me up that people claim I didn't try to coach those guys," Ryan said after the 1992 season. "We worked our ass off trying to coach those guys, but they just couldn't play. All I ever said was that I wanted my guys to stick together. If they were going to stay out, I wanted them to stay out together. That's what they did, and it meant a lot to our team. I really believe the fact that they had some guys coming in and some guys staying out is what blew that Dallas team apart. You can't have that in this league."

When the Eagles veterans returned to work, they were charged with emotion and united in their loyalty to Ryan. In their first game, Ryan ordered Cunningham to fake a kneel-down and then throw a long pass that set up a touchdown on the final play of a 37-20, run-it-up victory over those same Cowboys.

That was a pivotal moment for Ryan. When he ordered that touchdown against the Cowboys, he was crossing a bridge and burning it behind him. He was letting everyone know he wasn't going to turn back.

In a sense, Ryan was declaring his independence. He had clearly sided with the players during the strike, effectively estranging himself from management. Now, he was tweaking the nose of Cowboy coaching legend Tom Landry and violating the coach's unwritten code of conduct. From that point on, the Eagles under Buddy Ryan were the bad boys of the NFL. Ryan didn't care. He felt he had a team that was good enough to make enemies, and the players adopted his air of brazen confidence. "This team came back from the strike with the belief that it could beat anybody," said tight end John Spagnola, the Eagles' union representative during the strike. "Buddy and the coaches were waiting for us, and we're just going out there with something to prove."

The Eagles won six of 10 games after returning from the strike. They finished with a 7-5 record in games played by the veterans, although officially they were 7-8 because of the three losses by the replacement team.

At his press conference on the day after the season finale, Ryan presented "scab rings"—oversized replicas of the rings given to Super Bowl champions—to player personnel director Joe Woolley and front-office executive George Azar, who had been responsible for the formation of the replacement team. "We didn't start putting our [replacement] team together until a week before the games," Ryan said after the 1992 season. "Other teams already had their teams picked. They were telling guys in training camp, 'Here's $1000, stay in shape, we'll call you when the strike hits.' We didn't do any of that. And then we go and get a bunch of guys that couldn't play dead."

Ryan's Eagles were wildly unpredictable, talented enough to beat the best teams in the NFL, inconsistent enough to lose to the worst. Followers of the team came to expect the unexpected. Before Ryan arrived, the Eagles had played six overtime games in their history. They played six more in Ryan's first two seasons and a total of eight in his time with the team.

Ryan was always making news off the field. On November 30, 1988, Ryan nearly choked to death on a piece of pork chop during a dinner with his coaching staff in the press lounge on the fourth floor of Veterans Stadium. He was saved by offensive coordinator Ted Plumb, who jumped up and performed the Heimlich maneuver. Linebackers coach Ronnie Jones said he walked in during the excitement, saw Plumb wrapping his arms around Ryan from behind and had this immediate reaction: "I thought Buddy had made one comment too many about the running game."

Four days later, Ryan ran off the field with 0:04 left in the game after Washington's Chip Lohmiller made a 43-yard field goal to give the Redskins a 20-19 lead. Ryan said he went to find the officials' dressing room to complain about a call, but in fact he ducked into the Eagles' locker room. Before he left, though, Ryan told special teams coach Al Roberts to run the "Cal-Stanford deal" on the ensuing kickoff, referring to the famous lateral-filled touchdown return in a college game a few years earlier. "We practice that every Saturday," Ryan said.

In the summer of 1989, the Eagles traveled to London to play the Cleveland Browns in the American Bowl. After a week of practices and sightseeing, the Eagles scored a 17-13 victory in the exhibition game in Wembley Stadium. Ryan was doing his press conference in a small, low-ceilinged room after the game when a sweaty, breathless Braman barreled through the crowd of reporters, carrying a trophy. "Buddy, Buddy, look what they gave us for winning the game," Braman exclaimed.

"Ain't that nice," Ryan drawled sweetly, winking at reporters after Braman turned away.

During the 1989 regular season, the Eagles played host to the Minnesota Vikings on November 19. That week, the city of Philadelphia had honored Lech Walesa, the leader of the Solidarity movement in Poland. The Eagles won the game 10-9. They needed only to get off a punt in the final seconds to secure the victory, so Ryan sent 15 players on the field to ensure that the Vikings wouldn't be able to block the kick. A penalty didn't matter. Ryan only wanted to run off the final few seconds on the clock. "Our Polish punt team," Ryan called it. That off-season, the NFL outlawed the intentional use of extra players.

In the summer of 1990, the Eagles played a scrimmage against the Atlanta Falcons in Macon, Georgia. That was the Falcons' first season under coach Jerry Glanville, who was known as "The Man in Black" because he tended to dress like Johnny Cash. Not to be outdone, Ryan arrived for the scrimmage wearing a black shirt, black shorts, black socks, black shoes and a black hat.

"We had fun," Ryan admitted, looking back at his tenure after the 1992 season. "It was a lot of hard work, but it was fun. We weren't boring. We weren't a boring team to play for, and we weren't a boring team to watch. We were unpredictable. Teams would walk out of the huddle against us, looking over to see what we would do.

"I worked hard. I worked seven days a week, but it was worth it because I called all the shots. And what made it really fun was that everything worked out. We were right on schedule. Things were falling into place just like I thought they would."

In a 1990 book, Giants coach Bill Parcells compared Ryan and the Eagles to "Neanderthals." Parcells said the Eagles under Ryan were strong but unsophisticated, relying on power and intimidation as opposed to strategy. Ryan responded with a press statement in which he said he wasn't a descendant of the Neanderthals but of the Cro-Magnon men. "Cro-Magnons were smarter than Neanderthals," Ryan said at the time. "They hunted in teams, and they always came out on top."

The Eagles became an NFL power in 1988. Ryan had drafted defensive tackle Jerome Brown in the first round in 1987, and he selected tight end Keith Jackson and cornerback Eric Allen in the first two rounds in 1988. All three would become Pro Bowl players.

Following a slow start, the Eagles burst into prominence with a 24-13 victory over the New York Giants on a Monday night in October 1988. That was the night Randall Cunningham passed for 369 yards and three touchdowns and made the most famous play of his career: maintaining his balance despite a hit from Pro Bowl linebacker Carl Banks and firing a touchdown pass to Jimmie Giles.

Still, a letdown loss the next week in Cleveland and a stunning home loss to Atlanta—which was coached by Campbell—had the Eagles and Ryan in serious trouble. The Eagles were 4-5, and there were rumblings about Ryan's job security. "That will be their mistake," Ryan replied when asked about speculation that he might be fired.

The Eagles took off. They won six of their final seven and captured their first NFC Eastern Division title since 1980 when they beat Dallas and the Giants lost to the New York Jets in a stunning span of several minutes on the final day of the regular season. After a week off as division champions, the Eagles traveled to Chicago to play Ryan's old team, the Bears, in Soldier Field. On the day before the game, Ryan ordered the team buses to honk their horns on the way past Soldier Field from the airport to the team hotel. "We're not going to sneak into town," Ryan said.

The Eagles lost 20-12 in a game that became famous for the fog that rolled over the edge of the stadium in the second half.

So was set the theme for Ryan's final three seasons: late-season surges followed by playoff flameouts. The Eagles won six of their final seven regular-season games in 1988, five of their final six in 1989, and six of their final eight in 1990. Ryan's teams were at their best when things seemed worst. They fought out of corners with raging fury. But they lost their first playoff game each year. In 1989, Ryan might have had his best team. The Eagles started 6-2—their best mid-season mark in any season from 1982 to 1992—but stumbled in a Week Nine game against 2-6 San Diego. They flattened out the next week in a 10-3 loss to Washington.

The Eagles won their next four but lost command of the NFC East when they dropped a 30-20 decision in the Superdome in New Orleans. They won their finale against Phoenix, but their 11-5 record was good for just second place behind the 12-4 Giants.

The Eagles spent three days practicing at the Atlanta Falcons' training facility in Suwanee, Georgia, before their 1989 playoff game. At the end of one group interview, Ryan was asked about Greg Bell, the standout running back for the Los Angeles Rams, who would play the Eagles in the wild card playoff game. Ryan said something nondescript about Bell, then walked from the podium. He saw a group of writers from Philadelphia and whispered, "Greg Bell, my ass." Unfortunately for the Eagles, Bell and the Rams played a great game. Los Angeles won 21-7, and Bell ran for 114 yards and a touchdown.

Frustrated, Ryan chalked up the loss to injuries to Byars and tackle Matt Darwin and compared the soft, shifting zone defense that the Rams used to baffle Cunningham to a "junior-high defense in Texas."

Once again, Ryan made news at his press conference on the day after the final game. Asked if he would be comfortable coaching the 1990 season in the final year of his original, five-year contract, Ryan replied, "Why would I do that?" Clearly, he expected a contract extension. "You know me, I think I've done a great job," Ryan said. "I mean, you'd have to be blind."

But Ryan wasn't about to approach Braman, and Braman wasn't about to be pressured by Ryan. So neither side made the first move, and Ryan went into 1990 without a new contract.

Always a players' coach, Ryan angered management with his actions and comments during Keith Jackson's bitter contract holdout in the summer of 1990. Ryan was openly supportive of Jackson, who held out of training camp and missed the first two regular-season games in a futile attempt to force the Eagles to renegotiate his contract. When Jackson decided to return, Ryan sent a limousine to pick up the prodigal tight end at the airport and then presided over a bizarre press conference in which Jackson said he was back because of a "front-office conspiracy" to get rid of Ryan.

The Eagles had lost their first two games without Jackson. They lost twice more in his first four games of that season. But then they got hot: winning five in a row, losing two, winning three more to finish 10-6, and earning the homefield advantage against the Washington Redskins in the wild card playoff game.

The Eagles prepared for the playoff game against the Redskins by spending three days practicing in Tampa. Ironically, the Eagles' first and last practices under Ryan were in Tampa—the minicamp in March 1986 and the pre-playoff workouts on the first days of January 1990. But like the previous two, that playoff game ended in disaster. The Eagles lost 20-6, and Ryan created another stir when he benched Cunningham for three plays in the third quarter and replaced him with a rusty Jim McMahon. "We were logjammed," Ryan said of the Eagles' offense. "I had to do something. I wasn't going to sit there and not do anything."

Three days later, Ryan was fired. To this day, Ryan swears he was surprised by Braman's decision to dismiss him. Ryan said he was down in his office on the first floor of Veterans Stadium, looking at film of Tennessee offensive tackles Antone Davis and Charles McCrae, when Braman walked in with the bad news. "I know some of my assistants have said they thought it was coming," Ryan remarked after the 1992 season. "But I never did. I just never thought they would fire someone with a record like I had. I built a winner up there."

At the time, Ryan expressed his surprise in typically cocksure fashion: "I've been fired before, but always for losing. I've never been fired for winning." Braman said he felt the Eagles needed more "discipline and precision." He noted the team's renegade image, its team-record number of penalties in 1990. "You can win in this league without being a bad boy," Braman said. He also said that he expected the Eagles to take the "quantum leap" forward to legitimate Super Bowl contenders, adding, "It's time to stop being the bridesmaid and become the bride."

Ryan said after the 1992 season that if he had to do it all over again, he would make more of an effort to talk directly with Braman. He had let Gamble serve as an intermediary, and he felt a lot was lost in translation. "I should have talked to him more," Ryan said of Braman. "But I was a working head coach. I didn't have time to sit around and call up the owner every time I wanted to make a decision. I left that to somebody else. I think he [Braman] was misinformed about me. I don't think he would have made the decision if he wasn't misinformed."

Ryan's dismissal drew howls of displeasure from many of the team's veteran leaders, including White, Byars, Joyner and Jackson. "You built something up and then they tear it apart," White protested. "It's just not fair." Added Joyner: "It's like we're being torn apart limb from limb." Vowed Byars: "My grandkids will know about Buddy Ryan. I won't let him be forgotten."

There was something about the earthy, outspoken Ryan that touched a nerve among the sports fans in the Philadelphia area. Two years after he was fired, Ryan still was a hot topic on the radio talk shows. Ryan was the only Eagles coach ever to do his own live radio call-in show. He would banter with fans, laughing, joking, bragging. A week after he was fired, Ryan did his last radio show from a Center City restaurant. The place was packed with people who chanted "Buddy . . . Buddy . . . Buddy" and brought him flowers and other gifts. He was touched by two hours of homage from callers, most of whom said the team would never be the same without him. "I could be mayor of this town," Ryan said, "but they won't let me coach the football team."

Two weeks after he was fired, Ryan interviewed for the head coaching job in Tampa Bay. But Tampa Bay owner Hugh Culverhouse decided to stick with former receiver coach Richard Williamson, who had served as head coach for the final five games of 1990 on an interim basis. After the 1991 season, there were nine openings for head coaches in the NFL. Ryan was interviewed for just one: Tampa Bay again, and this time Culverhouse decided to hire former Cincinnati Bengals coach Sam Wyche.

"I might have had the Tampa job if I agreed to take it the way Wyche took it," Ryan said, referring to Wyche's agreement to keep Floyd Peters in charge of the Buccaneers' defense. Ryan hoped to bring in veteran coaches such as Dan Henning and Ron Erhardt and to reassemble part of his old staff with the Eagles. He also had plans to make changes in the Bucs' personnel and scouting staffs. "I know I would have done a great job down there, and they know it, too," Ryan said after the 1992 season. "But I was only going to take it the way I wanted it. If I was going to be responsible, I was going to make the decisions. I was going to build a winner."

When Ryan arrived in Philadelphia for the celebrity auction on the night of December 4, 1992, he had been out of coaching for 23 months. He was living with his wife, Joan, on their 176-acre horse farm in Lawrenceburg, Kentucky. Ryan had bought the farm back in the mid-1970s, using his playoff shares and the Super Bowl check he earned as an assistant coach with the Minnesota Vikings.

After he was fired by the Eagles, Ryan earned his trainer's license. He was the hands-on owner of about 40 thoroughbred horses. His days were filled. On most of them, he would get up about 5 a.m. and arrive at the Kentucky Trainer Center by 6:00. He would work with his horses until about noon, then return to do chores around the farm unless he had a horse running that afternoon or evening.

Asked about his horses that night, Ryan said they were "doing OK, but I'm still looking for that Super Bowl winner." Ryan stayed all evening, shaking hands and slapping backs and telling old stories with his old players. He talked briefly with Braman but not Gamble or Kotite. He flew back to Kentucky the next day.

On Sunday, the Eagles put their 7-5 record on the line against the 9-3 Vikings, one of the surprise teams in the league. Under first-year coach Dennis Green, the Vikings already had topped their victory total from 1991, when they went 8-8. It was a fascinating game for Eagles running back Herschel Walker, who had played two and a half seasons for the Vikings before they released him on May 29. The Eagles signed him as a free agent three weeks later. "I'm really looking forward to it because I practiced against those guys," Walker said of the Vikings' defense. "They're aggressive. They'll test you but that's what I like, a challenge." Asked if he had anything to prove to the Vikings, Walker replied, "I never look at things that way. That would be looking back. I never look back." But this was a weekend for old Eagles, not new ones. Walker gained just 44 yards on 13 carries and wasn't really a factor in the Eagles' 28-17 victory. Of Walker, Ryan said after the season, "If they gave Heath Sherman the ball as much as they gave the other kid, he would have gained twice as many yards. Sherman, he's a running back. The other one [Walker], he's just a big guy with speed."

On a cold, windy day, the Eagles breathed some life back into their season. The victory improved their record to 8-5 and greatly improved their chances for an NFC wild card playoff berth. The Eagles needed the victory to keep pace with the other conference playoff contenders. New Orleans (10-3), Washington (8-5) and Green Bay (7-6) also won that weekend, leaving the Eagles with little margin for error.

Dallas (11-2) also won to stay three games ahead of the Eagles in the NFC Eastern Division race. The Cowboys ended the day needing just one more victory to clinch the division title. "We had to have this one," Eric Allen said after the game. "It's getting to that point in the season. We know if we win all our games, we'll be in the playoffs, and once we get there, whoever we're playing is going to be in trouble."

The victory echoed of the Eagles' past. Cunningham played the way he did when Ryan was the coach. Offsetting the Vikings' fierce pass rush with scrambles and bootlegs, Cunningham ran 12 times for 121 yards and scored two touchdowns on 1-yard sneaks. The 121 yards was the second-highest total of Cunningham's career and the first time he had run for more than 100 yards since a 1990 game against New England. For one game, Cunningham really was back scrambling. The Eagles took a 14-10 halftime lead and then increased their advantage to 21-10 when Cunningham capped an 84-yard drive in the third quarter with a plunge into the end zone.

But the Vikings came back, driving 70 yards behind running back Terry Allen, whose development had helped convince them to discard Walker. Allen, a third-year player, would finish with 82 rushing yards and another 31 receiving yards. His second, 3-yard touchdown run of the game pulled the Vikings to within 21-17 with 6:44 left in the game. Rising up, the Minnesota defense forced a punt when Al Noga sacked Cunningham on third down. After a short Jeff Feagles punt, the Vikings took possession at their 30 yard line, trailing by four points with 4:42 left to play.

The Vikings' hopes were dashed in one play. Dropping back, Minnesota quarterback Sean Salisbury tried to loft a soft swing pass in the left flat to Allen. But Joyner, who was rushing into the backfield from that side, stopped, reached back with his left hand, grabbed the football and raced 24 yards into the end zone with a game-clinching interception.

Joyner raced through the end zone. He stopped in front of a huge banner that was hanging over the wall, a banner that read "Jerome Is Watching." After the season, Joyner said that he remembered seeing that banner during the pregame warmups. "I was jogging before the game and I ran down to that end zone," he recalled. "I noticed the banner, and something just told me that I was going to get in that end zone. I tell people that, and they don't believe it. But it's true. I just knew something was going to happen."

After the game, Joyner declined to comment to reporters. But defensive tackle Mike Golic noted that Joyner had told some of his teammates that he was going to make a big play before they trotted on the field for that series. "He called it," Golic said. Reflected Joyner after the season: "It was just something that popped into my head. It was weird. I knew it was going to happen. I just knew it."

After crossing the goal line, Joyner circled through the end zone. He held off his excited teammates with one hand. He turned to the banner, held the football aloft and saluted. It seemed more than a simple salute to a banner. It seemed a salute to the past, which had been so present that weekend. It seemed a salute to a teammate and a friend that was gone and to a time that was gone, too.

· 14 ·

TIGHT SPOT

This time, Keith Byars didn't fight the switch. He moved between running back and tight end. He changed positions for the good of the team, although this time he got $100,000 in the bargain to help smooth the transition.

The last time, Byars was entering his junior year in high school. He was a tight end in those days, and that's where he wanted to stay. "I loved tight end," Byars recalled. "That was my first position, tight end and outside linebacker. But we were running sprints, and I was faster than most of the guys on the team, and the coach said he wanted more speed in his backfield. I didn't want to go. I hated the move. But the coach changed my number on me. I had to go."

This time, Byars moved in the other direction. He still was wearing No. 41 on his game jersey, but he was the Eagles' starting tight end as they prepared for the December 13 game against the Seattle Seahawks.

There was another big difference: Byars endorsed the move. He had approached Eagles coach Rich Kotite after the team's stunning loss to the Green Bay Packers on November 15 and suggested the switch, in large part because of the productive play of reserve running back Heath Sherman. "Heath has the hot hand, so we have to stick with him," Byars said shortly after the switch. "I told Richie that. I told him that I'm willing to play tight end. I never said I didn't want to play tight end."

Still, there was a nagging sense around the team in 1992 that Byars was a little unhappy, frustrated and annoyed. He was outspoken at times in his criticism of Kotite and in his contention that the team needed to make better use of his talents.

It all began back in the spring. Byars had been starting in the Eagles' backfield since his rookie season in 1986. He was an established player, a team leader and a versatile, valuable member of the offense. But Byars' role was that of an all-purpose player. He was a receiver and a blocker and even an occasional passer, but he wasn't used much as a runner. He had carried the football just 131 times for 524 yards in the 1990 and 1991 seasons.

So the Eagles went looking for running backs in an effort to upgrade their ground game. In April, they used their first draft pick to select Alabama running back Siran Stacy. They used their third pick to select Notre Dame running back Tony Brooks. Then in June, after a breathless, three-week pursuit, the Eagles signed running back Herschel Walker to a two-year, $2.8 million contract. Walker had been released by Minnesota and wasn't generating much interest from other teams. But the Eagles agreed to pay him $1.3 million in 1992—nearly $400,000 more than they were scheduled to pay Byars.

Proud and competitive, Byars wasn't upset as much by the money as by the implication: the Eagles needed better running backs. They needed rookies to upgrade the position. They needed Walker, an athlete vilified in some corners of the NFL, to serve as their featured running back. "I said it before and I'll say it again: I felt they should have concentrated on improving the offensive line in the off-season instead of worrying about the running backs," Byars remarked in training camp.

Looking back after the season, Byars had other thoughts: "The only thing that bothered me was that people would say, 'Well, you have to have a 1,000-yard rusher.' I've been saying this for years: give me the ball 'X' amount of times, and I'll produce. Every time I got the ball, I put the numbers up. I was just upset that I was never given the same opportunity. You can't give one guy an 'A' test and another guy a 'B' test and say that's how you compare them."

But the off-season acquisitions of big-name players at his position were only the beginning of a tumultuous season for Byars. Things got more complicated. The Eagles got nowhere during the summer in contract negotiations with star tight end Keith Jackson, one of Byars' closest friends on the team. In fact, when Byars' wife, gospel singer Margaret Bell Byars, recorded an album in 1991, Jackson and Byars sang backup vocals.

Jackson never re-signed with the Eagles. On September 29, he fled to the Miami Dolphins as an unrestricted free agent. "That was difficult because I really felt that Keith should have been here," Byars said after the season. "He had been part of what we had built here. He was one of the stones we had built this whole thing on, and then he was gone. I said it at the time, I felt from talking with him that in his heart he wanted to be back with us but that from a business standpoint, he felt he had to go." Beyond the personal loss, Byars would feel a tremendous professional impact from Jackson's departure. It would be a turning point in his career.

Byars had dabbled at tight end for several seasons. At 6-foot-1, 240 pounds, he was big enough and strong enough to play tight end. He had lined up as the second tight end in certain formations, so he wasn't completely unfamiliar with the position. Early in training camp, Kotite had been raving about a Byars-Walker backfield combination. But as Jackson's absence became more and more noticeable, Byars began to take more and more practice repetitions at tight end.

Byars started at tight end in the last exhibition game on August 27 against the New York Jets. But he was convinced that he would soon be back at running back, that Jackson would return to the team and reclaim the tight end spot. "I'm just a couple of aspirin, temporary relief," Byars said after that game. "Keith Jackson is the cure."

On September 1, the Eagles claimed tight end Pat Beach on waivers. Beach had been released the previous day by the New York Jets. The 31-year-old Beach was a nine-year NFL veteran, having played his entire career with the Baltimore/Indianapolis Colts before signing with the Jets during the Plan B free agency period in the spring of 1992.

Beach started the September 6 season opener against New Orleans. Beach and Byars both played tight end in that game and again the next Sunday in Phoenix, as the Eagles used a lot of two-tight-end formations, with Walker as the lone running back. The power formation helped Walker run for 114 yards against the Saints and 112 yards against the Cardinals.

But as the running game bogged down, and Walker's effectiveness began to decrease, the Eagles started to feel the effect of Beach's limitations as a receiver. Beach had caught just 31 passes in his previous three seasons with the Colts and was much more accomplished as a blocker than as a receiver. "I'm not a tight end like Keith Jackson," Beach admitted. "I'm not the receiver he is, I'm not as fast as he is, and I don't run the routes he runs."

Beach caught just seven passes in the Eagles' first six games. He did not catch a pass in the Eagles' 7-3 victory over Phoenix on October 25, after which quarterback Randall Cunningham attributed the team's offensive woes to "not having Keith Jackson." Cunningham was accustomed to having a tight end with speed and good receiving skills. From 1988 through 1990, when Cunningham was putting together three consecutive Pro Bowl seasons, Jackson caught 194 passes—more than the combined total of any two Eagles wide receivers.

Beach couldn't fill that role. Neither could the team's other veteran tight end, Maurice Johnson. But Byars, a speedy, soft-handed athlete who had caught 283 passes as a running back from 1988 through 1991, was the perfect candidate.

There were just two problems. One was that Byars had complained loudly about his role as a tight end in the 31-14 victory over Phoenix on September 13 in Sun Devil Stadium. "I was a tackle," Byars said three days after that game. "We can't win many games without having me more involved in the offense. I'll do whatever I have to do to help the team, but it's not the best thing for the team for me not to have the ball in my hands." The other problem was that Byars had cracked a bone in his right hand during the October 18 game in Washington. He sat out the next week's game against Phoenix, and the injury limited his blocking and pass-catching ability for the next several weeks.

Byars' injury provided an opportunity for increased playing time for Heath Sherman, who had carried the football just 15 times in the first eight games. Sherman ran for 81 yards, including a 30-yard touchdown, in the 31-10 victory over the Los Angeles Raiders on November 8 in Veterans Stadium. The next week in Milwaukee, Sherman ran for a 17-yard touchdown and took a screen pass 75 yards for another score in the Eagles' 27-24 loss to the Green Bay Packers.

On the plane ride home from Milwaukee, Byars made a decision: he would volunteer to play tight end on a full-time basis to free up a spot in the backfield for Sherman. "Things got misinterpreted," Byars said at the time. "After the first two games, I told Richie we can't have success with me at tight end for 60 minutes. Everybody automatically interpreted that as, 'He doesn't want to play tight end.' But that's not what I said. I told Rich we needed to have our best players on the field at one time. I told him if I was in the backfield and Heath was on the bench, you're not going to have your best players on the field. I said, 'Leave Heath in there. He's got the hot hand. Let him stay in there and I'll go to tight end and make some plays there.' " Earlier in the season, Byars' increased action at tight end led him to approach Eagles management. He noted that the incentives in his contract were geared for a running back. He could earn bonuses based on his total of rushing yards. But he felt he was being short-changed of the chance to earn some more money because he was playing tight end as much as running back.

The Eagles agreed. Mindful that Byars would be a free agent after the 1992 season, they gave him a $100,000 bonus. "I was a running back with running back incentives," Byars noted. "When you don't play it, it's like you're in limbo. You don't have the opportunity to earn the incentives that you negotiated into your contract. It was very simple. They said, 'OK, let's do it.' "

Still, the bonus and some of Byars' statements about his diminished role in the offense led to some criticism of him. Byars' image took a little bit of a beating in the tumult over his switch to tight end. It was just a few comments from radio hosts and callers, a few lines in a few newspaper stories. But it was out there: the notion that Byars was unhappy with his role, that he wanted the ball more, that he was being a little selfish.

Byars wasn't the kind of man who worried about fan or media perceptions of him. But he had been above reproach for most of his career. Now, there were questions about him being protective of his own self-interests. "That's not the case at all and the people in this locker room know it," Byars said shortly after his switch to tight end. "Selfish and Keith Byars will never be in the same room."

After the season, Byars said, "My only concern is winning ballgames. I felt at times that there wasn't any urgency to get me the football. It wasn't about being selfish. It was about winning. When it's time to win ballgames, you have to have the ball in your big players' hands. There were times when I wasn't involved until we got in trouble. In San Francisco, I was a decoy in the first half. My number never was called. Then, at halftime, I was like, 'Hey, get me the ball.' It's not a secret. That's one of the things I was upset about, off and on, during the season. I'm not saying I was the forgotten man but at times I was."

Byars had been Buddy Ryan's first draft pick as head coach of the Eagles in April 1986. Byars had been an All-America running back at Ohio State, where he finished second in the balloting for the Heisman Trophy as a junior. But Byars broke a small bone in his right foot early in his senior season. He had led the nation in rushing with 1,764 yards and in scoring with 24 touchdowns as a junior. But he was in and out of the lineup as a senior because of the injury, and he finished the season with just 213 rushing yards and four touchdowns.

Ryan called Byars a "medical reject" on the night before the 1986 draft, trying to convince other teams the Eagles weren't interested in the injured running back. But with his first draft pick, the tenth overall selection, Ryan grabbed Byars and said the Eagles passed a "gut check" by taking such a risk.

Byars had been a legendary athlete in his hometown of Dayton, Ohio. He was a starter on two state championship basketball teams at Roth High School, hit close to .500 as a centerfielder for the baseball team, ran on a state champion 400-yard relay team and collected 1,701 rushing yards as a senior running back for the football team. The fourth of five children, Byars once said he learned to play sports by tagging along with his older brothers, Russell and Reggie. His late father, Reginald, was a minister. Byars often credited his father with developing his strength of character and religious faith.

Byars had majored in social work at Ohio State and was extremely active in community service through his professional career. He was the Eagles' 1990 nominee for the NFL's Man of the Year award. He earned a community service award from the Big Brothers/Big Sisters of Philadelphia in 1991. That same year, he was named Humanitarian of the Year by the Philadelphia Sports Writers Association.

Ryan called Byars a "franchise back" when he drafted him. Ryan envisioned Byars as a 20-carry-a-game, 1,200-yard-a-season running back, the featured member of a punishing, clock-controlling ground game. But Byars slowly developed into something else: an all-purpose player with more pass receptions (283) from 1988 through 1991 than any other NFL running back. Byars was a receiver, a blocker, even a passer, with four touchdown throws in four attempts during the 1990 season. A left-hander, Byars often fooled defenses by running to his left and throwing a perfect pass. "It's a right man's world," Byars said. "Not a white man's world. A right man's world."

Byars also had developed into an unquestioned team leader, a voice of reason and perspective in the locker room, the guy who had started and served as "commissioner" of the Eagles' 36-man, Monday-night bowling league during the 1990 season. "The ultimate team player," Kotite had called him.

Byars was married to gospel singer Margaret Bell, who occasionally performed the national anthem before Eagles games. Once, after hearing his wife sing, Byars exclaimed, "She was so good I was going to ask her to marry me. Except I already did."

The Eagles had an 8-5 record as they prepared to travel to Seattle. This was, on paper, the softest game on the schedule. The Seahawks had a record of 2-11 and were generally regarded as one of the two worst teams in the NFL along with the New England Patriots. Seattle had the NFL's worst offense, based on rankings by total yards. The Seahawks' quarterback, Stan Gelbaugh, was a journeyman who had tried out for eight different teams in three different leagues during his undistinguished career. But the Seahawks did have an imposing defense, thanks in large part to the presence of tackle Cortez Kennedy, a 300-pound reminder of what fate had taken from the Eagles just six months earlier.

Kennedy was a run-stopping, quarterback-sacking, walking, talking, hitting image of the unforgettable player the Eagles had lost forever. He wore the same jersey number, came from the same college and played the same position with the same remarkable combination of strength, quickness and intensity as his late, great close friend: former Eagles Pro Bowler Jerome Brown. "He's the closest thing you'll see to Jerome in a long time," Byars said on the Wednesday before the game.

The game against the Eagles in the Kingdome in Seattle promised to hold special significance for Kennedy, the very best player on a very bad team. Kennedy had invited Brown's parents, Willie and Annie Brown, to spent the weekend with him in Seattle and attend the game. "He was like the older brother I never had and a father figure," Kennedy said of Brown. "He was somebody I could talk about life with." Kennedy changed his uniform number to 99 before the 1992 season to honor Brown, who wore that number for the Eagles. Kennedy had worn 96 in his first two seasons in Seattle. "I wanted to pay tribute to him and his family and friends," Kennedy stated. "I couldn't let a great person like that—not a football player, but a great person—just leave this league."

The uniform number was just one similarity between Kennedy and Brown. Kennedy also had become the kind of disruptive interior force that made Brown so valuable to the Eagles. The 6-foot-3 Kennedy led the Seahawks in tackles with 90 and quarterback sacks with 10.5 after 13 games. He was well on his way to his second consecutive Pro Bowl, and he was regarded by many as Brown's successor as the best defensive tackle in the NFL. By the end of the season, he would be voted NFL Defensive Player of the Year.

Eagles left guard Mike Schad, who would square off with Kennedy, said before the game that the Seattle player was remarkably similar to Brown. "He's just like Jerome Brown was," Schad noted. "He's a big, strong kid, a 300-pounder with a low center of gravity. He plays hard, and he covers a lot of ground. I'm going to have my hands full with him." Rich Kotite also had a high opinion of Kennedy: "He's the best defensive tackle in football. He inspires the people around him. He loves playing the game. He never is blocked. He never stops. He's a true leader."

Kennedy said he met Brown during his junior season at the University of Miami. At the time, Brown was a third-year NFL player and one of the most famous products of the Miami program. Kennedy recalled that Brown stormed into the weight room at Miami one day, looking for the player they were comparing to him. "He said, 'Where's this guy who's supposed to be just like me?' Then he just gave me a big hug."

Kennedy talked with Brown on the telephone just a couple of hours before Brown was killed in a car accident in his hometown of Brooksville, Florida. "I couldn't believe it when I heard about it," Kennedy said. "A guy at the Seahawks called me and I told him it couldn't be true because I just got through talking to Jerome. I just couldn't believe it. I was [home] in Arkansas and I was going to fly to Miami to see him the next day."

Led by Kennedy and the rest of an inspired defense, the Seahawks made things miserable for the Eagles in the Kingdome. The Eagles didn't help themselves, playing their sloppiest game of the season: they set a team record for penalty yardage, committing 17 infractions for 191 yards.

The tone was set on the opening kickoff, when Eagles return man Vai Sikahema dashed 66 yards to the Seattle 31, only to have the play nullified because of an illegal-block penalty.

The Eagles' offense struggled against an unrelenting Seattle defense.

Quarterback Randall Cunningham was sacked 10 times and lost a fumble that was returned 52 yards for a touchdown in the fourth quarter by Seahawks cornerback Dwayne Harper. "They just had our number," Cunningham said after the game. "I have to give them credit. They have a great defense and they played hard. They had a great scheme and gave us a lot of different looks." Center David Alexander added: "I think they blitzed on every second down. They did a great job with it."

The Seahawks got sacks from six different players. Safety Robert Blackmon and linebacker Rufus Porter each had 2.5 sacks. Kennedy—who sat out the latter stages of the fourth quarter and all of overtime with a back injury—had two sacks and was credited with seven tackles. "He had problems," Kotite said of Cunningham. "He was getting hit a lot. They were just getting too much penetration at the line of scrimmage. It [the problem] was the offensive line."

The Eagles' problems were doubled by their penalties. They committed six infractions on kick returns, ruining their chances for good field position. The 191 yards in penalties was a team record, far exceeding the old mark of 157 set in 1952. "We just kept having to go 90, 85, 80 yards," Kotite recalled. "It was tough. The penalties took us out of a lot of things."

The Eagles held a staggering advantage in most statistical categories. They had 466 yards to 87 for Seattle, and 25 first downs to 11 for the Seahawks. They also held an 18-minute edge in time of possession. The Eagles defense was all over Gelbaugh, who completed only 9 of 31 passes for 66 yards. Seattle running back Chris Warren managed just 49 yards on 19 carries. Defensive ends Reggie White and Clyde Simmons each had two sacks. Cornerbacks Eric Allen and Mark McMillian each had an interception. The Seahawks converted just two of 15 third downs. "The defense was magnificent," Kotite said. White agreed: "We didn't take them lightly. We played hard on defense. I think we did a pretty good job."

Despite the statistical domination, the Eagles needed all 75 minutes to beat the Seahawks. It was the longest game in Eagles history, ending only when Roger Ruzek made a 44-yard field goal as time expired in overtime to secure a 20-17 victory. "We should have put them away in the second quarter," Alexander complained. "But that's the way we are. We wait until we have our damn backs against the wall until we do anything. It's very frustrating. We're out there with our backs against the wall against a team that was 2-11. I'm thinking, 'The heck with this.' It was just getting ridiculous."

Seattle pulled into a 10-10 tie late in the first half when Gelbaugh tossed an 11-yard touchdown pass to fullback John L. Williams. That concluded an 89-yard drive that included 80 yards of pass-interference penalties against the Eagles. Next, Seattle went in front 17-10 when Harper scooped up a Cunningham fumble and rambled down the right sideline and into the end zone. Harper celebrated too soon and dropped the football at the 4 yard line, but it bounced up to him in the end zone. The first defensive touchdown of the season by the Seahawks gave them a 17-10 lead with 13:50 left in regulation. Two possessions later, the Eagles tied the score by going 93 yards for a touchdown. Byars made the big play, displaying the receiving skills and speed that he brought to the tight end position.

On first down from the Seattle 7, with the Kingdome crowd in full roar and the Seahawks' defense starting to smell an upset, Byars reached back and caught a high pass from Cunningham. Byars whirled, stepped away from a diving Rufus Porter and raced 46 yards to the Seattle 47 yard line. "The biggest play of the game," Kotite recalled.

"That was another example," Byars said after the season. "We had a lot of numbers that day, but we really weren't doing anything offensively. We had so many chances. But when we got in trouble, then we started to look to put the ball in my hands. That was one of the things that bothered me, that we didn't seem to have that urgency until we got in trouble and then it would be like, 'Hey, let's get Keith the ball.'

"When you play the Redskins, they get Gary Clark the ball. When you play Dallas, they give the ball to Emmitt Smith. When you play San Francisco, they get the ball to Jerry Rice. I mean, that's what teams do, they get the ball to people who can make plays, and at times I felt like we didn't do enough of that."

Eight plays after Byars' 46-yard catch-and-run, the Eagles were looking at a fourth-and-two from the Seattle 15. But Cunningham beat a blitz by Robert Blackmon and dumped a perfect pass on the left side to Vai Sikahema, who got a first down at the Seattle 8. "I just ran a little out pattern and turned back and the pass was there," Sikahema said. On the next play, Walker cut outside, got good blocks from Byars and wide receiver Fred Barnett and raced into the right corner of the end zone. It was 17-17 with 4:52 left in regulation.

Both teams had chances late in regulation and through the first 12 minutes of overtime. But Seattle's best drive was ended when Simmons sacked Gelbaugh, and the Eagles kept stalling as Porter and Blackmon kept racing into the backfield and sacking Cunningham. Finally, the Eagles took over at their own 20 with 2:55 left in overtime. They got one first down, then they got a big play from veteran wide receiver Roy Green, who caught a 20-yard pass from Cunningham.

On the next play, Cunningham stepped up in the pocket and shoveled a pass to Byars just before he was tackled for another sack. Byars shook off Blackmon's attempted tackle, turned upfield and raced 21 yards to the Seattle 29. "Randall and I have an understanding of each other," Byars said after the game. "When he gets in trouble, he looks for me. I just try to get open. I know to expect anything when he starts running with the ball."

After two Walker runs gained two yards, the Eagles called time out with 0:03 left. Roger Ruzek trotted on the field. The snap, hold and kick were good. The football split the uprights just as the clock winked to 0:00. "You live for those situations as long as you don't face them every week," Ruzek noted. "That could be treacherous. It was a rush like I can't explain."

In the standings, the inelegant victory counted just as much as a dominating performance. The Eagles jacked their record to 9-5 and set the stage for a pivotal game the following Sunday with the Washington Redskins in Veterans Stadium. The Redskins had beaten the NFC Eastern Division-leading Dallas Cowboys earlier in the day to tighten up the division race. Dallas was 11-3, and Washington was tied with the Eagles with a 9-5 record. The Eagles still had an outside shot at the division title—they needed to win their final two and have Dallas lose its final two—but the team from Philadelphia didn't look much like a champion in the Kingdome.

In the locker room after the game, reporters crowded around linebacker Seth Joyner. In that day's editions of the *New York Times*, Joyner had called Kotite a "puppet" of team owner Norman Braman. "I should learn my lesson," Joyner said in the locker room. "Things always seem to get misconstrued or misread, and I'm the bad guy."

In the article, Joyner was quoted as saying that Cunningham had "lobbied" owner Norman Braman for then-offensive coordinator Rich Kotite to be promoted to head coach.

"Randall lobbied for Rich to Braman and deserted Buddy," Joyner argued. "Buddy gave Randall a chance as a black quarterback that no other coach in this league would. Buddy built the entire offensive around Randall. I told Randall that he would pay for what he did, and I don't know if him missing all of last year with the knee injury was it, but God works in mysterious ways."

Joyner also was quoted as saying that Braman fired Ryan and promoted Kotite from offensive coordinator because he wanted a coach he could control: "Buddy cared about winning, and Braman cared about making money. Buddy did not get the chance to complete the job. Braman wanted a puppet and that's what he got. Much of what Buddy said has come to roost. We lost Keith Jackson because of money. Free agency is coming and this team could be ripped apart." Joyner's published comment sent shock waves through the team. Asked about the "puppet" reference during his post-game press conference, Kotite grimaced and said, "I have nothing to say about that. It's ludicrous."

A little while later, Byars sat in front of his locker. He had caught five passes for 93 yards, a season-high. His 46-yard reception would be his longest of the season. In the four games since becoming a full-time tight end, Byars had caught 15 passes for 216 yards and two touchdowns and the Eagles had gone 3-1. Trying as usual to put a positive spin on a negative situation, Byars noted, "It's going to be a long flight home. But it would have been a lot longer if we hadn't won."

· 15 ·

REKINDLING THE FLAME

This was it. The long season, the special season, was down to one game. If the Eagles were going to make good on their promise—to themselves, to their fans, to the memory of their fallen teammate—they had to win this game.

It was that simple, that serious. A season of great expectations, a season of unprecedented urgency, was resting on one game against the defending Super Bowl champion Washington Redskins.

More than a season was at stake, too. Since they first emerged as an NFL power in 1988, the Eagles had been on the verge of greatness. There was something special about them, something charismatic. They were young and talented and colorful. They were convinced of their own destiny. They were certain to take their place among the most memorable professional teams in sports history. But something always went wrong. They lost three times in a row in the playoffs. Then the coach got fired. Then the star quarterback got hurt. Then the star defensive tackle was killed. Then the star tight end left the team through a legal loophole.

This was their last chance. Too much had happened. Too much was going to happen. It might already have been too late, but nobody on the team wanted to believe that. They still were talented. They still were motivated. They still were determined to break through in 1992.

Seth Joyner sat back in his airplane seat and wondered, "What have I done now?" The long post-game flight home from Seattle to Philadelphia on the night of December 13 would provide Joyner with plenty of time to study the situation. Fiercely competitive and frustrated by the team's past failures, Joyner wanted nothing more than to win the Super Bowl this season. With a perpetual scowl on his face, Joyner was brooding and intense in the best of times.

These weren't the best of times. Joyner had vowed to honor his late friend with a championship. Plus, he had been with this team since 1986—the beginning of its climb to fame. He knew this probably was his team's last chance.

But now things were spinning out of control. Again. The Eagles were supposed to be focusing on the biggest game of the regular season, the game that could define this period in franchise history, the showdown with the defending Super Bowl champions, and the spotlight had shifted to Joyner. "I guess my timing wasn't too good," he would say after the season.

Controversy was nothing new to Joyner, nothing new to the Eagles. Outspoken and passionate, Joyner had created stirs all season with his withering criticisms of the Eagles organization, head coach Rich Kotite, his teammates and himself. In the middle of November, after an especially inflammatory tirade following an especially frustrating loss, Joyner had vowed not to speak with the media anymore.

He made one exception. He talked with Thomas George of the *New York Times* for an article that Joyner thought would focus on his background, personality and playing skills. But when the article appeared on Sunday, December 13, the day of the Eagles' game against the Seattle Seahawks in the Kingdome, Joyner was stunned. "Uh, oh, here we go again," he said to himself.

Although there was a lot in the article about Joyner's background, personality and playing skills, two items leapt off the pages of the most prestigious newspaper in America. In one, Joyner called Kotite "a puppet" of team owner Norman Braman. In the other, Joyner suggested that Randall Cunningham's devastating 1991 knee injury was punishment from God for the quarterback's role in the dismissal of former coach Buddy Ryan. "Why now?" Kotite wondered when he was told of the article. "Why would he do this now? It doesn't make sense."

As usual, Cunningham had other concerns. The comments by Joyner really didn't bother him. Cunningham figured that stuff had been worked out during a historic players-only meeting back on April 1, 1991, when he got to hear his teammates tell him he was arrogant, selfish and preoccupied with his own stardom. That was old news. Cunningham was sore on the plane flight back from Seattle but his ailments were physical, not psychological or emotional. He had been sacked ten times by the Seattle defense and he had nearly lost the game when his fumble was returned for a go-ahead touchdown in the fourth quarter.

This would be a pressure-packed game for Cunningham, whose career had seemed on the verge of careening out of control at times during the 1992 season. He was back in the starting lineup, but the aura of superstardom had been stripped away from him during his traumatic time on the bench in the middle of the season. There was no denying Cunningham's talent, but he was maddeningly inconsistent and he had shown a tendency to play poorly in late-season games of this magnitude.

The Redskins were his most difficult opponent, too. He had started twelve games against them in his career and lost eight times. He was benched for one series in a playoff loss to the Redskins two seasons earlier. Because they varied and disguised their pass coverages and concentrated on containing him in the pocket, the Redskins always presented big problems for him. "They know me," Cunningham once said. "They know how to contain me. It's like their defense is designed to stop me."

Cunningham was doing his best to stay cool. Tall and thin with a high, flattop haircut, Cunningham would walk through the locker room with a confident, casual air. He was 29. Three years earlier, *Sports Illustrated* magazine had proclaimed him the NFL's "Ultimate Weapon."

On the morning of Wednesday, December 16, four days before the game against the Redskins, Cunningham had a large selection of tailor-made, $1500 suits delivered to him in the locker room. He tried on his new wardrobe as some of his teammates played dominoes, read newspapers, played video baseball or studied the game plan. That night, Cunningham went to Graterford Prison in rural Montgomery County to tape his television show. "The Randall Cunningham Show," which aired on Sunday mornings on the local CBS affiliate, normally was taped at the WCAU studio. But this episode would be shot at the prison. The wardrobe, the television show—these were the trappings of Cunningham's success. He reveled in his own celebrity. He was the kind of professional athlete who marketed his own recovery from the knee injury with a customized line of baseball caps, who promoted his own namesake candy bar, who favored the lifestyle of the rich and famous. Kotite called him "Arsenio," after talk-show host Arsenio Hall, and his teammates often complained about his preoccupation with his own popularity. But Cunningham's celebrity was built on the increasingly rickety foundation of his status as a star quarterback. That foundation was in danger of cracking as the Eagles prepared to play the Redskins.

"There's pressure on all of us," Cunningham said on the Thursday before the game. That was his style, to try to deflect the harsh glare of a pivotal situation. It infuriated many of his teammates that Cunningham was so anxious to accept credit but so reluctant to assume responsibility. "It's not just me," Cunningham said. "We all have to play well to beat the Redskins."

Reggie White had a lot on his mind. It occurred to him, in private moments, that the next time the Eagles played the Redskins, he might be wearing a Washington uniform. White was scheduled to become an unrestricted free agent on February 1, which meant he would be able to sign with any NFL team. In September, he had been the lead plaintiff in a class-action lawsuit against the NFL, which had helped to force the resolution of long-standing labor differences between the league owners and the NFL Players Association.

White was an immense man, 6-foot-5, 295 pounds. He would turn 31 on Saturday, the day before the big game against the Redskins. He had been with the Eagles since 1985 and was generally regarded as the greatest defensive player in their history. He was a sure Hall of Famer, one of the most dominant defensive linemen ever to play the game.

At that point, White had 122 quarterback sacks in 119 games. He was the only player in NFL history to have more sacks than games played. He was an accomplished run defender as well as pass rusher, and he had never missed a game because of injury.

The Eagles had lined up White as their starting left defensive end in every game since October 6, 1985. Back then, Marion Campbell was the Eagles' coach, Ron Jaworski was the quarterback, Paul McFadden was the place-kicker and Roynell Young and Herman Edwards were the cornerbacks. Those were names from the Eagles' distant past, dim reminders of another era. White had started 118 consecutive games for the Eagles, and now, his career with the team might be nearing its end. "I try not to think about it," White said on the Wednesday before the game against the Redskins. "But I am human."

White's past problems with the Eagles front office were no secret. He had haggled with the team's management for 18 months before finally agreeing to a four-year contract back in the summer of 1989. That deal was reached on the day his lawsuit against his former agent, an Eagles executive named Patrick Forte, was scheduled to go to trial. Like many of his teammates, White seemed to regard Eagles owner Norman Braman as typical of the breed—distant, aloof, condescending. "They think we're big dumb cats that come out of college and all we can do is play ball," White once said of the NFL owners.

White felt the Eagles were on the precipice as the game against the Redskins approached. One more disappointment and all his old wounds—his bitter contract problem in 1989, his dismay at the firing of Buddy Ryan, his disillusionment at the workings of the team's front office—could open up again.

In an ironic twist, the team that most interested White was the Redskins. He respected and admired Washington coach Joe Gibbs, an evangelical Christian who was regarded as one of the best coaches in NFL history. He regarded the Washington organization as one of the best in the league. He saw its new, state-of-the-art practice and training facility as a sprawling, glittering monument to their commitment to excellence. "When you go to Washington, you don't hear players there say they want to leave," White once said. "Something must be going on there that's right."

Eric Allen knew the stakes of the upcoming game. The Eagles' 27-year-old cornerback always described himself as a "football fan," who studied the summaries and standings in the newspapers every Monday and loved to watch "Monday Night Football" and "Inside the NFL" on television.

At 5-foot-10, 190 pounds, with bright green eyes, Allen was a gifted athlete. He was blessed with remarkable speed, quickness and anticipation. But Allen also was a student of the game. A two-time Pro Bowl selection, Allen knew playing his position was a matter of playing the odds and the angles. He spent the week watching film of the Redskins' offense. "Sometimes I feel like I overprepare," Allen once said. "I feel like I can run those guys' [opposing receivers'] patterns for them. But that's the most important part of the game at this level. You have to prepare. So many guys have the physical talent. You have to do your work during the week."

For most NFL teams, a normal work week involved film review and a short conditioning run on Monday; a day off on Tuesday; film study, meetings and practices on Wednesday, Thursday and Friday; and a brief, walk-through practice on Saturday morning. But many of the Eagles—especially defensive players such as Allen and Joyner—insisted on supplementing their preparation by staying late after practice to watch additional film. Joyner was notorious for watching film late Saturday night in the team hotel.

Allen watched about 20 to 25 hours of film a week. He often brought film home to watch at night. It was during just one session that Allen noticed the tendencies of the Redskins' offense during pressure situations. "They always look for Gary Clark," Allen said of the Redskins' veteran wide receiver.

The Eagles' record was 9-5 but nobody was celebrating. With two games to play in the regular season, the Eagles had little chance of catching the Dallas Cowboys for first place in the National Football Conference's Eastern Division. Instead, they were locked in a struggle with several other teams for the three NFC wild card playoff berths.

One of those teams was the Redskins. As the defending Super Bowl champions, the Redskins had experienced some typical problems with the emotional letdown from the high of the previous season. They had struggled through an awkward, injury-marred season in 1992 but they had won three in a row. They were sporting a 9-5 record, too, and they seemed to be gathering some momentum.

The Eagles were coming off their sloppiest game of the season. They had set a team record for penalty yardage in an inelegant 20-17 overtime victory over Seattle. The Eagles had committed 17 penalties for 191 yards in the Kingdome. They had surrendered another 89 yards on the 10 quarterback sacks. They had needed all 15 minutes of overtime to finally beat the Seahawks, whose 2-12 record was reflective of their undisputed status as one of the worst teams in the National Football League.

"I was trying to stay positive," Kotite said of his thoughts during the four-and-a-half-hour flight back to Philadelphia. "We were terrible in Seattle. We stunk. But I thought, if we can commit that many penalties and give up that many sacks and still win the football game, it must mean that we were a good football team. That's the way I looked at it and that's the way I wanted the whole team to look at it."

It wasn't easy. The season had been supercharged with excitement when the Eagles won their first four games. They romped over Dallas on a nationally televised, Monday night game in early October to establish themselves as the hottest team in the league. Everything was so bright and clear back then. This season was going to be so different, so memorable. Filled with urgency, touched by tragedy, this aging, unfulfilled team was determined to make something special of this season.

"I remember how well we were clicking," Eagles defensive tackle Mike Golic said after the season. "We never really were a team that started off fast. We always seem to have to rally in the second half of the season. Now, we were 4-0, with that big win over Dallas, it just seemed like anything was possible at that point."

But storm clouds filled the middle of the season. The Eagles lost five of their next eight games after that 4-0 start. Their mighty defense, regarded as one of the best in NFL history during the 1991 season, began to buckle. Cunningham was benched for a game and a half. Kotite's tactics came under heavy criticism from team leaders such as Joyner and tight end Keith Byars. Injuries mounted along with the losses and the special season began to lose its promise. "We lost our way there for a while," Byars would say afterward. "Things kind of snowballed on us. One thing went wrong, and then another and then another. We lost track for a little while just what the season was supposed to be all about."

The Eagles had dedicated the season to Jerome Brown, the boisterous, unforgettable star defensive tackle who had been killed in an automobile accident on June 25. They kept his locker just as he left it in Veterans Stadium as a sort of shrine. They wore patches on their uniforms inscribed with "J.B. 99"—his initials and jersey number.

Brown's memory was a source of strength and inspiration to many of them. Joyner spent the season with "99" shaved out of the hair on the back of his head. White and others would put their hand on Brown's locker before they left the dressing room to play a game. But it was a long season, and a lot of things went wrong.

"Remember what we're playing for," Eagles safety Andre Waters pleaded to his defensive teammates during an emotional speech in early November. "Remember that we're playing for No. 99. Remember that this is for him."

The Eagles began to right themselves in December. They beat Minnesota. Then they beat Seattle. But that victory had done little to lift their spirits. A win was a win but this was ridiculous. Great teams don't need every last second of overtime—the game lasted a full 75 minutes, the longest in Eagles team history, and was decided when kicker Roger Ruzek made a 44-yard field goal as time expired—to dispatch lesser opponents.

Things were coming to a boil. Joyner, a Pro Bowl player following the 1991 season and regarded by many as the most complete outside linebacker in the NFL, had barely been able to control his emotions. Joyner had been devastated by Brown's death and had spent much of his time trying to come to grips with the loss.

In training camp, Joyner lashed out at the Eagles front office for their handling of the aftermath of Brown's death and at some of his teammates for failing to attend the funeral. He ripped Kotite following losses to Kansas City and Green Bay. Joyner's most inflammatory comments were published in the *New York Times*.

"It was a very, very difficult season for me," Joyner recalled afterward. "There were so many things that happened, and I had a hard time dealing with the Jerome situation. That was with me all year. I was emotional, maybe even more emotional than I usually am, because I felt we had to dedicate the season to him. Whenever something went wrong, I reacted strongly."

On Tuesday, December 15, Joyner met with Harry Gamble and then with Kotite at Veterans Stadium in Philadelphia. "I want you to understand what happened here," Joyner told the team president, and then the head coach, during separate meetings. "I'm not trying to create problems." Joyner then took the unprecedented step of calling his own press conference. He met with about 30 reporters from newspapers and radio and television stations in the press room on the fourth floor of Veterans Stadium.

Joyner said his "puppet" reference to Kotite was in response to a question about his feelings following the January 8, 1991 dismissal of Ryan and promotion of Kotite from offensive coordinator. He said he didn't really think Kotite was a puppet. "If I felt that way, I would have walked in his office and told him that," Joyner said at the time.

Joyner said he was concerned that his teammates would lose faith in him as a leader. He didn't want to distract the team at this critical point in the season. He wanted to focus on football, on renewing the quest to make the Super Bowl.

"There was a feeling of mine that the coaching staff, the players and management kind of felt that I was trying to be disruptive in bringing up these points," Joyner said at the time. "I just wanted to come forward and let everybody know what happened and how it happened.

"Not for one second did I try to do all this and be disruptive because at this point in time there really is no need for it. I came in today and watched film as usual and sat down and talked with Harry and talked with Richie and explained to them the situation.

"It's important, more than anything, for my teammates to understand that I'm not trying to stir up anything. Had I known that this was the direction that this article was going and this is what the article was going to bring about, I would have never even did the interview. Nobody wants to win more than Seth Joyner."

After the long trip back from Seattle, which was the Eagles' second cross-continental journey in three weeks, Kotite gave the players Monday and Tuesday off. He met with his assistant coaches on Monday to begin formulating the game plan for the Redskins.

Washington had long been the Eagles' archfoe. Since 1988, Philadelphia had compiled a record of 27-12 against their four NFC Eastern Division rivals. They were 24-5 against Dallas, Phoenix and the New York Giants. They were 3-7 against Washington, including a playoff loss that ended the 1990 season.

With their big, strong offensive line and disciplined defense, the Redskins had been able to neutralize the Eagles' two biggest strengths: their powerful pass rush and Cunningham's big-play ability. "They're the team that gives us more trouble than any other," White noted. "They are the one team that has always had success against us. We have to turn that around. We have to get the upper hand this week. This is our playoff game. As far as I'm concerned, if we don't win this game, we won't be in the playoffs."

As an organization, the Redskins stood in sharp contrast to the Eagles. Joe Gibbs had been their coach since 1981. In that period, the Eagles had been coached by Dick Vermeil, Marion Campbell and Fred Bruney (for one game), as well as Ryan and Kotite. Washington had won three Super Bowls and compiled a 15-4 playoff record under Gibbs; the Eagles were 0-4 in playoff games during that same period. This Washington team had struggled more than most of its predecessors. Injuries to stars such as defensive back Darrell Green and offensive tackle Jim Lachey, plus the poor play of quarterback Mark Rypien, the Most Valuable Player in the team's Super Bowl victory over Buffalo back in January, had doomed the Redskins to a disappointing season. "We're just another team scrambling to get into the playoffs," Gibbs said on the Wednesday before the game against the Eagles. "We don't look at ourselves as the defending champs. That was last year. That means nothing. We're just another team that's scrapping and fighting and just trying to get something going."

Both the Eagles and the Redskins were in position to salvage the 1992 season. The stakes were the same for both teams: the winner of Sunday's game would clinch a playoff berth, the loser would have to scramble just to qualify for post-season play. But there was considerably more pressure on the Eagles. The Redskins had been to the Super Bowl and won it. They weren't trying to prove anything. They also had not dedicated their season to a late, great teammate. The Redskins were just trying to win a game and get into the playoffs. The Eagles were trying to keep alive a dream, to rekindle a flickering flame.

"That was the biggest game of the regular season," Allen said afterward. "Not just because of the position we were in, with both teams tied and the winner qualifying for the playoffs, but also because it was the Redskins. They were the one team that really had been our nemesis. They were the team that always blew out the candles whenever we got hot. They had been a brick wall in our path."

"That was the key game in the regular season," Joyner added. "They always had been our toughest team to beat and we knew going into that game that if we were going to do anything that season, we had to beat the Redskins that day."

Game day was overcast and windy. A mist was in the air. The temperature was 45 degrees. As usual, a capacity crowd of 65,000 spectators filled Veterans Stadium, the gigantic concrete bowl in South Philadelphia. The Redskins seized control early in the game. Their defense, led by linebacker Wilber Marshall, stuffed Eagles running back Herschel Walker for no gain on a fourth-down play. They drove into Philadelphia territory behind Rypien's passing and Earnest Byner's running and they took a 3-0 lead on a Chip Lohmiller field goal on the second play of the second quarter.

The Eagles struck back. Cunningham passed 33 yards to wide receiver Fred Barnett to move the team into Redskins territory. Next, running back Heath Sherman—who had supplanted the loudly heralded, highly paid Walker as the team's top ball-carrier in the second half of the season—broke three tackles on a stumbling, lunging, 21-yard touchdown run. But then the Redskins responded. Three plays later, Rypien glanced to his left, saw Clark covered, and then looked downfield to see wide receiver Ricky Sanders two steps behind Allen. Sanders caught Rypien's perfect pass at the 22 yard line and raced into the end zone for a 62-yard touchdown. Washington was out front, 10-7.

Cunningham had been solid but unspectacular for much of the first half. But now he made a mistake: his third-down pass for wide receiver Calvin Williams was intercepted by cornerback A.J. Johnson, who gave the Redskins possession at the Philadelphia 30. But Joyner got Cunningham off the hook. On the next play, Joyner intercepted a Rypien pass to get the Eagles' offense back on the field. Joyner also had a sack and 12 tackles in the game, and he would be named NFC Defensive Player of the Week for his performance.

"Anybody that knows me knows that no matter what is happening, I'm always going to be prepared," Joyner said after the season. "There was a lot going on that week, a lot of pressure and circumstances that could have been distracting. But I don't lose my focus. If anything, situations like that make me prepare even better, to be ready for anything."

After Joyner's interception, the Eagles got one first down and punted. The Redskins drove 50 yards—overcoming sacks of Rypien by Joyner and White—and added another Lohmiller field goal on the last play of the first half for a 13-7 lead. "We're a second-half team," Kotite told his players at intermission. "We've done it all year. We'll do it again."

The Eagles took the second-half kickoff and drove 80 yards for the go-ahead touchdown. The big play was Cunningham's 24-yard bootleg around left end, a misdirection play that completely fooled the Washington defense. It was a telling play because it took full advantage of Cunningham's running ability and it caught the Redskins, normally the most disciplined of defensive teams, badly out of position. With his long legs gobbling up ground, Cunningham moved the football from the Eagles' 37 yard line to the Redskins' 39. "That was the big play of the game," said Redskins linebacker Andre Collins, who had been caught inside on the play. Three plays later, Cunningham lofted a 28-yard touchdown pass to Williams, a third-year player who leaped and beat Redskins defenders Johnson and Brad Edwards to the football. After Ruzek's extra point, the Eagles were in front, 14-13.

Midway in the fourth quarter, Philadelphia's Vai Sikahema returned a punt 47 yards to the Washington 25. From there, the Eagles drove to the 1, but a false-start penalty on tackle Ron Heller pushed the team back to the 6. On third down, Cunningham threw incomplete, and the Eagles were forced to settle for a short Ruzek field goal and a 17-13 lead. "I thought that was going to come back and haunt us," Kotite said of Heller's penalty.

It looked costly at the time. If the Eagles had scored a touchdown, their lead would have been 21-13. The Redskins would have needed a touchdown and a field goal in the final four minutes to win the game. But now the Redskins only needed a touchdown when they took possession after the ensuing kickoff with 3:35 to play. As his teammates waved towels above their heads to incite the crowd, Heller felt his stomach tighten into knots. "You try not to think about your own situation," he said after the game. "But I was dying inside."

For one series, the Redskins of 1992 looked like the Redskins of 1991. Rypien was confident, sharp and precise with his passes. The offensive line was providing plenty of pass protection. The running game was strong. In all, the Redskins ran 17 plays, including 10 in the final 69 seconds. The clock kept ticking, and they kept driving, generating 85 yards and picking up six first downs. The Eagles kept backing up and backing up, to the edge of the end zone, to the edge of the cliff.

"I don't know how to describe it," Mike Golic said after the season. "I was out of the game because we had put in some new [defensive] fronts that week. So you're standing there, and you're just dying. You're just watching them march down the field, play after play, and you're just praying that somebody will do something to stop them. But it's excruciating."

Rypien got the drive started with a 10-yard strike to Clark. Byner added 20 yards on an 8-yard reception and a 12-yard run. The next big play was a 1-yard gain on a quarterback sneak by Rypien on fourth and one at midfield. Then Rypien tossed a short pass to running back Ricky Ervins, who slipped away from Philadelphia linebacker Byron Evans and ran for a first down at the Eagles' 31. "They have so many weapons," Kotite said after the game. "They strike the fear in you."

Rypien scrambled for nine yards to the 22, then executed another quarterback sneak for two yards and a first down at the 20. But then the Redskins were forced to use their third and final timeout with 0:35 left. From the 20 yard line, Rypien threw three consecutive incompletions. The most memorable one was the second-down pass in the left corner of the end zone to Clark, who broke away from defensive back John Booty and got both hands on the football. But Clark lost control as he fell to the ground. "It was a great throw," Clark said after the game. "I just didn't have enough time to pull the ball in."

On fourth down, with 0:21 left, Rypien dumped a short pass to Ervins, who rumbled to the 5 yard line. There was a mad scramble—some of the Eagles on the field were celebrating, thinking the game was over, while the Redskins raced to get set at the line of scrimmage—and Booty admitted to picking up the football. "I thought the game was over," he said afterward.

Because Booty picked up the football, referee Dale Hamer stopped the clock at 0:07, allowing the Redskins a chance to get set at the line of scrimmage. When Hamer restarted the clock, Rypien spiked the football to stop the clock at 0:02. "Those final seconds took a year off my life,"

Joyner said after the game. "My heart rate must have been up to 200 beats."

The Eagles' sideline was a sea of churning emotion. Everything had been down to one season. Then everything was down to one game. Now everything was down to one play. Heller said he was "going crazy" inside. Cunningham knelt down in prayer next to tight end Keith Byars. Kotite, who left the defensive calls up to assistant coach Bud Carson, also was "doing a lot of praying." The capacity crowd was on its feet, roaring in anticipation.

On the final play of the most important game of the regular season, Rypien took the snap from center and tried to roll to his right. But the quarterback was forced inside by pressure from White, who drove Washington's 300-pound right tackle, Ed Simmons, into the backfield. "I just reached back and gave it everything I had left," White said of his final pass rush of the game.

Rypien said he was looking first for Ervins, but the quarterback's attention quickly turned to Clark, who had run a hook pattern in the middle of the field. For an instant, Clark was open in the end zone. "I knew they would look for Clark," Allen said, recalling the moment. "I recognized the formation. I had seen them in that situation so many times. It's just a matter of watching film and just being around the league and having a sense for how teams are going to attack you. I just knew they would look for Clark. I've seen them do it in other games. I just wanted to make sure my zone was OK and then I went looking for him. You have to know the Redskins. That's what they do. They say, 'OK, here's what we run. If you can stop this, you can stop us.'"

Rypien's pass was low and hard. Clark was two yards deep in the end zone. He was on his knees, arms out, ready to cradle the pass that would have seized the game for the Redskins and shattered the Eagles' season. Allen came across from Clark's left and knocked the ball away at the last instant. It hit the ground and bounced away. Allen kept running and running, out of the end zone, all the way to midfield, as teammates poured on the field in celebration, as fans in the stands yelled and danced, and as Redskins walked dejectedly to their locker room.

"Pure adrenalin" was the way Allen described it. He said his mind was filled with snapshot images: of Jerome Brown, of the Redskins' Super Bowl title from the previous season, of joyous fans in the stadium, of all the hard work and fervent hopes that he and his teammates had poured into this season.

The Eagles were in the playoffs for the first time since 1990. They had won 10 games for the fifth season in a row. They had beaten the Redskins, the defending world champions, in a pressure-packed game on a cold December afternoon.

This season might be something special after all.

─── ▪ **16** ▪ ───

GOODBYE, PHILADELPHIA

O n the night of December 20, just a few hours after the Eagles clinched a playoff berth with a dramatic victory over the Washington Redskins, the telephone rang in Reggie White's house. His stepfather had been murdered.

It was the third tragedy to rock the 1992 Eagles. First, star defensive tackle Jerome Brown was killed in an automobile accident. Then, head coach Rich Kotite returned home from the team's final exhibition game to find the lifeless body of his mother-in-law, Stella Corkum. Now, White was stunned to learn that his mother's husband had been beaten to death in an apparent robbery attempt outside of a recreation center in Chattanooga, Tennessee. Leonard Collier, 44, was attacked while sitting in his car outside the St. Elmo Recreation Center, where his stepson's illustrious sports career had begun. Police in Chattanooga said Collier had been beaten to death with a blunt object.

White flew home to Chattanooga on Monday. He was in the middle of one of the most distracting times of his professional life. His team was getting ready for the last game of the regular season, to be followed by a berth in the playoffs, and his status as a future free agent was tied to ongoing labor discussions between NFL owners and the representatives of the NFL Players Association.

But now White was needed far from Philadelphia, far from football. He was needed at home, with his mother and other family members and friends. "It wasn't easy," White recalled, looking back after the Eagles' final regular-season game on December 27 against the New York Giants.

172

"If he had died a natural death, it would have been easier. But to die from somebody murdering him is not easy. My mom has been very strong through this. But it's been very difficult for all of us. I'll tell you one thing this ordeal has taught me and that's to appreciate family more. You have to judge people not by how they are or what they do, but just by looking deep into their hearts and seeing the good and not just the bad."

White had been raised in Chattanooga. His father was a semi-pro baseball player who never married his mother. One year, when White was about nine, his mother and stepfather went away and left him and his older brother with his grandmother. White's grandmother, Mildred Dodds, was a deeply religious woman who led him along a path that resulted in his being ordained as a Baptist minister when he was 17. White said he can remember sitting on the couch with his grandmother in a small home in the projects in Chattanooga and watching the Reverend Billy Graham, the evangelical preacher, on television. "My grandmother is a big fan of Dr. Graham's," White said. "She loved to watch him on TV when we were kids."

Ironically, White's first chance to preach at one of Billy Graham's Crusades came in June 1992. White was at Veterans Stadium, preparing to make his first public appearance with one of his childhood heroes, when he was notified of the death of Jerome Brown. White went on stage that night as planned. With tears in his eyes, he broke the news of his friend's death to thousands of people in Veterans Stadium. "It was hard and yet it was a comfort somehow," White said before the start of the 1992 season. "I cried that night for Jerome. I still cry for him. But I must learn to accept it. We all must. Things happen for a reason."

White attended Howard High School in Chattanooga. He was a big, strong but slightly awkward athlete when he began his high school career. But he would develop into an All-America selection in football and an all-state choice in basketball. "The first time I met him, he was an eighth grader," recalled Robert Pulliam, who was the head football coach at Howard High School at the time. "I asked him what his ambitions were, and being the football coach in the high school, I thought he was going to tell me he wanted to be a big ferocious professional football player. Instead, he said he wanted to go into the ministry."

Pulliam remembers White as a "big, old, Bible-toting young man" who resisted the lure of trouble in school and on the hard streets of the neighborhood. "In that environment, there was a lot of peer pressure, a lot of picking on kids if they were different," Pulliam noted. "I didn't want Reggie to lay that Bible down because of peer pressure. But the strength was his. He played in a program that, prior to his arrival, hadn't had a winning season in 8 to 10 years. Physically and morally, he built that program."

Henry Bowles, the basketball coach at Howard High, said White came to him as a "big, clumsy tenth grader. But he wanted to play and he wasn't afraid to work. I'll tell you how hard he worked: by his senior year, he was all-state."

White was a two-time All-America selection as a defensive lineman at the University of Tennessee. He was named the Southeastern Conference's Player of the Year as a senior, when he registered 15 quarterback sacks. That was the brief heyday of the United States Football League, and White jumped immediately into professional football following his senior season at Tennessee. He signed a five-year, $5 million contract and began his professional career with the Memphis Showboats of the USFL in January 1984. White played two seasons in the USFL. He was used mainly as a nose tackle by the Showboats, which limited his opportunities to rush the passer. But he still managed 23 quarterback sacks in his career in the winter/spring league.

In June 1984, the NFL held a supplemental draft to allow teams to claim the rights of players who had signed with the USFL. The teams used the same selection order as in the regular 1984 draft two months earlier, so the Eagles were picking fourth, behind Tampa, Houston and the New York Giants. Tampa took quarterback Steve Young. Houston took running back Mike Rozier. The Giants selected offensive tackle Gary Zimmerman. The Eagles took White, and then-coach Marion Campbell told the press, "I wish I could put him in the lineup right now."

It would be September 1985 before White would join the Eagles. He still had three years remaining on his original contract with Memphis. But the Eagles, with first-year owner Norman Braman anxious to make a major move for the franchise, bought out the remainder of White's contract with the Showboats and signed him to a four-year contract. Or so White thought. In fact, the contract included an option for a fifth season, which would have bound White to the Eagles in 1989 for just 10 percent more in base salary than he made in 1988—from $400,000 to $440,000.

That option year, as well as a life insurance policy that named the Eagles as beneficiaries in the event of White's death, would serve as the point of contention in a long, acrimonious dispute that would bring White and the team to the chambers of a U.S. District Court judge in Philadelphia before they finally settled on a new contract in the summer of 1989.

White's distrust of the Eagles front office, especially Norman Braman, was developed during his 18-month struggle for a new contract. If 1992 was to be his last season in Philadelphia, and he would sign with another team as a free agent, it might be said that the end of his career with the Eagles was foreshadowed by the beginning. His first deal with the team set in motion a chain of events that would lead to his last. "It went bad from the beginning," said Jim Sexton, who became White's agent in the fall of 1986. "If you could have seen his reaction when we started looking over the documents and realizing what had happened when he first signed with the team. It was just a bad way to start a relationship between a team and a player."

White had become an adversary of NFL owners in general and Braman in particular during the 1987 players' strike. White was an outspoken, passionate leader of the Eagles veterans who refused to cross the picket line and participate in the so-called replacement games. White had been a quiet player during his first two seasons in Philadelphia, regarded as a bit of an oddity because of his strong religious beliefs by some members of that older, established Eagles team. But White emerged as a team leader during the throes of that emotional 24-day strike, when a younger Eagles team—which was being remade by coach Buddy Ryan—began to establish its identity.

But that was a team struggle. That was a fight waged by most of the NFL players against the NFL owners. White's battle with Braman and others in the Eagles front office in 1988 and 1989 was personal. He felt he had been deceived by his old agent, who later was hired by the Eagles as a front-office executive. He felt he had been lied to by Braman and team president Harry Gamble and played for a fool by the franchise's power brokers.

"You have to understand how Reggie is," Sexton once said. "Everything is personal with him. It's not just business. It's personal. How you treat a person in business is a personal thing with him. The Eagles probably thought they were just doing business, just trying to get the best deal for themselves. But Reggie didn't look at it that way. It became personal with him, and it's not the kind of thing that he forgets."

When White was playing for the Memphis Showboats, he was represented by Patrick Forte, a glib, confrontational agent who was based in Flint, Michigan. During the complicated negotiations to get White out of his contract with the Showboats and into the NFL with the Eagles, Forte once told a roomful of reporters on a telephone conference call that the problem was that Philadelphia's management was displaying a "classic case of no balls."

Forte made an impression on the Eagles. In February 1986, five months after negotiating White's contract, he was hired by the team as a vice president and chief contract negotiator. Forte was still an Eagles executive when White filed a $1.5 million civil suit against him three years later. In a deposition, White said he believed Forte and the Eagles "cut a deal" during those negotiations in the summer of 1985. Forte, Braman and Gamble all have denied that Forte's future employment was ever discussed during the White negotiations. But White believed it. Part of his lawsuit against Forte was based on his contention that during the contract negotiations, Braman had told Forte, "When this is over, there's a job here for you."

White filed suit against Forte on March 2, 1989, after months of haggling with the Eagles over the existence of the option year in his contract. White charged Forte with negligence, breach of contract and breach of fiduciary duty for failing to strike the option-year clause from the last year of the contract and for failing to notify him of its existence.

All standard NFL player contracts cover one year. When a player signs with a team for three years, he really signs a series of three, one-year contracts. Each contract includes an option year for the following season, which would bind the player to the team for 110 percent of his salary from the previous season. But in nearly every instance, the option-year clause is deleted from the contract by the player or his representative.

The option-year clause wasn't deleted from the last year of White's four-year deal with the Eagles. And while the Eagles were willing to sign White to a new contract starting in 1989, they also were making clear to him and his agent that the basis for the negotiations was the fact that White was under contract for 1989. "Reggie White is not a free agent," Braman said pointedly while he watched his team practice at the Crystal Palace Sports Centre outside London in preparation for the American Bowl exhibition game in early August 1989. "He is under contract for 1989."

White was also livid about the terms of an annuity that the Eagles had purchased for him as part of his original contract with them. Since the annuity included a life insurance policy, White cancelled a policy that he had purchased for himself. But when Sexton became White's representative in the fall of 1986 and began studying the conditions of his client's contract, he discovered that the beneficiary of the life insurance policy was not White's wife, Sara, but the Eagles. According to Sexton, the Eagles were using White's money to buy a life insurance policy that would protect the team in the event of White's death. "That bothered me more than the option year," White stated during the 1992 season. "That put my family at risk in the event that I would have died. You're talking about my family in that situation."

White's lawsuit against Forte was scheduled to go to trial in U.S. District Court in Philadelphia on August 21, 1989. That morning, in the chambers of judge Charles Weiner, White and the Eagles agreed to a new, four-year contract worth $6.1 million that would make him the highest-paid defensive player in NFL history. The contract was fully guaranteed, a fact noted by tight end Keith Jackson when he tried to force the Eagles to offer the same protection in his contract four years later. It included a $400,000 bonus for signing and yearly base salaries that would escalate from $1.225 million in 1989 to $1.525 million in 1992.

Not that White was happy. The deal nearly fell apart the next day when the Eagles insisted that White pay $29,000 in fines for missing 29 days of training camp. According to Sexton, the two sides haggled for five hours before White agreed to donate $29,000 to the Fellowship of Christian Athletes in Memphis.

At a press conference on the evening of August 22, White was a barely controlled bundle of anger as he sat next to Gamble. It was a weird, awkward scene. At one point, Gamble said "bitter negotiations are not unique" between players and teams in the NFL. White was then asked if he felt he would have gone through the same process with any other NFL team. "No," White said pointedly.

Before the 1992 season, White looked back at that period and swore, "I can't go through that again. I won't go through that again. I can't sit at home wondering how much these guys want to win. I can't come back with that mindset. The last time, I came back that way and I wasn't right the whole season. I can't come back and think about what they did or what they said." Later in the 1992 season, White had this to say about the Eagles front office: "A lot of times, they'll say things and then when you sign, they'll say, 'Don't forget, it was just business.' To me, business doesn't consist of lying to a person. Reggie White doesn't handle business that way. I would never lie to my employees."

This strong undercurrent of unhappiness was significant because White was one of the best defensive players in the NFL. In his first game with the Eagles, on September 29, 1985, White registered three quarterback sacks and tipped a pass that cornerback Herman Edwards returned for a touchdown against the New York Giants.

White managed 13 sacks in 13 games as an NFL rookie in 1985. But he blossomed under Ryan, who replaced Campbell in January 1986. Ryan made White the cornerstone of his "46" defense, using him at left defensive end but occasionally lining him up over the opposing center, where he would disrupt the middle of the line of scrimmage. "That way, you can scare more than one player," Ryan explained. "Let them all worry about him."

White was in the Pro Bowl by the end of the 1986 season. He earned the Most Valuable Player award in that all-star game in Hawaii when he registered four sacks, a game record. White's most remarkable season probably was 1987, when he tied an NFC record with 21 sacks, just one short of the league record of 22 set by Mark Gastineau of the New York Jets in 1984. But while Gastineau had set his record in a 16-game season, White managed his 21 sacks in just 12 games, since he missed four because of the players' strike.

Inspired by the strike and the solidarity shown by the Eagles on the picket line, White was a nearly unstoppable force that season. He had more than one sack in nine games. He also made one of the most memorable plays of his career, sacking Washington quarterback Doug Williams, grabbing the football and racing 70 yards for a touchdown.

At 6-foot-5 and 290 pounds, White was a remarkable blend of speed and power. He had the agility of a much smaller player. Asked to name the best defensive lineman in the NFL, the San Francisco 49ers' Jim Burt replied, "Reggie White. Who else? Did I hesitate when I said his name? No, nobody would. He's unbelievable."

Starting in 1986, White was named a starter to the Pro Bowl in six consecutive seasons. He would make it seven in a row in 1992. He never managed fewer than 11 sacks in a professional season and averaged 19 sacks in the three seasons from 1986 to 1988. White also was a tremendous defender against the run. He wasn't a one-dimensional pass-rusher who sacrificed run support in his pursuit of the quarterback. Excluding the strike-shortened 1987 season, White made 100 or more tackles in four of his first six NFL seasons and 98 in another one.

An important source of White's value was his durability. In a violent, dangerous sport, White seemed almost immune from injury. He never missed a game in his NFL career, starting his 120th in a row in the 1992 regular-season finale against the New York Giants. "I've been around a lot of great defensive linemen and Reggie's the best of them all," Ryan once said. "You don't see 300-pound guys with that kind of speed and quickness."

White was a rarity off the field, too. A licensed minister, he attributed his physical prowess to divine blessing and found no disparity between his gospel of peace, love and understanding and his tenacity on the football field. He spent his Sunday afternoons delivering punishment in the Lord's name. On the football field, the Minister of Defense never turned the other cheek. "People think Christians have to be wimps," White sermonized. "Jesus wasn't a wimp. Jesus was strong. He was tough. I play as hard as I can to honor the Lord. I'm not trying to hurt anybody. But intimidation is part of the game. If I get a chance to hit a guy, I'm going to hit him as hard as I can. I'm not going to hold up. I play this game to glorify the Lord and that means playing it as hard and as well as I can. The Lord wouldn't want me to play any way but as hard as I can play."

Throughout White's career, offensive linemen have reported that he never cursed when he felt he was being held or blocked unfairly. But when his temper rose, White would coil into his three-point stance, announce that "Jesus Is Coming," and explode with a combination of speed and power that was remarkable even by NFL standards.

Proud, energetic and filled with a sweeping vision, White was extremely active in the community. On Friday afternoons during the football season, he would preach on the street corners or in small community centers in troubled neighborhoods in North Philadelphia and Camden, New Jersey. He disqualified himself from the NFL's Player of the Week and Player of the Month award because they were sponsored by a beer company. With his wife, Sara, White started his Alpha and Omega ministry with the goal of improving life for underprivileged youth, especially those in the inner cities. "We're losing too many of our black youths," White once said. "They are dying young. Too many of them are dying young. We have to do something. We have to make a difference."

In a locker room filled with young, liberal players, White often sounded like a loud voice from another time. His religious beliefs led him to rail against drug and alcohol abuse and racism, but also homosexuality and abortion. Along with his wife, White in 1991 opened Hope Palace, a second home on their property in Knoxville, Tennessee, to serve as a shelter for unwed mothers. He was working with investors to establish a chain of non-profit enterprises to help train poor people to rebuild their communities.

Like most ministers, White preached that today was fleeting, a wisp of time in eternity. His tomorrow was everlasting. But when it came to football, it was now or never. White believed that this season represented a last chance for the Eagles, who had been one of the NFL's strongest teams since 1988 but still were looking for their first playoff victory since the 1980 season. White felt the Eagles had endured too many disappointments to survive another one. He knew the team's nucleus had been together since 1986 and that time passes quickly in the fast-paced world of the NFL.

White was talking about the urgency of the 1992 season in May. When Jerome Brown was killed on June 25, White raised the stakes: the Eagles had to win not only because this was their last chance, but also because they had to honor the memory of their fallen teammate. White sensed that the team was slowly disintegrating. He had loved being a part of the special camaraderie that developed on the team as its identity was formed under Ryan in the late 1980s. Then Ryan was fired. And Brown was killed. And Keith Jackson was gone. And now Andre Waters and Wes Hopkins were hurt. It just wasn't the same anymore. White was trying to stay focused, trying to concentrate on this week's game against the New York Giants, on the challenge that lay ahead for the Eagles in the playoffs. But it was hard not to look beyond that, to the freedom and the opportunity that awaited him after the season.

White was anxious to test his freedom. He had gone to NFL Players Association representatives in September and volunteered to serve as the lead plaintiff in a class-action lawsuit against the NFL. When he filed suit on September 21 to have every player whose contract expired at the end of the season declared a free agent, he called the action "the football equivalent of the Emanicipation Proclamation." The symbolism was obvious: White considered the current system in the NFL a form of slavery. He called it "bad and dehumanizing."

White wanted change. He wanted to see what kind of money he could command. He wanted to see how he would be treated in the open market. White tried to concentrate on football, but these thoughts kept intruding. He was so close to being free that it was hard not to daydream about it. What would it be like to play for the Redskins? Or the 49ers? Or the Cowboys? Would Atlanta and Detroit make huge offers for his services? What about Miami? They had stepped up and snatched Keith Jackson away from the Eagles. Would they do the same with him?

On Tuesday, December 22, with White in Chattanooga attending to family matters following the murder of his stepfather, the NFL and the Players Association jointly announced a "tentative agreement" to end their bitter five-year labor dispute and bring a form of free agency to the league. Under the terms of the agreement, players would become free agents after five years in the NFL. Players with fewer than five years of service would remain bound to their old team even when their contract expired. There would be a salary cap that would kick in when player costs reached 67 percent of the NFL owners' gross revenue. Under the terms of the agreement, gross revenue would include money generated from ticket sales and television rights but not merchandising sales from NFL Properties, the league's marketing and licensing arm. When the salary cap kicked in—and most experts expected it would by 1994—the term for free agency would drop from five years to four years.

The agreement would cut the annual college draft from 12 rounds to seven rounds and allot each team $2 million to use to sign draft choices. That provision was designed to keep teams from lavishing millions on unproven college players at the expense of veterans. For example, the Eagles paid rookie offensive tackle Antone Davis, their No. 1 draft pick, a $2 million signing bonus as part of a five-year, $4.7 million contract before he played a down for them in the summer of 1991. That year, as he was surrendering 12 sacks and being called for 12 penalties, Davis made more than any other Eagles player except quarterback Randall Cunningham.

The agreement also would allow teams to designate one "franchise" player who would be unable to sign with another team. The "franchise" player would be required to earn a salary that was among the top five for players at his position. In addition, NFL teams would be allowed to match contract offers to two players in 1993 and to one player in 1994. This right-of-first-refusal clause would allow teams to retain players who had fielded offers from other teams. In general, those terms would allow teams to keep most of their star players in the first two years of the agreement.

But the Eagles were an exception. The reason was that all plaintiffs in various lawsuits against the NFL were exempt from any restrictions in their status as free agents and could not be stopped from signing with other teams. The NFL agreed to this "plaintiffs' clause"—over Braman's strong objections—because they wanted a universal settlement, one that would end all ongoing lawsuits against the league.

There were 16 players with their names on various lawsuits against the NFL, and three of them were stars for the Eagles—Reggie White, Seth Joyner and Clyde Simmons. As a result, the tentative agreement meant that the Eagles would not be able to restrict White in any way when his contract expired after the 1992 season, nor Joyner and Simmons when theirs expired the following year.

White had volunteered to put his name atop the class-action suit in September. But at the time, he had no idea that such an action would prove so important to his hopes of becoming an unrestricted free agent. Joyner and Simmons also had stumbled into good fortune. They had signed three-year contracts just days before the start of the 1991 season, but they resented what they considered the superior, confrontational attitude of the Eagles organization during the negotiations. They also felt the old restricted free-agency system in the NFL was unfair and led to the Eagles' hard-line approach.

So in June 1992, Joyner and Simmons put their names on a lawsuit that was filed in U.S. District Court in Philadelphia. Seven other players from other teams had their names on the lawsuit, which was really only a variation of the *McNeil v. NFL* antitrust suit scheduled to start later that month in Minneapolis. "Basically, it was more just a symbolic act than anything," Joyner said on Wednesday, December 23, in the Eagles locker room. "We were looking for damages, but mostly we just wanted to protest what we felt was an unfair system that needed to be changed. It was either take their best offer or hold out for the [1991] season and that wasn't right. But I guess something else has come out of this now. We'll be in good position." According to Jim Solano, the agent for both Joyner and Simmons, "We never expected that this would result. These guys sued because they were disgusted with the way negotiations went. It was a protest. But it's put them in the driver's seat now."

White returned to his home in South Jersey on Thursday evening, Christmas Eve. He had missed practice on Wednesday and Thursday. He attended practice on Christmas morning and again on Saturday, but it was tough for him to concentrate on the Giants, on football.

On Saturday night, the Eagles assembled at the Hilton Hotel in Mt. Laurel, New Jersey, as they always did on the eve of a home game. As the defensive players gathered for a meeting, White let slip just how far his mind was from the next day's game against the Giants. He mentioned free agency and the future and the fact that his career with the Eagles might soon be over. "Where's your head at, Reggie?" cornerback Eric Allen snapped.

White was taken aback. An unquestioned team leader and future Hall of Fame inductee, he wasn't used to criticism from other players. Allen's comment hit home. "He was right," White said the next day. "He checked up on me. I have to keep my head in this organization. That's the type of guy Eric is. He had enough guts to say it to me. It tore down my pride a little but that was OK. I realized that he was right. That's what accountability is. We have to be accountable to each other as teammates and as Christians. It made me think." After the game, Allen commented: "It's checks and balances. Sometimes a guy has to approach the upper level guys and suggest something. That's what makes a team. It's not the coaches. It's the relationships."

White entered the game against the Giants with 123 quarterback sacks in his career. The NFL record was 126.5 sacks, set by Giants linebacker Lawrence Taylor, whose illustrious career appeared to be over when he tore his Achilles tendon in November. Previously, Taylor had announced that 1992 would be his last season.

White had dominated the Giants throughout his career. He had sacked the Giants' Phil Simms—who would sit out this game with an injury—16 times, more often than any other NFL quarterback. His play was a big reason the Eagles had won eight of nine games against the Giants since the start of the 1988 season. In the Eagles' 47-34 victory over the Giants back on November 22 in Giants Stadium, White had registered three sacks, his season high.

The Eagles made short work of the Giants on a sunny, 32-degree day in Veterans Stadium. It would be the final game for Giants coach Ray Handley, who would be fired two days later. The Giants, Super Bowl champions after the 1990 season, went 8-8 in 1991 and 6-10 in 1992 in their two seasons under Handley.

The Eagles built an impressive lead at halftime behind quarterback Randall Cunningham, who passed for one touchdown and ran for another. Cunningham passed 34 yards to wide receiver Calvin Williams for the game's first touchdown and raced 20 yards into the end zone for another score midway in the second quarter. Roger Ruzek's 45-yard field goal on the last play of the first half gave the Eagles a 17-0 lead.

Cunningham was another reason for the Eagles' dominance of the Giants. His elusive scrambling style had frustrated the Giants' defensive players for several seasons. His touchdown run in the second quarter was the eighth of his career against the Giants. He didn't have more than four against any other NFL team. "The guy is a seed between my teeth," Giants linebacker Carl Banks once said of Cunningham.

The Eagles also got a big game from running back Herschel Walker, whose role had diminished in the second half of the season. Walker ran 16 times for 104 yards, lifting his season total to 1,070. He became the first Philadelphia player to run for 1,000 yards in a season since Earnest Jackson in 1985.

With the victory, the Eagles finished unbeaten and untied at home for the first time since 1949. With an 8-0 mark in Veterans Stadium, the Eagles were the only team in the NFL to go unbeaten at home in 1992. "Playing at home has been great," Walker said after the game. "But we have to carry that spunk and carry that swagger on the road with us. My philosophy is to try to take over the stadium."

In the locker room after the game, the mood was one of relief and pride in the accomplishments of the regular season. The Eagles had clinched a playoff berth the previous week against Washington. The team just wanted to beat the Giants to keep perfect their home record and continue to build some momentum for post-season play.

The Eagles had finished the regular season with an 11-5 record, a one-game improvement over 1991 and their best mark since they went 11-5 in 1989. They also managed to come full circle: four consecutive victories at the beginning of the regular season and four consecutive victories at the end. During the middle eight games, the Eagles lost five times. And all five of those had been on the road, where they would find themselves in the playoffs, starting with next Sunday's wild card game against the New Orleans Saints in the Louisiana Superdome. "We're going to have to be road warriors," tight end Keith Byars remarked. "We've been a great road team in the past. We're going to have to get that back. We're going to have to get back to taking control of hostile environments."

Reggie White had a solid, unspectacular game. He wore wristbands with the words "Step Dad" written on them to honor his slain stepfather. He was part of a defensive surge that held the Giants without a first down in the first half. He was credited with three tackles and one quarterback sack, the fourteenth of his season, the 124th of his career. "His body was here in Philadelphia but his heart and mind was down in Chattanooga, Tennessee," Byars noted. "He wanted to be down there with his mom, with his family. It's a credit to him that he was able to play the way he was."

On several occasions during the game, White heard the cheers from the Veterans Stadium crowd, which chanted, "Reggie . . . Reggie . . . Reggie," as if to acknowledge that the best defensive player in the team's history might be bound for another team after this season. "I guess if it was up to them, I would be here next season," White commented.

White sat in front of his locker for a long time after the game. There was a chance, he knew, that this was his 64th and final game in Veterans

Stadium. But he was determined not to think that way, to focus on football, on the opportunity before the team in the upcoming playoffs. He felt he owed that to his teammates. "I've allowed it to distract me," White admitted. "That's not fair to my teammates. I have to stay focused. I have to stay focused on the Philadelphia Eagles. We have an opportunity here to do something. I can't be thinking about anything else but the opportunity we have here. I have to go out and play hard for God, No. 1, and also for this team and the guys around here. Hopefully, we've got four games left. The most important thing is the team, so I'm not going to let anything distract me."

POST-SEASON

— • 17 • —

FREE AT LAST

Hhistory sat heavily on the Eagles' shoulders as they prepared for the January 3 playoff game against the New Orleans Saints in the Louisiana Superdome.

The trilogy of playoff tragedy following the 1988, 1989 and 1990 seasons had come to symbolize this talented but unfulfilled team as much as the individual exploits of athletes such as Randall Cunningham, Reggie White and Seth Joyner. The lopsided losses to Chicago, the Los Angeles Rams and Washington in post-season play formed a dark shadow over the team's past. "I think back on all three losses," tight end Keith Byars reflected on Wednesday, December 30, as the players returned to Veterans Stadium from a two-day break and began earnest preparations for the game against the Saints. "I don't want to forget them. I want to remember how I felt because I don't want to feel that way again."

The Eagles had 10 starters who were veterans of all three playoff losses. That group formed the nucleus of the team and included leaders such as Byars, Cunningham, David Alexander and Ron Heller on offense, and White, Joyner, Clyde Simmons and Eric Allen on defense.

For those prominent athletes—most of whom were in their sixth, seventh or eighth NFL season—the wild card playoff game in the Louisiana Superdome represented perhaps their last chance to break free of the haunting reminders of missed opportunity and unrealized potential. "All you can ask for is an opportunity," Allen said. "That's what we have here: another chance. We have to make the most of it."

Each playoff loss had been fascinating in its own way, marked by "some weird circumstance," according to Alexander. Strange weather patterns, flukish injuries, devastating officials' calls—they all combined to doom the Eagles in their previous playoff appearances, to create the impression that this team was cursed. "It didn't seem like any of them was a normal game," Alexander added. "There was always something strange, something weird."

The first playoff loss came to be known as "The Fog Bowl," one of the most famous post-season games in NFL playoff history. It was a game played on a smoky, surrealistic sound stage as thick fog rolled into Chicago's Soldier Field off nearby Lake Michigan. The Eagles were a young, vibrant team back in 1988. They had won six of their final seven games to capture the NFC Eastern Division title when the New York Giants lost to the New York Jets on the last day of the regular season. Cunningham was 25. White was 27. The Eagles had a rookie Pro Bowl tight end named Keith Jackson. Their outspoken coach, Buddy Ryan, was in just his third season.

"I don't think we were mentally capable of beating that Chicago team," Allen conjectured, looking back on his rookie season. "I think we probably had more athletic ability than they did. But I remember talking to [former Chicago defensive end] Al Harris, who was on that team, and he talked about how they had prepared to beat us by just making sure they did the things that they could do."

The Eagles had plenty of chances to win the game. The Bears were an aging, flawed team that would get blown away the next week by San Francisco, losing 28-3 at home. By 1989, the Bears would be a 6-10 team. The Eagles moved the football with remarkable ease. They were inside the Bears' 25 yard line eight times, but they only managed four Luis Zendejas field goals in a frustrating 20-12 loss.

Cunningham passed for 407 yards with three interceptions. Jackson dropped a potential touchdown pass in the end zone, and another touchdown pass to star wide receiver Mike Quick was nullified by an illegal-motion penalty on third-year fullback Anthony Toney.

The skies were sunny on New Year's Eve, 1988, when the game started. But the fog rolled in just before halftime. Visibility was limited to about 15 to 20 yards in the second half. Most of the spectators in the stadium couldn't see the action on the field. Reporters were escorted out of the press box and down to the field, where they stood on the sideline and watched the players shift in and out of sight.

"We got down early [17-9 at half] and the next thing you know the fog rolled in," Byars remembered. "You couldn't see. It was frustrating because I think we would have won the game." "That one hurts me the most," Allen added. "It was my first year and it was Buddy's homecoming back to Chicago. But we were so young. It was an experience just to be there."

In 1989, the Eagles played their first playoff game on New Year's Eve again. This time, they were home for an NFC wild card game against the Los Angeles Rams, a high-powered passing team. The Eagles limped into the game. Three weeks earlier, one day before the Eagles played Dallas in what was dubbed "The Bounty Bowl," Allen was wrestling in the locker room with reserve cornerback Sammy Lilly. It was the kind of roughhousing that Ryan encouraged in the locker room, just good-natured, boys-will-be-boys stuff.

But Allen went down hard. He severely sprained his ankle. He played sparingly the next day, a 20-10 victory memorable mainly for the barrage of snowballs that spectators in Veterans Stadium unleashed on both teams. Allen sat out the next game—a 30-20 Monday night loss in New Orleans. That loss cost the Eagles the NFC Eastern Division title. They finished second to the Giants with an 11-5 record. That meant a wild card playoff game against the Rams in Veterans Stadium.

Injuries were a problem for the Eagles as they spent three days in Suwanee, Georgia, preparing for the game. Allen couldn't practice. Byars was sitting out with sore ribs. Left tackle Matt Darwin was hurt, too, forcing Alexander to move outside. Dave Rimington replaced Alexander at center. Not that Ryan was worried. When asked about Rams running back Greg Bell in the last question of a press conference, Ryan gave a bland answer, then walked away, stopping to stage-whisper to the Philadelphia reporters in the room, "Greg Bell, my ass."

It was a warm, misty New Year's Eve. The Rams broke to a 14-0 lead as quarterback Jim Everett threw a 39-yard touchdown pass to Henry Ellard and a 4-yard touchdown pass to Damone Johnson in the first quarter. Allen finally entered the game in the second quarter after the Rams had taken advantage of cornerbacks Eric Everett and Izel Jenkins to move the ball with ease. The Rams would finish with 409 yards. "My ankle wasn't right until the middle of the next season," Allen said. "It was weird. I could run straight ahead, but I couldn't cut. Now, when we see guys fool around in the locker room, guys always say, 'Ask Eric what can happen.'"

The Eagles got within 14-7 on a one-yard touchdown run by Anthony Toney early in the fourth quarter, but the Rams finished them off with a long scoring drive. Bell went 54 yards around left end to the Eagles' 10. Two plays later, Bell scored from seven yards out. He finished with 124 yards.

Another key in the Rams' 21-7 victory was their defense, which baffled Cunningham and the Eagles with a series of soft zone coverages. The Eagles managed just three first downs in the first half. "A junior high defense," Ryan later called it. Remembered Byars: "The Rams played a simple defense, dropped everybody back and we didn't take advantage of it."

The Eagles were ready in 1990. The team had been under enormous pressure all season as rumors circulated about Ryan's job security, but they overcame a 0-2 start to finish with a 10-6 record. Once again, they would be home for the playoff opener. This time, the opponent was the Washington Redskins, a team the Eagles had dominated by a 28-14 score on a Monday night game in Veterans Stadium six weeks earlier.

That game came to be known as "The Body Bag Game," because some of the Eagles had chanted "body bags, body bags" as one injured Redskin after another had been carted away. In all, nine Redskins needed assistance to leave the field. "You guys got enough body bags?" some of the Eagles yelled.

The Eagles had spent the week practicing in Tampa, which was more than a little ironic. Their first practices under Ryan were held in Tampa during a spring minicamp in 1986. Injuries were a concern again. In the regular-season finale the previous Sunday in Phoenix, center David Alexander had damaged his knee and defensive tackle Jerome Brown had torn his right rotator cuff.

It was January 5, 1991 when the Eagles took the field for the last time under Ryan. They broke to a 6-0 lead, but the Redskins went in front 10-6 at halftime. The key play came late in the first half when Eagles cornerback Ben Smith upended Redskins running back Earnest Byner, caused a fumble, picked up the loose ball and rumbled 94 yards for an apparent touchdown. Ironically, Ryan had predicted earlier in the week that Byner would fumble. Told that Byner had lost just one fumble despite handling the ball 297 times during the regular season, Ryan had said, "Is that right? Well, maybe he'll lay it down three times for us."

Byner lost a fumble just once and it appeared to be the big play of the game. But after a lengthy delay, the play was overturned by the instant replay official, who ruled after further review that the ground had caused Byner's fumble. As a result, the Redskins kept possession. "You need breaks and that was the break that we needed," Byars said. "That changed the whole game."

Once again, the Eagles' offense was sputtering under Cunningham. Late in the third quarter, with Washington in front 13-6, Ryan yanked Cunningham and replaced him with Jim McMahon. McMahon threw three incompletions and left the game. The Redskins then drove for another score. By the time Cunningham returned to the game, the Redskins were in front 20-6 and that was how it ended. "Seven points down in the third quarter and he embarrasses Randall on national television," Eagles owner Norman Braman was quoted as saying after the game.

Brown took six injections of pain-killers to play. He wore a harness that pinned his left arm to his side. Alexander tried to play one series in the third quarter, but his knee gave way and he limped off the field, throwing his helmet to the sideline. "That was so frustrating because I had to sit there and watch the team lose, and I couldn't really help them," he said. "It's just been one thing after another for us, always some strange situation that seemed to turn against us." A memorable post-game scene remains from that playoff loss to the Redskins: linebacker Seth Joyner, sitting alone on the Eagles' bench long after his teammates had retreated to the locker room and the stadium had emptied of spectators.

"In all three of them, we made a lot of mistakes," Byars said of the playoff losses. "We made mental mistakes, and we made physical mistakes. It just leaves you with such a bad feeling because you work so hard in the off-season and during the season and you get to that point and then you just let it get away."

Despite their past, the Eagles were confident as they prepared to face the Saints, who had finished second to San Francisco in the NFC Western Division with a 12-4 record. Some of the confidence was based on faith. Quarterback Randall Cunningham, who tended to have his own unique perspective on things, suggested after the regular-season finale against the Giants that it was the Eagles' "destiny" to win the Super Bowl. "We have a destiny," Cunningham claimed. "That destiny isn't just to win a playoff game. It's to get to the Super Bowl and win the Super Bowl."

But most of it was based on the matchup: the Eagles had fared well in the past against sturdy but basic teams such as the Saints. With their methodical offense and linebacker-oriented defense, the Saints were reminiscent of the good New York Giants teams of the late 1980s, teams the Eagles swept in 1988 and 1989.

"I feel a lot different than I have in the past about the situation," Allen said in the locker room after the Eagles had beaten the Giants in the regular-season finale. "I don't want to look past New Orleans or anything but, man, it would be very hard to conceive of us losing to New Orleans." Joyner had his own thoughts: "You have to be good and you have to have some good luck. We've endured all the bad luck. In the past, I think we had something missing, but now all the pieces are in place. The offensive line is strong enough for us to compete, and the defense hasn't been giving up the big plays."

The odds were stacked against the Eagles making it to the Super Bowl, which was set for January 31 in Pasadena, California. No NFC team had made the Super Bowl as a wild card since the playoff field in each conference had been expanded from four teams to five in 1978.

The Eagles would need to become the first NFC team since Washington to win three playoff games to make the Super Bowl. Washington won the Super Bowl tournament after the strike-shortened 1982 season. But the Redskins played all three of their playoff games at RFK Stadium.

The Eagles were looking at the likelihood of three road playoff games—at New Orleans, at Dallas and at San Francisco. That would have been a lot to ask from a team that was 3-5 on the road during the regular season and hadn't beaten a team with a winning record away from home. "Our only concern right now is winning the first one," defensive tackle Mike Golic stated on Thursday, December 31. "We don't want to look at it like, 'We have to do this, this and this.' We just have to beat the Saints. That's the only goal we have right now."

The game was packed with pressure for both teams, which were remarkably similar in their recent histories. Only the Eagles knew how the Saints felt as they prepared for the pivotal game, and only the Saints could identity with the Eagles. These were two proud, talented, experienced teams with the same fatal flaw: both had been good when they had needed to be great. Both teams had been to the playoffs three times during their current phases of development. Both had won one division title and qualified twice as a wild card. Both were 0-3 in post-season games. One team was sure to break free by early Sunday evening in the Superdome. One team was sure to walk off the field, suddenly lighter, looser, a weight of expectations and disappointment lifted off their shoulders.

The Eagles had won 52 regular-season games since 1988. That was more than every team except Buffalo and San Francisco. The Eagles had provided their fans with great plays, great games, great weeks of anticipation and speculation. So why were most of their fans feeling so unfulfilled? And why was there such pressure on this team to win the wild card game in the Superdome? The Saints knew why. The Saints had won 62 regular-season games since 1987. That was more than every team except Buffalo, San Francisco and Washington. The Saints had also given their long-suffering fans moments of joy and wonder.

The New Orleans franchise never even had a winning season in their first 20 years of existence, much less made the playoffs. Jim Mora arrived as head coach in 1986—after negotiating briefly with Norman Braman about becoming head coach of the Eagles—and the Saints had gone 7-9, 12-3, 10-6, 9-7, 8-8, 11-5 and 12-4. So why were most of their fans feeling so unfulfilled? And why was there such pressure on that team to win? The answer was expectations. Both teams had been just good enough to promise more than they had been able to deliver.

"We prepared hard for those playoff games, we just lost," defensive end Clyde Simmons said on the Thursday before the game against the Saints. "But as you get older, you start to realize that nothing is promised you. When you're younger and you go to the playoffs a couple times, you start thinking you're going to go there every year. But after we missed it last year, you start to realize you have to make the most of your opportunities. This might be a last opportunity."

These were two good teams. The Eagles and Saints had won a lot of games. They had beaten other good teams. They regarded themselves, with some justification, as among the elite franchises in the NFL. But neither team had been able to finish what they had started. Both had merely hinted at their potential, never once following through.

The Eagles won the NFC Eastern Division title in 1988. They were a playoff team, a young, rising power, in 1989 and 1990. But they lost all three of their playoff games. The Saints were a wild card team in 1987 and 1990. They won the NFC Western Division title in 1991. But they also had lost all three of their playoff games.

Something had to give Sunday in the Superdome. Somebody had to finally win. After all these years, after all that work in training camp and in the off-season and all those struggles during the regular season, somebody finally had to break the spell that had bound them. Somebody had to win. But somebody had to lose, too. Somebody had to walk away a loser in their first playoff game for the fourth time in their recent history, to face being branded as a talented team that choked in the playoffs. "Believe me, however bad it [the pressure] is up there, it's worse down here," Mora said in a conference call with Philadelphia-area reporters on the Wednesday before the game. "The fans, the media, they all want to know why we haven't won a playoff game."

The Eagles arrived in New Orleans on Saturday, January 2. The night before, Alabama had stunned top-ranked Miami in the Sugar Bowl to capture the college football national championship. "Roll, Tide, Roll," Alabama fans yelled on Saturday night on Bourbon Street in New Orleans' famous French Quarter.

When the Eagles players walked in the visiting dressing room in the Superdome early Sunday afternoon, they were greeted by a startling sight: a locker had been set aside for Jerome Brown. "I couldn't believe it," defensive end Reggie White said after the game. "We just walked in and there it was."

All season, the Eagles had kept Brown's locker stall in Veterans Stadium just as he had left it. His framed jersey was hung up in the back of the stall. His helmet and shoulder pads sat on a top shelf along with his favorite fishing hat and Bell of Pennsylvania hard hat. A few practice shirts were hung in the locker. Some of his shoes were stacked neatly on the floor.

It became a shrine of sorts in the locker room. Some players would touch it on the way out to the field for the start of a game. When safety William Frizzell became a father, he put a cigar in Brown's undisturbed locker. "It's just a reminder," safety Andre Waters reflected during the regular season. "You look over there, and you remember Jerome. You remember when he would be sitting there, cracking on everybody, laughing and making jokes."

Now, the shrine had been moved. Earlier in the week, Braman had suggested bringing Brown's locker to the Superdome. Kotite had equipment manager Rusty Sweeney wait until the players left the locker room in Veterans Stadium on Saturday to board the buses for the trip to the airport. Sweeney loaded Brown's belongings into a separate trunk. A stall was set aside for Brown in the visiting dressing room in the Superdome. A strip of tape with "99," Brown's number, was pasted across the top of the locker. When the players walked into the dressing room in the middle of the afternoon, the shrine was waiting for them. "It was very moving," defensive tackle Mike Pitts commented. "It just reminded us again what we're playing for this season."

Just before the Eagles took the field for the start of the game, the Buffalo Bills completed the greatest comeback in NFL history. Down by a 35-3 score early in the third quarter of their AFC wild card game against the Houston Oilers, the Bills scored five consecutive touchdowns, forced overtime and won by a 41-38 score. It was an omen.

The Eagles played horribly in the first half against the Saints. All those playoff ghosts seemed to be dancing along the Philadelphia sideline as the Eagles missed tackles and blocks, dropped passes, crossed signals and generally moved a step slower than the aggressive Saints.

New Orleans took the opening kickoff and drove 73 yards for a touchdown. The Saints set the tone on the first play, as quarterback Bobby Hebert faked a handoff and lofted a long pass for wide receiver Quinn Early, who was racing down the middle of the field. The pass fell incomplete, but the Saints had served notice that they planned to attack.

On third down, Hebert avoided a pass rush and shoveled a short throw to fullback Craig Heyward, who raced 25 yards for a first down. Passes of 10 yards to Early and 19 yards to Eric Martin moved the Saints deep into Eagles territory. Next, Hebert lofted a pass in the end zone for Martin, who got tangled up with Eagles' cornerback Mark McMillian. Pass interference was called on McMillian, giving the Saints a first down at the one yard line. On the next play, the 260-pound Heyward, nicknamed "Iron Head," crashed into the end zone.

The Eagles struck back two possessions later when Cunningham threw a 57-yard touchdown pass to wide receiver Fred Barnett. The first playoff touchdown pass of Cunningham's career was a perfect throw—traveling more than 60 yards in the air—and Barnett caught it in stride two steps behind Saints cornerback Toi Cook.

But that was it for the Eagles' offense in the first half. The running game was anemic as Herschel Walker and Heath Sherman combined for just 25 yards. Excluding the long pass to Barnett, Cunningham completed just four of 14 passes for 20 yards. He had three passes knocked down at the line of scrimmage. The Eagles converted just one of six third downs. They looked disorganized during a hurry-up drill at the end of the first half as both Barnett and wide receiver Calvin Williams failed to get out of bounds to stop the clock after catching short passes.

Meanwhile, the Saints looked strong. They rolled up 14 first downs to just four for the Eagles and generated 250 total yards in offense. Hebert completed 13 of 19 passes for 187 yards, exploiting open areas in the middle of the Eagles' zone defense.

The Saints drove 71 yards to set up a 35-yard Morten Andersen field goal for a 10-7 lead midway in the second quarter. After an Eagles punt, the Saints drove 53 yards for a touchdown. Hebert passed 20 yards to Early, and rookie running back Vaughn Dunbar slashed 24 yards to move the Saints deep into Eagles territory. Hebert finished the drive with a seven-yard touchdown pass to Early, who beat Eagles cornerback Eric Allen to the football in the left corner of the end zone.

It was 17-7 at halftime. The Eagles were in trouble as they trudged to their locker room. During the entire regular season, they had rallied to win just once after being behind at halftime. "Remember the Bills," Kotite told his players before they returned to the field for the second half. "They were down 30. We're down 10. What's the big deal?"

The second half started ignominiously for the Eagles. They took the kickoff and drove to the Saints' 25, but then New Orleans linebacker Rickey Jackson swept around Eagles tackle Antone Davis and sacked Cunningham, forcing a fumble that defensive end Wayne Martin recovered. On the next play, Hebert threw a short pass to Dunbar, who raced past Eagles linebacker William Thomas for a 35-yard gain. Four plays later, Andersen kicked a 42-yard field goal for a 20-7 lead.

The Saints got the football back with 5:15 left in the third quarter. They were still ahead 20-7. But rather than try to establish a running game and work some time off the clock, the Saints went for the kill: Hebert faked a handoff and lofted a long pass for Early. But the pass went right to Allen, whose interception was the first in a flurry of big plays for the Eagles. Philadelphia drove 39 yards and pulled within 20-10 when Roger Ruzek hit a 40-yard field goal with 1:01 left in the third quarter.

"That's when it started to shift," Eagles defensive coordinator Bud Carson noted after the game. "This group, when one of them makes a play, they all want to make a play. We just came out and played a little more aggressively in the second half. We were dogging [blitzing] a little more because we had to. We needed to make something happen."

The fourth quarter belonged to the Eagles. They would end up scoring 26 points, the third-most ever scored in a single quarter in NFL playoff history. It also was the most scored in the fourth quarter of an NFL playoff game since the New York Giants scored 27 against the Chicago Bears in 1934.

Suddenly, all the Eagles were making plays. Linebacker Byron Evans knocked down a Hebert pass on third-and-1. Cunningham completed passes of eight and seven yards on crucial third-down plays to Williams and Byars, respectively. Then Cunningham lofted a high pass for Barnett, who made a leaping catch in the end zone to pull the Eagles to within 20-17. "It was great coverage," Barnett said after the game. "But I kept my eye on the ball and it went through my mind that nothing was going to stop me from catching the ball."

By now, the Saints were panicking. They had blown leads in the fourth quarter in three of their four losses during the regular season, and in the playoff loss to Atlanta last season. Now, they were doing it again.

The Superdome crowd was filled with high anxiety. On first down, Hebert rolled to his left and tried to throw across his body to Martin crossing the middle. Eagles linebacker Seth Joyner stepped in front of the pass, intercepted it and raced to the Saints' 26.

The Eagles were in control. The offensive line was firing off the football. Heath Sherman was weaving his way into the Saints' secondary. Sherman carried four times, the last a six-yard sweep around left end for a touchdown that gave the Eagles a 24-20 lead with 6:48 left in the fourth quarter.

The Eagles were just getting started. The Saints' next possession ended when White barreled over tackle Stan Brock and sacked Hebert in the end zone for a safety. It was 26-20, Eagles, with 5:24 left. White jumped up, raised his arms and half-skipped, half-danced across the end zone. "I can't tell you how good that felt," White admitted after the game. "We had waited so long, so long. We waited five years to win a playoff game and to come and finally come back and win the way we did, it was just a great feeling."

After a free kick by the Saints, Sherman gained 11, 6 and 16 yards to move the Eagles into New Orleans' territory. The Eagles worked the clock down to the 2:36 mark, and Ruzek kicked a 39-yard field goal for a 29-20 lead.

Allen finished off the Saints. On the second play of the Saints' ensuing possession, he intercepted a Hebert pass and raced 18 yards into the end zone for a touchdown. Down 20-10 at the start of the fourth quarter, the Eagles had scored 26 points in an 8:20 span, getting two offensive touchdowns, a defensive touchdown, a field goal and a safety.

The comeback set off a wild celebration on the Superdome field in the final minutes. It was a catharsis for the Eagles—all the frustration and anxiety seemed to wash away. The Eagles were free at last—free of the suffocating air of their own unfulfilled expectations, of the constant reminders of their horrible playoff past, of the burden of their unwanted status as talented, enigmatic underachievers.

They had buried the Saints and their own bad memories under an avalanche of big plays. They had won by bigger scores, staged bigger comebacks, but never before had they risen to the occasion in such grand and dramatic fashion. "Finally, finally, finally," White exclaimed moments later in the locker room. "People doubted us but we hung together and we just played a great ballgame when we needed it most." Joyner chimed in: "We got the monkey off our backs. People said we couldn't win a playoff game, that our quarterback couldn't win a playoff game. We proved a lot of people wrong."

Down the hall, the Saints were a shattered team. Cornerback Vince Buck wondered if the Saints' playoff failures were the result of some "Louisiana voodoo curse." Six weeks later, Mora would tell a New Orleans television station, "I still think about it numerous times during the day. I wake up in the morning, and it's on my mind. I go to bed at night, and it's on my mind. It's hanging in my gut like a big piece of weight."

The Eagles' locker room was a cauldron of relief and excitement. The weight of past playoff failures had been lifted from their shoulders. They were loose. They were confident. They were going to Dallas to play the Cowboys in an NFC semifinal game in Texas Stadium. "Dallas—that's just where we want to be," Byars said. "I've only lost one game there in my career. That's a good place for us to be going." All around the locker room, the Eagles were wearing looks of joy and relief. The playoff jinx finally was broken. They had proven they could win in post-season play.

Near the entrance to the locker room sat reserve quarterback Jim McMahon. He was 33. He was the second-oldest player on the team. He was the only one who had ever been where they all wanted to go. In his last playoff game in this building, McMahon had led the Chicago Bears to a Super Bowl romp over the New England Patriots in January 1986. McMahon was trimming his toenails. To no one in particular but to everyone associated with the team, he said, "Don't mean anything unless you win them all."

· 18 ·

FUTURE SHOCK

Not Dallas. Not the Cowboys. Anybody but the Cowboys. The Redskins, maybe. The 49ers, maybe. The Bears, the Rams, the Giants—anybody but the Cowboys.

Dallas? The Eagles laughed at the Cowboys. They ran up the score on them. They set bounties on their heads. They bombarded them with snowballs. They said, "Boo," and the Cowboys fell down.

It was so easy. It was so much fun. The Eagles were sure of one thing when they became an NFC power back in 1988. They could count on one absolute certainty: they would beat the Cowboys.

"We know we're going to win, and they know we're going to win," Eagles coach Buddy Ryan used to say before his team would play the Cowboys. "They just don't know how."

Everybody beat the Cowboys in those days. Once they were America's Team, the most glamorous franchise in the sport, the haughty, highfalutin symbol of all that was so neatly packaged and promoted in the NFL.

But they got old and slow. The only coach they ever had, a legend in a suit, tie and fedora named Tom Landry, got old and lost his touch. Once, midway in the 1988 season, Landry lost track of the line of scrimmage and cost his team the chance for a game-winning field goal. The Cowboys lost by a point in the final four seconds of that game. The Eagles were the team that beat them that day.

The Cowboys went 3-13 in 1988, their final season under Landry, who had been their coach since they were formed in 1960. His final game was December 18, 1988 in Texas Stadium. Only 46,131 spectators showed up that day, more than 16,000 below capacity.

Who could blame the Dallas fans for staying home? The Cowboys lost 23-7 to the young and cocky Eagles, who clinched the NFC East division title that day when the New York Giants lost to the New York Jets. The Eagles danced and sang and celebrated—Jerome Brown was hugging reporters in the locker room—and the Cowboys slinked off into the sunset.

An oil man named Jerry Jones bought the Cowboys in 1989. He hired Jimmy Johnson, who had just won a national championship at the University of Miami, as the new head coach. But it got worse before it got better for the Cowboys: they went 1-15 that season.

Everybody beat the Cowboys, but only the Eagles made such a sport of it. On Thanksgiving Day, 1989, the Eagles beat the Cowboys 27-0 in Texas Stadium. After the game, Johnson accused Ryan of putting bounties on the heads of rookie quarterback Troy Aikman and kicker Luis Zendejas, a former Eagle. Johnson said Ryan had offered money to any player who knocked Aikman or Zendejas out of the game with an injury.

Ryan laughingly denied everything. "Why would I put a bounty on a kicker who hadn't been making anything?" Ryan asked, zinging Zendejas. But the Cowboys insisted on an NFL investigation, since Zendejas had sustained a concussion from a blow from Eagles linebacker Jessie Small after the second-half kickoff. NFL officials ultimately ruled there was no basis for the Cowboys' charges.

A week later, Eagles players started parading around the locker room with green T-shirts with the words "Buddy's Bounty Hunters" written on them. Oh, the Eagles had such great fun at the Cowboys' expense. It became part of their identity. Ryan was so smug, so sure of the Eagles' superiority. And the Philadelphia players, they just knew that Dallas was no match for them. "We dominated them for so long," Eagles linebacker Seth Joyner said after the 1992 season. "It was like you could always put stars next to those games because you knew they were going to be victories."

Two weeks after the 1989 Thanksgiving Day game, the Cowboys arrived in Philadelphia for a rematch. The Eagles won 20-10 in a sloppy, listless game that was played one day after the team was stunned by the death by heart attack of popular quarterbacks coach Doug Scovil. The Eagles couldn't work up much emotion for the game, so the fans in Veterans Stadium took over—pounding the Cowboys with snowballs. His head down, running hard with a police escort by his side, Jimmy Johnson was splattered with snowballs and a cup of beer on his way off the field after the game.

From December 14, 1986 to September 15, 1991, the Eagles won nine consecutive non-strike games against the Cowboys. The only Dallas victory in that period came during the 1987 strike, when a Cowboys team that included picket line-crossing veterans Danny White, Ed Jones and Tony Dorsett whipped a team composed entirely of "replacement" Eagles. Three weeks later, the Eagles got revenge when Ryan ordered a run-it-up touchdown in the final seconds of a 37-20 romp over the Cowboys in the first game back for the union players.

Nine consecutive victories. The Eagles lost seven times to the Washington Redskins in that period. They lost three times to the St. Louis/Phoenix Cardinals. They lost to weaklings such as Atlanta in 1988 and San Diego in 1989 and Indianapolis in 1990 and Tampa Bay in 1991. But they could always count on beating the Cowboys.

Dallas started to become a good team, too. Johnson traded Herschel Walker, a star-crossed running back who would find his way to Philadelphia before the 1992 season, to the Minnesota Vikings for a ransom of high draft picks during the 1989 season. The Cowboys would use those draft picks to reinvent themselves.

Troy Aikman was the No. 1 overall pick in the 1989 draft. He would become a star quarterback. The Cowboys traded up in the 1990 draft to select Florida running back Emmitt Smith, who would lead the NFL in rushing in 1991 and 1992. Johnson and Jones would orchestrate an incredible total of 46 trades in their first four years in Dallas, rebuilding the Cowboys into a team of tremendous speed, skill and youth.

Dallas got better and better. In 1990, the Cowboys were 7-7 and in contention for a playoff berth when they traveled to Philadelphia for a game against the Eagles. But on the first series of the game, Philadelphia defensive end Clyde Simmons landed hard on Aikman, separating the quarterback's right shoulder and ending his season. Dallas lost that game by a 17-3 score as reserve quarterback Babe Laufenberg was overwhelmed by the Eagles' defense. Without Aikman, the Cowboys would lose the next week, too, to finish with a 7-9 record.

"Back then, we just didn't think they could beat us," Eagles defensive tackle Mike Golic commented. "We just knew we were going to win. We seemed to knock them around pretty good back then, too. I think it came from Buddy. He had that attitude toward them, that we were tougher and we were going to intimidate them. They hated Buddy and he loved it."

Even without Ryan, though, the Eagles continued their dominance of the Cowboys. For one memorable game, anyway. On September 15, 1991, the Eagles rode into Texas Stadium with a 1-1 record. Randall Cunningham was out for the season with a knee injury. The Eagles had lost the previous week by a 26-10 score to the Cardinals.

As the team buses made their way down a ramp into the bowels of

Texas Stadium, Cowboys fans gathered around the entrance and started jeering at the Eagles. They held up rubber chickens with little No. 12 Eagles jerseys on them. They pointed thumbs down. They screamed obscenities.

Suddenly, Jerome Brown was on his feet, yelling out the window, pointing. "Kiss my black ass," screamed Brown in his high-pitched voice. "Kiss my big black ass." Everybody laughed. That was Brown. Even Kotite, who had replaced Ryan eight months earlier with orders to improve the team's outlaw image and to tone down the boisterous Brown, cracked a smile.

Brown never lost a game in Texas Stadium. The Eagles were 4-0 on the Cowboys' home field with Brown in the lineup at defensive tackle. And his last game was his best: Brown had two quarterback sacks as the Eagles produced one of the most dominating defensive performances in their history on that September 15, 1991 day.

The Eagles set a team record with 11 quarterback sacks. Clyde Simmons tied a team record with 4.5 sacks. The Cowboys, with young offensive stars such as Aikman, Smith and wide receiver Michael Irvin, managed just 90 total yards that day, a franchise low.

That was the Eagles' ninth consecutive non-strike victory over the Cowboys. The Eagles never suspected, not after their 24-0 victory, that their dominance of the series was coming to an end.

"That might have been the best game we ever played on defense," Eagles safety Andre Waters once said of that game. "I mean, we went in there and just shut them down. They couldn't do anything. Eleven sacks! Eleven sacks is just unheard of."

Sixteen months later, confidence was not a problem for the Eagles as they prepared to play the Cowboys in an NFC semifinal playoff game on January 10, 1993 in Texas Stadium. The Cowboys were the NFC Eastern champions, thanks to a 13-3 record. They had been given a bye the previous weekend when the Eagles rallied for that resounding 36-20 victory over New Orleans.

But the Eagles had momentum. They had confidence. They were playing the Cowboys, the team they had dominated for so long. "I don't think they want to play us," Waters remarked on the Monday before the game. "Dallas is worried. I think they remember what we've done to them in the past."

Waters' return was a fascinating subplot to the game. Waters had been out since October 18 with a fractured left fibula and ligament damage in his left ankle. Just the previous week, he had announced that he wouldn't play again that season, that he would concentrate on rehabilitating his leg and getting ready for 1993.

But that was before the Eagles beat the Saints, and the Redskins upset the Minnesota Vikings. That set the NFC semifinal pairings: Washington at San Francisco, Philadelphia at Dallas.

"Emmitt Smith is mine," Waters screamed as the triumphant Eagles filed into their Louisiana Superdome locker room following the victory over the Saints. Waters wanted to play against the Cowboys. But mostly, he wanted to play against Smith. Shortly after Waters was hurt, Smith was quoted in newspapers in the Dallas area as saying that the Philadelphia safety "deserved" to be injured. Smith called Waters the "dirtiest player in the NFL." He said he had the injury "coming to him."

Waters was livid. A highly emotional man who was sensitive about his image as a "dirty" player, Waters vowed to extract revenge.

"He made a mistake," Waters said in November. "He thought I would be out for the season. But I'll be back. I'll see him in the playoffs. And when we meet, two of us are going to walk on the field, but only one of us is going to walk off. They're going to have to carry him off."

Waters had made gradual progress in his rehabilitation. The broken bone healed quickly, but he was slowed some by the ligament damage in his ankle. On Tuesday, January 5, Waters worked out in Veterans Stadium before Kotite and defensive coordinator Bud Carson. On Friday, two days before the game, Waters was activated off the injured reserve list, which meant he would be in uniform in Texas Stadium. "It's a personal challenge between me and him," Waters said of Smith. "He talked the talk. Now he's got to walk the walk."

Many of the Eagles' defensive players felt Waters' return would make a difference against the Cowboys. Smith never had run for 100 yards against the Eagles when Waters was in the lineup. His highest total in four games against a Waters-led Eagles run defense had been 75 yards. Back on November 1, when Waters was out with an injury, Smith had run for 163 yards. "When Andre's in there, he doesn't come through that line quite so fast," Joyner noted. "He's looking for 'Dre' instead of looking where to run."

Waters' scheduled return was just another reason for the Eagles to feel confident about their game against the Cowboys. The Eagles also felt they had history on their side. This was the same team they had beaten nine times in a row, the same team they had devoured by a 24-0 score just last year, the same team they had whipped by a 31-7 score on a Monday night showdown just three months earlier. "Nobody put it on them like we did and they know it," Eagles linebacker Byron Evans said in the locker room after the victory over the Saints. "If they were home, watching TV, they know what to expect. Run for the lifeboats . . . the Eagles are coming and they're bad."

The Cowboys had won two of the last three in the series, but the Eagles believed there were extenuating circumstances. Dallas won 25-13 in Veterans Stadium on December 15, 1991, clinching a playoff berth and eliminating the Eagles from playoff contention. But the Eagles were down to their third quarterback, Jeff Kemp, since both Randall Cunningham and Jim McMahon were out with injuries. And Dallas had won 20-10 in Texas Stadium back on November 1, 1992. But that was the low point of Cunningham's slow, steady slide. He played perhaps the worst half of his career, completing just three of eight passes for 13 yards.

Cunningham was playing a lot better now. He had led the Eagles to five consecutive victories. And he had cleared a major hurdle the previous weekend in New Orleans—winning his first playoff game as a starting quarterback, throwing his first touchdown passes in post-season play.

"This group is extremely focused and confident," Kotite said, sitting at the glass table in his office on January 7. The next day would be the two-year anniversary of what Joyner called "the big change"—the dismissal of Buddy Ryan, the promotion of Kotite from offensive coordinator to head coach.

"I think they're ready," Kotite said. "They've been through a lot. It's been a long year, and a lot of things have happened. But these guys, when their backs are up against it, they respond.

"That's a great team we're going to be playing down there. Dallas is strong on offense, defense and special teams. No weaknesses. But these guys are confident. I can sense it. I see it in the way they're going about their business, the look they have in meetings, on the practice field. They're got a good feeling about themselves."

Earlier that day, tight end Keith Byars expressed his view: "I don't care where we play these guys. Hey, man, I've lost one time at Dallas. You're telling me I'm scared to go to Dallas? I don't care where we play. We can go play in a parking lot in Dallas, it doesn't matter to me."

The Philadelphia area was alive with excitement over the Eagles. The Sixers and Flyers had losing records. The Phillies were out of sight. None of the local college basketball teams was doing anything special. It was all Eagles—all day on WIP, the all-sports radio station. The newspapers that covered the team were running four or five Eagles-related stories a day. The Philadelphia television stations all sent crews to Dallas for breathless updates on the buildup to the big game.

On Wednesday, January 6, the Eagles opened their locker room to the media at 11 a.m. By 11:10, there were 47 media people in the room and three players. "You play for situations like this," Eagles cornerback Eric Allen remarked. "This is what you work for, when there's only a few teams left and everything is focused on a couple games that weekend." Recalled Joyner after the season: "I was confident. We all were confident. I really thought we had crossed a hurdle by winning in New Orleans. To me, that seemed like a tougher team than Dallas. That was the win we needed, the first playoff win. I really thought we were going to build on that."

Early on the morning of Sunday, January 10, the Eagles' team buses pulled into Texas Stadium. As usual, a group of Cowboys fans waited by the ramp, taunting and teasing the Eagles as they rode by. It occurred to Joyner, to defensive end Clyde Simmons, to some others, that this was the same situation that greeted the team back on September 15, 1991, that Jerome Brown jumped up that day and cursed at the fans and let them know that, hey, the Eagles were here. Now, there was only silence.

The game wasn't close. The Eagles took a 3-0 lead midway in the first quarter, but the Cowboys dominated the rest of the game. Dallas took a 7-3 lead after the first quarter, a 17-3 lead at halftime, a 27-3 lead at the end of three quarters and finally, shockingly, a 34-3 lead before the Eagles scored a meaningless touchdown in the game's final minute.

It was stunningly easy for the Cowboys. They just overwhelmed the Eagles with speed and talent. They were superbly prepared, a step or two ahead of the Eagles at every turn. "For them to dominate the way they did, it was just so tough to swallow," Joyner said after the season. "I knew they had improved and they had a lot of great players, but no way I thought they were so much better than us that we wouldn't even compete. But they just turned it up and turned it up and we didn't respond. It's a game of challenges. They challenged us and we didn't even answer."

These were the Cowboys, remember. The team the Eagles used to dominate. Just last season, the Eagles had sacked Aikman 11 times in a 24-0 win in this stadium. Just three months ago, the Eagles had whipped the Cowboys by 31-7 on "Monday Night Football."

The reversal of fortunes left the Eagles dizzy as well as beaten. They were future-shocked. The Cowboys had blown past them with stunning speed. When the Eagles looked up, the Cowboys were gone, so far ahead that it might take years to catch them.

"The biggest thing, I think, was that maybe some of us didn't want to admit that Dallas was a good team," White said in the locker room after what would be his final game for the Eagles. "I know I didn't. I didn't want to admit it. But I have to now. I'm not happy about it but I have to admit it. They have my respect." Byars admitted after the season: "It was a shock for us to lose that way, especially to Dallas. But I guess you have to give them credit. I hate to do it, but they deserve it. They busted the norm. The NFL is a bunch of copycats and they didn't follow anybody else. They weren't afraid to make moves and it paid off for them."

The Cowboys did pretty much whatever they wanted that day. Aikman completed 15 of 25 passes for 200 yards and two touchdowns. Smith ran for 114 yards and a touchdown. Dallas rolled up 346 yards and 22 first downs and controlled the football for more than 35 of the game's 60 minutes.

"It was just methodical, what they did to us," Mike Golic said in the locker room. "They kept pulling away and pulling away and there was nothing we could do about it. It was a feeling we weren't used to. It was agony." Six weeks after the game, Golic looked back and commented, "We had never been in that position before, and I just think we were shocked. Guys were just looking at each other like, 'What is this?' That had never happened to us before."

The 34-10 final score marked the Eagles' worst playoff loss. Ever. Overall, it was their worst loss in a non-strike game since they fell 35-3 to the New York Giants on October 12, 1986, a span of 106 games. That loss came during Cunningham's and White's second season. Joyner, Simmons and Byars were rookies. Ryan was a first-year coach. That was the beginning of this era in Eagles history. This looked like the end.

"That was the only time in my career I ever wanted a game to end," Allen said after the season. It was five weeks later, and there still was shock and dismay in his voice. "I just wanted to get out of there," Allen continued. "I just wanted it to be over, for everybody to go home. I never felt like that before. I would never have believed it. I never, ever, would have believed the Cowboys could do something like that to us."

After the Eagles took a 3-0 lead, Dallas got a 46-yard kickoff return from Kelvin Martin. On the Cowboys' sixth play, Smith burst through a huge hole in the middle of the line for 16 yards. Four plays later, Aikman lofted a one-yard touchdown pass to tight end Derek Tennell.

Late in the second quarter, Aikman completed a 41-yard pass to wide receiver Alvin Harper, who got a step on Eagles cornerback Mark McMillian. That put the football at the Philadelphia 14. Aikman scrambled for eight yards then threw a six-yard touchdown pass to tight end Jay Novacek, who made a diving catch in the end zone.

On the ensuing kickoff, Philadelphia return man Vai Sikahema lost his first fumble of the season. Dallas' Thomas Everett recovered. The Cowboys drove to the Eagles' 2-yard line, and rookie Lin Elliott kicked a 20-yard field goal as time expired for a 17-3 lead at halftime.

The Eagles had been a second-half team all season. They outscored their opponents 197-111 in the second half during the regular season. They outscored New Orleans 29-3 in the second half the previous week in the wild card playoff game. But the younger, quicker, fresher Cowboys dominated the second half on this day. The Cowboys took the kickoff and drove 70 yards in six plays to take a commanding 24-3 lead.

First, Aikman completed a 24-yard slant pass to Michael Irvin. Just after that play, Waters ran on the field for the first time, taking his place in the Eagles' secondary. Two plays later, Aikman faked the football to Smith and threw a 20-yard pass to Novacek, who was two steps ahead of Waters.

Two plays after that, Smith burst through the middle, cut outside and raced 23 yards for a touchdown. It was so easy. Smith was casually motioning to his blockers during the run. He was so relaxed, so confident. He scored standing up, untouched by an Eagles defender. "I never said he wasn't a good running back," Waters said of Smith after the game. "I just didn't like the comment he made about me getting hurt. He proved he's a great running back." Two series later, Smith ran for five yards. And 12 yards. And 11 yards. And six yards. And two yards, to move the Cowboys into position for a 43-yard Elliott field goal that jacked their lead to 27-3. "He's the best back in the NFL," White admitted after the game. "I didn't believe it, and I told him that after the game. It took a long time for him to prove it to me, but he finally did."

Smith carried one time for five yards in the fourth quarter. He left the game with more than 11 minutes to play. The Cowboys didn't need him. His replacement, a former practice squad player named Derrick Gainer, ran nine times for 29 yards as the Cowboys drove down the field. When Gainer scored on a one-yard run with just 3:19 left in the game, it was 34-3 in favor of the Cowboys. "It was a butt-kicking that seemed to last forever," Eagles safety Rich Miano said in the locker room. "It was like a bad nightmare, only we couldn't wake up and end it."

The Eagles' offense did nothing. Cunningham completed just one pass for more than eight yards in the first three quarters, a 12-yarder to Williams. Cunningham seemed hesitant to run, indecisive, baffled. On a key third-down play just before halftime, Cunningham made the wrong motion in the shotgun formation, causing center David Alexander to snap the ball with the quarterback not ready. The ball glanced off Cunningham and he recovered, but another possession was lost. "One of those days," Cunningham called it after the game. "Give Dallas credit. They played a great game."

The Eagles' running game, which averaged 149.3 yards during the regular season to rank second in the league, managed a measly 63 yards against the Cowboys. And 33 of those yards came on the Eagles' first possession.

In the second and third quarters, the Cowboys had more first downs than the Eagles had yards. The Cowboys had 223 yards and 13 first downs. The Eagles had 10 yards and one first down. "I never dreamed the score would be what it was," Kotite confessed. "In my wildest imagination, I never thought we'd lose this game," Byars agreed. "Never—not in a million years," added White.

The Eagles had lost playoff games before, but this was different. In previous playoff losses to Chicago, the Los Angeles Rams and Washington, the Eagles could tell themselves they lost because of their own mistakes. They were young and they were improving. They would be back.

This was different. The Eagles weren't young anymore. The young team was on the other side of the field. The Eagles didn't lose this game because of mistakes or inexperience or fog or injuries or bad calls—they were completely outplayed by a younger, faster, sharper, more physical opponent.

It ended in the cold gloom of a north Texas winter day. The Eagles filed slowly to the locker room as Cowboys fans jammed the front rows behind the blue wall of the lower deck of Texas Stadium, leaned over the railing and screamed at them. "Randall, Randall, Randall," they mockingly chanted at the Eagles quarterback. "Hey Joyner, you suck!"

The locker room was a tomb. Players walked to the showers and back with stunned expressions on their faces. Equipment men hurriedly filled up bags and trunks, packing away a season, an era.

It was over. The promise had been broken. There was no sense talking about next year, not after so many disappointments, not with free agency on the horizon, not with the Cowboys—so young, so fast, so sure of themselves—in complete command of the NFC Eastern Division.

Suddenly, the Eagles looked old. They looked like a team of players whose time had passed. They probably wouldn't collapse—teams usually fade slowly from prominence, just as players gradually slide down the far side of their peak—but they would never be the same.

Reggie White sat in front of his locker. His massive shoulders were slumped. He kept looking down at the floor. His contract would expire in three weeks. He would soon be free to sign with any team in the NFL. "I'm just not prepared to right now," White said in response to a question about free agency. "Let me get over this first."

As the Eagles boarded their chartered jet for the flight back to Philadelphia, they were struck by a final irony. Since the plane was still on the ground, a live feed of the NBC-TV broadcast of the Miami Dolphins' playoff game against the San Diego Chargers was being shown on the monitors throughout the cabin. Tired, dejected, stunned by the ease with which the Cowboys had whipped them, the Eagles trudged on the plane. As fate would have it, they settled into their seats just in time to watch Keith Jackson catch a 19-yard touchdown pass from Dan Marino. "Oh, my," NBC announcer Dick Enberg shouted.

The Dolphins quickly forced a turnover and took possession again. They had won the AFC Eastern Division title. Now they were on their way to a 31-0 romp over the Chargers in a conference semifinal playoff game. Suddenly, there was Jackson again, making a wonderful, diving catch of a 30-yard Marino pass for another touchdown, racing to the back of the end zone, celebrating with the fans in Joe Robbie Stadium. "The best receiving tight end in the NFL," Enberg shouted. "He got away from the Philadelphia Eagles and the Dolphins came up with the money and now they have him."

Joyner was overwhelmed. Players were screaming to shut off the game, but a couple of flight attendants reported that the coaches up in the first-class section wanted to watch. The game would stay on.

Joyner couldn't take anymore. He grabbed a blanket from the overhead compartment and hung it over the screen. Then he walked back to his seat and sat down for the long flight home.

EPILOGUE

· 19 ·

THE TEAM THAT WAS

They had it all. They had talent. They had confidence. They had style. They had a boisterous Pro Bowl defensive tackle, a future Hall of Fame defensive end, an all-purpose offensive star and the best pass-receiving tight end in the NFL. They had a superstar quarterback, an intense outside linebacker, a silent storm of a defensive end and a double-barrel burst of big hitters in the deep secondary.

They were brimming with promise and bursting with pride. They had color, character, energy, and plans. Big plans. They had youth. They had enthusiasm. They had time. Plenty of time.

The broken nucleus of The Team That Was gathered together again on a sunny Saturday morning in May 1993. They met on a high school football field in Brooksville, Florida. The circle was closing. They were there to participate in the second annual Jerome Brown "For the Kids" Football Camp, and to remind themselves of a teammate, a team, and a time that was just a memory.

"It's just not the same," said Keith Byars, the versatile, valuable offensive star who was investigating the possibility of signing with another team. Once he had been the consummate Philadelphia Eagle, the "ultimate team player," in the words of his coach. Now, Byars was a player without a team, uncertain of the future, unsatisfied with the past. "The change has been so great, you can't even measure it," Byars remarked. "But one of my favorite sayings is, 'Football can bring us together, but football can never tear us apart.' Football did bring us together. But we're not going to let football or anything else tear us apart."

Jerome Brown was there that soft spring day. He was there in spirit, anyway—that being his hometown, his high school, and his camp. The Eagles Pro Bowl defensive tackle, once and forever the symbol of The Team That Was, had been killed 11 months earlier in a car accident. His former teammates and friends from around the NFL had vowed to keep the camp going in his honor.

Reggie White was there. The future Hall of Fame defensive end, who had played eight remarkable seasons for the Eagles, was wearing a white Green Bay Packers T-shirt. Just five weeks earlier, White had ended his association with the Eagles by signing with the Packers as a free agent. Keith Jackson was there. The best receiving tight end in football had spent his first four seasons with the Eagles. But he had left as a free agent, too, signing with Miami after some deft legal maneuvering the previous September. Seth Joyner and Clyde Simmons were there. Brown's closest friends on the Eagles, key members of The Team That Was, they would still be tied to Philadelphia for at least one more season. But they knew their team would never be the same.

"We had something special," said White, sitting in the hot sun on the concrete stands of the Hernando High School football field. "It's hard to get together with these guys again and realize that we're not on the same team anymore, that what we had there in Philadelphia is gone now. It didn't have to be that way." Reflected Simmons: "I remember how good things were in the past. We had a good team and we had a lot of close friends and good relationships. Things happen, I guess. Things change."

It had been, perhaps, the most tumultuous off-season in the history of the franchise. Free agency had come to the NFL, and had changed every team. But nowhere was the upheaval more dramatic than in Philadelphia. The team that won 11 games during the 1992 regular season, that won a wild card playoff game, that was regarded as one of the best in the NFL, was torn apart and reconstructed. It bore only a slight resemblance to the Eagles of the recent past.

White was gone to Green Bay. Backup quarterback Jim McMahon was gone to Minnesota. Starting offensive tackle Ron Heller was gone to Miami. Third-string quarterback David Archer was gone to the Sacramento franchise of the Canadian Football League. John Booty, Leon Seals, Daryle Smith and Izel Jenkins all were gone to other NFL teams. Byars was an unrestricted free agent. He was strongly considering leaving the Eagles. Defensive tackle Mike Golic was an unrestricted free agent, looking hard at the possibility of signing with Miami. Free safety Wes Hopkins' career was in doubt. He was recuperating from February knee surgery, uncertain of his future. The Eagles had made plans to replace him. Strong safety Andre Waters had nerve damage in his left leg. Like Hopkins, Waters was rehabilitating, hoping to stick around for one more season. Simmons and Joyner were scheduled to be unrestricted free agents after the 1993 season, and the recent developments had greatly increased the likelihood that they, too, would be gone.

"We were so close for six or seven years," recalled Golic, who joined the rest of the gang that May day in Brooksville. He sat on the burnt grass of the football field where Brown had been a star for the Fighting Leopards of Hernando High. One year earlier, Brown organized his first camp. Many of his teammates had been there. They were all Eagles, all teammates, all together. But now The Team That Was had been broken apart by tragedy and free agency and the relentless, accelerated pace of life in the NFL. "It's just one of those things that you take for granted," Golic said. "You're together and you think you're always going to be together. You know the end is coming but when it happens, so quickly and so suddenly, it's hard to accept." Added Byars: "We were so close to being on the verge of something big happening. In a year's time, it's changed a great measure, to say the least. There are various reasons why. It seems like management wants to break the program down and start over again. That's their prerogative. You look back over the last year and you realize everything that's happened. It makes you sad but you have to realize that we'll always be friends. You want it to stay the same but it never does."

On January 11, the day after the playoff loss to Dallas, Joyner had walked through the locker room and removed name plates from above the stalls of his defensive teammates. The 34-10 loss to the Cowboys still stung like salt in an open wound. There was still a lot of shock and hurt on a lot of faces as Joyner went about collecting plastic pieces of the past. "I have a case hanging up in my basement," Joyner would say later. "I have an Eagles helmet that all the defensive guys signed. I wanted to hang up all the nameplates of all the guys I played with. There was such a large air of uncertainty around the team. Nobody knew what was going to happen."

Dallas won the Super Bowl. On January 17, one week after they dominated the Eagles, the Cowboys whipped the San Francisco 49ers by a 30-20 score in the NFC championship game in Candlestick Park. Two weeks after that, the Cowboys annihilated the Buffalo Bills by a 52-17 score in the Super Bowl in Pasadena, California. Dallas' victory marked the ninth consecutive time the NFC representative had won the Super Bowl, and the third consecutive time a team from the NFC Eastern Division had been crowned champion of the league.

In late January, just as the Cowboys were driving to the Super Bowl, the decision-makers in the Eagles organization gathered in Miami. Team president Harry Gamble and coach Rich Kotite huddled with owner Norman Braman at Braman's home and took a long, hard look at the roster. They looked at the past. They looked into the future. And they decided that it was time for a change. "Last year was our year," Braman declared. "We didn't do it. You can go into the whys, and it probably starts with Jerome [Brown's death], to God knows what else. But the bottom line is that last year was our year and we just didn't do it. So now we have to move forward. We have to change. I've seen teams stay pat with older players, fail to make moves, and they just fall off the edge of a cliff. And it takes them years to climb out of it. We're not going to do that. We're not going to repeat the mistakes of the past. We have a plan. We have a game plan for the future and we're going to follow it."

Braman's grand plan included subtractions as well as additions, a restructuring of the roster of a team that had won 10 or more games in each of the previous five seasons. The Eagles' total of 52 regular-season victories since 1988 was the third-most in the NFL, behind only San Francisco and Buffalo. But Braman was convinced it was time to break up the nucleus of The Team That Was. The strategy was clear: follow the Cowboys' blueprint. Get younger. Get faster. Substitute new players with youth and speed for older players whose experience and know-how was compromised by their old legs and worn-down bodies. "We're going to have a lot of new, young players," Braman vowed. "We're going to balance that with some seasoned veterans that we get from free agency. But we have to get younger and faster. Old legs are old legs. Old bodies are old bodies. This is a fast-paced sport. You play four or five preseason games and it's a long season. People wear down. You have to get younger and faster to stay competitive."

Braman made no secret of his desire to rebuild the Eagles following the formula made famous by the Cowboys, who had used draft picks and trades to infuse youth and enthusiasm into a team that had gone 1-15 as recently as 1989. The Cowboys had used the blockbuster trade of running back Herschel Walker to acquire a ransom of high draft picks to remake their roster. Braman planned to inherit a similar bounty, thanks to the conditions of the NFL's new labor agreement. In essence, Braman planned to use his past problems in player relations to his team's advantage. Because Reggie White, Clyde Simmons and Seth Joyner were named plaintiffs in lawsuits against the NFL, they were allowed to reject any restriction placed upon them as free agents. The Eagles could designate them as franchise or transition players under the terms of the labor agreement, but they could reject those labels and become unrestricted free agents.

Braman saw opportunity in this system. He lobbied hard behind the scenes to assure the Eagles of compensation for lost free agents. The team designated White its franchise player on February 25, but White rejected that status, making himself an unrestricted free agent. As a result, the Eagles stood to receive two No. 1 draft picks as compensation if White signed with another team. Joyner was named a transition player, and the Eagles would receive draft-pick compensation if he, as expected, rejected that designation when his contract expired after the 1993 season. The team's plan also called for designating Simmons either a transition or franchise player after the 1993 season, and receiving compensation if he, too, rejected that status.

Braman saw the prospects of a mother lode of high draft picks—young, talented, ambitious players—in exchange for the loss of older, disgruntled athletes. It made perfect sense. White, Joyner and Simmons were Buddy Ryan loyalists, prominent members of The Team That Was. So was Keith Jackson, who had signed with Miami as a free agent the previous September. Braman lobbied hard with the NFL's labor committee to secure compensation for the Eagles for the loss of Jackson. In fact, when NFL officials declined to award the Eagles an extra draft pick for the loss of Jackson, Braman hired Los Angeles attorney Max Blecher and filed an objection to the settlement of the new labor agreement. The objection was based on Braman's contention that the new agreement violated antitrust law, but it clearly was designed to force the league to fork over compensation for the loss of Jackson.

Jeff Kessler, an attorney for the NFL Players Association, called Braman's objection "a ruse, an outrage. The lowest of the low. It's even worse than the $7.5 million salary he took while he was charging his players for sweat socks." While not nearly as critical, U.S. District Court Judge David Doty agreed that Braman's objection was unfounded when Doty gave final approval to the labor agreement on April 30. In his ruling, Doty noted that "There is evidence before the court that the Eagles' objections are nothing more than an attempt to obtain compensatory draft selections."

But Braman wasn't completely foiled. The Eagles still would receive two No. 1 picks for the loss of White, including the 13th overall selection in the 1993 draft. They still were likely to receive compensation if they lost Joyner and Simmons after the 1993 season. They still were in position to exchange older players for draft picks, veterans for rookies, old for new. They still were in position to imitate the Cowboys. "The new standard of excellence in our division, in the entire NFL, is the Dallas Cowboys," Braman said. "If we don't do what we have to do, if we're not aggressive, if we don't have a definitive vision, we're going to have a hard time staying competitive. We're going to have a lot of draft picks. We need to make good picks. We need to have a good draft, to have players who are going to come in and make an immediate impact on this football team."

Braman was determined not to "repeat the mistakes of the past." He pointed to former coach Dick Vermeil, who has been accused of failing to inject youth into the powerful Eagles teams of the late 1970s and early 1980s. By 1982, the Eagles were beginning a run of six consecutive losing seasons. "Vermeil didn't address it, maybe that's why he got out," Braman said of the coach who resigned after the 1982 season.

Free agency arrived on March 1, 1993. More than 300 players were declared unrestricted free agents, including 15 Eagles. The league had entered a new world filled with opportunity and peril, and the most-watched development would be the courting of Reggie White. Publicly, the Eagles had expressed a desire to re-sign White. Braman said it in early February. Later that month, Harry Gamble wearily noted, "I've said this a thousand times: we're going to try to sign Reggie." But White had expected the Eagles to make him an offer between February 1 and March 1, the period during which teams had exclusive negotiating rights to their free agents. The Eagles never made such an offer.

"Norman called me," White said March 3 in a telephone conference call with reporters. "He said they would make an offer. But they never followed up. It seems to me they're more concerned with covering themselves than with getting me signed." Hard feelings between White and the Eagles bubbled to the surface. They drifted further apart. White said he couldn't understand why the team hadn't made an offer, why Kotite had not bothered to call him. White said he heard from defensive coordinator Bud Carson and from defensive line coach Dale Haupt, but not from Kotite. "That bothers me," White said. "That bothers me a lot."

White had mixed feelings about free agency. He relished his freedom, the opportunity to test the open market, to command more money than any non-quarterback in NFL history. But loyalty to the Eagles, to his teammates, and to the community tugged at him. On March 3, more than 2,000 people jammed JFK Plaza in Philadelphia on a chilly, overcast day to "Rally for Reggie," and express their support for the Eagles super-star defensive end. Sponsored by WIP, the all-sports radio station, the 35-minute rally was a public plea to White to re-sign with the Eagles and finish his career in Philadelphia. Beneath a canopy of green and white balloons, speakers ranging from former Eagles Garry Cobb and Herb Lusk to Philadelphia sports impresario Sonny Hill to ordinary fans took turns imploring White to return to the Eagles.

White was touched. On March 25, when it was clear that he would soon be signing with another team, White returned to Philadelphia to receive the Wanamaker Award as the athlete who best represented the city both on the field and off. When the crowd rose to salute him, White broke down in tears. "I promised myself I wouldn't do this," White said.

Soon after the start of the free-agency period, White embarked on a tour of NFL cities. He visited Cleveland on March 6. The Browns presented White's wife, Sara, with a $900 leather jacket as a gift. They showed the Whites around the team's new practice and training facility. Two days later, White went to Atlanta, saw the Falcons' facilities and took a tour of the Georgia state capital. He visited Detroit next. Since he was in the Midwest, he agreed to take a short trip to Green Bay to meet with Packers officials. His next stop was New York to talk with the Jets. Then he visited Washington. His last stop, on March 31, was San Francisco, whose team entered the running only a week earlier.

The 49ers had jumped in the race for White only after they lost defensive lineman Pierce Holt as a free agent. Under the terms of the new labor agreement, the top four finishers from the previous season couldn't sign a free agent until they lost one. Moreover, they could only sign a free agent for as much money as one of their free agents received from a new team. The so-called Rooney Rule, named after Pittsburgh Steelers president Dan Rooney, had restricted teams such as Dallas, Buffalo, Miami and San Francisco from pursuing free agents of White's caliber. But since Holt had received a three-year, $7.5 million deal from Atlanta, the 49ers had the opportunity to join the race for White. He visited their state-of-the-art complex in Santa Clara, California, saw their four Super Bowl trophies on display, met with 49ers owner Edward DeBartolo Jr. He came close to signing with San Francisco. "That was an organization that I always had a lot of respect for," White would say later. "And nothing really changed my mind about them. I was very impressed with everything about that team. They are committed to winning championships."

White narrowed his choices to four teams: San Francisco, Washington, Cleveland and Green Bay. On the night of March 5, as North Carolina was beating Michigan in the NCAA basketball championship game, White's agent, Jimmy Sexton, held extensive negotiations with all four teams. Washington's best offer was $13 million over four years. Cleveland's best was $14 million over four years. San Francisco offered slightly more than $19 million over five years. Green Bay's offer was tops: $17 million over four years, including $9 million in the first year.

White liked the Packers' offer. He also was impressed with Green Bay general manager Ron Wolf and especially with coach Mike Holmgren. A few days after his visit to Green Bay, Holmgren and defensive coordinator Ray Rhodes had surprised White by traveling to his home in Knoxville, Tennessee. They caught up with him at a luncheon where he was a guest speaker. He was struck by just how happy he was to see them. "We just hit it off," White remarked. "There was something there. I was surprised because I didn't really consider the Packers when this whole thing started. But I just had a good feeling about that whole organization."

Money was a factor. White made no secret of his desire to get as much as he could, to use his resources to fund his ministry. "The more I have, the more I can do for other people," White noted. "If I short-change myself, I'm short-changing others. I can't do that." San Francisco's offer was good, but flawed. Because of the restrictions of the Rooney Rule, the 49ers had to make an offer that increased in value every year. Because the offer wasn't guaranteed, and because the NFL salary cap was likely to kick in by 1994, White was concerned that the 49ers would be tempted to cut him after two seasons rather than pay more than $4 million per year for a defensive lineman in his mid-30s.

Green Bay made sense to White. He liked the idea of moving his family to a small, peaceful place. He planned to commute to Milwaukee, which is about a two-hour drive away, once or twice a week to work with the inner-city community. On April 6, White accepted the Packers' offer of $17 million over four years. The contract wasn't guaranteed, but it was structured to give White most of his money in the first two years. He would receive a $4.5 million signing bonus, plus a $1.5 million bonus upon reporting to training camp, plus $3 million in salary in 1993. That was $9 million in the first year. The rest of the contract called for salaries of $3.15 million in 1994, $2.85 million in 1995 and $2 million in 1996. "I may never win a Super Bowl with the Packers but I'm happy," White would say later. "I feel comfortable there. They are committed to winning. It's a good organization and I just have a good feeling about the people there. That's what really struck me."

White couldn't hide his disappointment in the Eagles front office. He was sure that the problems between the players and management had sabotaged the Eagles' chances, that the mistrust between the athletes in the locker room and the officials on the fourth floor ruined the team's ability to realize its potential. "I just think we never could overcome the gap with management," White remarked. "Not feeling comfortable in the locker room, especially when they were there. Going into every year wondering when are they going to get these guys signed. Mr. Braman is a businessman and he handles things the way he wants to handle them, and that's fine. But our frustration came from busting our behinds on the field. We were not satisfied with being paid. We wanted to win and it was hard for us to win. I met with a lot of other owners. To see the passion of these guys when they look you in the eye and say, 'My goal in life is to win another championship,' it's unusual when you've never experienced that."

White's flight was the most dramatic development of the spring of 1993. On the day White signed with Green Bay, Simmons said his famous friend's departure left the Eagles "like the lost children of Israel trying to find the promised land without Moses." But it was part of a pattern. McMahon signed a two-year, $3.2 million contract with Minnesota on March 24. He told reporters in Minneapolis that "if the Eagles want Randall Cunningham, they can have him. I'm going somewhere I can play." Defensive back John Booty signed with Phoenix. Defensive tackle Leon Seals signed with New England. Quarterback David Archer left for Sacramento of the CFL. Offensive tackle Daryle Smith signed with Minnesota. Then starting left tackle Ron Heller, another key member of The Team That Was, signed April 20 with Miami.

Heller said he made an "excruciating decision." The Eagles had offered him more money, about $3.3 million over three years as opposed to $3 million over three years from the Dolphins. But he liked the idea of finishing his career on a grass field in warm weather. He had a permanent residence in Tampa. He knew the Dolphins were a relatively young team that had gone 11-5 in 1992 and had reached the AFC title game. He sensed that the Eagles, by comparison, were moving in another direction. "I've been through a rebuilding program before," Heller remarked. "At this stage of my career, I don't want to go through another one."

At that point, the Eagles had lost seven free agents and signed just one, tight end Mark Bavaro, who had spent the 1992 season with Cleveland. But on April 21, the Eagles jumped into the free-agent market, signing defensive back Erik McMillan from the New York Jets and agreeing to contract terms with defensive lineman Tim Harris from San Francisco. Harris signed the next day. On April 24, the Eagles signed defensive tackle Keith Millard, who had been out of football since announcing his retirement midway in the 1992 season. The next day, during the NFL's annual college draft, the Eagles selected Jackson State offensive lineman Lester Holmes and Colorado defensive tackle Leonard Renfro in the first round, Missouri wide receiver Victor Bailey in the second round, and Texas A&M cornerback Derrick Frazier and North Carolina State safety Mike Reid in the third round. They also traded with San Diego for veteran offensive lineman Broderick Thompson.

"We had a great week," Eagles coach Rich Kotite declared late on the night of April 25. "We really improved this football team." Later that week, Kotite said, "I don't want to wake up one day and have this an old team. I don't want to wake up and have this a football team of good old boys. We are changing. We have changed. If we don't make changes, we're going to be left in the dust by other teams."

The signing of Harris was a surprise. Harris had finished second to Clyde Simmons among NFC pass rushers with 17 quarterback sacks in 1992. But the 49ers made only a half-hearted attempt to re-sign him, and few other teams expressed much interest in him. The reason was his history of off-the-field problems, which included a drunken driving conviction in April 1992. He also was regarded as one of the NFL's loudest, cockiest players. "I play with my mouth," Harris admitted before the start of his first minicamp with the Eagles. "I play with my emotions. I wouldn't call it trash-talking. But I wouldn't call it something nice, either." Eagles officials downplayed questions about Harris' background. "We did our homework on this guy," Kotite said of Harris. "I am really thrilled that he's here. I'm not one to hold anything against somebody. He's someone who has been playing in the NFL, who has had some sort of problem, and we're aware of it. The whole world is aware of it. He's made every effort to remain an NFL player and to get his life where it should be. I don't have any negative thing going into that. I will deal from the positive."

On May 6, Harris was arrested in Live Oak, California and charged with driving under the influence of alcohol. If convicted, he faced a suspension for up to six games by the NFL under terms of the league's substance-abuse policy. It was possible that he would begin his career with the Eagles on the suspended list.

On May 8, Randall Cunningham married Felicity de Jager in a ceremony that was held at the Taj Mahal casino hotel in Atlantic City, New Jersey. Cunningham paid a reported $1 million for the wedding, including $18,000 for a 14-tier cake. The Eagles quarterback invited close to 1,000 guests. He and his new wife held a press conference immediately after the ceremony.

One week later, on May 15, the shattered nucleus of The Team That Was gathered in Brooksville, Florida. Times had changed. Just four years earlier, in the spring of 1989, the Eagles were the defending NFC Eastern Division champions. They were a young, rising power, a gathering storm. The Dallas Cowboys were a team in disarray. Jerry Jones had purchased the team in February 1989, fired coaching legend Tom Landry and hired Jimmy Johnson. The Cowboys were on their way to a 1-15 season in 1989.

Now, the Cowboys were the defending Super Bowl champions. The new standard in the NFL. The Eagles were old by comparison, a team in transition, a team desperate to change to try to keep pace with their haughty, hated rivals. Reggie White and Keith Jackson were gone. Keith Byars was leaning that way. Wes Hopkins and Andre Waters were past their primes. Both veteran safeties were fighting against time to recuperate from leg injuries and salvage one more season. Seth Joyner and Clyde Simmons were less than a year away from free agency. Randall Cunningham was 30. He was more than two years removed from his last appearance in the Pro Bowl. He was no longer a young quarterback on the rise. Buddy Ryan was in Houston, where he had been hired as the Oilers' defensive coordinator.

Ryan had been a top candidate for the vacant New England Patriots head-coaching job after the 1992 season. He had an interview with Patriots owner James Orthwein. He had a supporter in the organization in Patrick Forte, the former Eagles executive and agent to Reggie White (and defendant in White's 1989 lawsuit) who now was a vice president for the Patriots. Orthwein settled on Bill Parcells, the former New York

Giants coach who, like Ryan, had been out of football for two years. "One of the few times he beat me," Ryan remarked, referring to his 5-1 record in his last six games against Parcells.

Ryan was 58. He had joined the staff of head coach Jack Pardee, whose Oilers team had blown a 35-3 lead in a January 3 playoff game in Buffalo. Later that day, the Eagles rallied from a 20-7 deficit to beat New Orleans 36-20. "I wanted to get back into football as a head coach," Ryan said. "But this is a good situation for me. That's a good football team. They've got players. They can go to the Super Bowl next year. I think I can make a difference. I'm back in football and I'm happy about that. I missed the camaraderie, the feeling around the players, 50 guys with a cause. But I wasn't sitting around moping because I wasn't coaching. I was training horses. That's hard work. I'm not the kind to sit around and mope and think about what didn't happen. I was happy working with my horses. But this is a great opportunity for me."

Ryan said he felt the Eagles were on the decline. He said he knew they were going "downhill" when Keith Jackson skipped off to Miami as a free agent back in September 1992. "That was terrible, just terrible," Ryan said. "We worked our ass off to get him in the [1988] draft and then we traded up to make sure we got Eric Allen in the second round. You don't just find those kind of players. It was just frustrating to see. I don't think they were as physical as they had been in the past. They just weren't the same team and it was tough for me to watch them."

Keith Jackson had a unique perspective on the Eagles, too. On February 7, 1993, he had played in the Pro Bowl for the fourth time in his five-year career. Jackson had been elected to the annual all-star game as the starting tight end for the American Football Conference after playing three times for the NFC team. He had caught 48 passes for 594 yards and five touchdowns in 13 regular-season games for the Dolphins, who won the AFC East title with an 11-5 record. He caught two touchdown passes in a 31-0 playoff victory over San Diego. That victory propelled the Dolphins to the AFC title game, where they lost to Buffalo.

"I went into a blind situation and it worked out so beautiful for me," Jackson declared. "I didn't know how things were going to go for me in Miami. It was a new situation. I knew what things were like in Philadelphia, but this was a totally blind situation for me. It worked out great. I made the Pro Bowl. I played for a team that won the division title. I played in the conference championship game, which is something I never did in Philadelphia. The Dolphins are a young, healthy team. We'll be back. And I realize now that God really does take care of his children. When I look at my situation, and I look at the disaster in Philadelphia, I can only say that I've been blessed."

Jackson was back with his old teammates for one day. He joined them in Brooksville for Brown's camp, for the unofficial reunion of The Team That Was. The free clinic was attended by around 450 youngsters, boys and girls. They got T-shirts, a small canvas bag, a miniature football and the chance to mingle with some of the best players in the NFL.

"Line up, line up," White yelled at the campers as they took the field for stretching exercises. "Let's go, let's go."

After warming up, the campers broke into groups with an NFL player or two in charge of each group. "In this group, you're going to learn how to be defensive linemen," said the 6-foot-6, 290-pound Simmons, towering over his charges. "I don't care about any other positions." Jackson and Byars, who used to represent the Eagles' most productive pair of pass catchers, worked together. They split up their group and tossed them passes, cheering every catch. The serious-minded Joyner gathered his group around him. Down on one knee, Joyner lectured his gang. "Pay attention," Joyner said to a youngster who allowed his eye to wander over to the action on the other side of the field. "Listen to me. I want you to pay attention to your coaches, pay attention to your teachers, pay attention to your parents and stay away from the drugs."

Cortez Kennedy and Russell Maryland, star defensive tackles who had followed in Brown's footsteps at the University of Miami, took their group down one end of the field. Then Kennedy, the NFL's Defensive Player of the Year in 1992, the athlete who had changed his uniform jersey number to 99 to honor his late friend, led his gang on a jog around the track. He was a 300-pound pied piper with a bunch of 80-pound followers. "Jerome had a ball with kids," Mike Golic said. "That's the way all the guys here feel about it. It's something he started, something we're all trying to keep going. We know how much kids and how much this town meant to him." Recalled Byars: "I wasn't here last year. My cousin was getting married that weekend and I remember telling Jerome, 'I can come down Friday and leave early Saturday morning.' He said, 'No, I'll catch up to you next year.' Who would have thought there wouldn't be a next year for him to be at his camp?"

Brown's death was the beginning of the end of The Team That Was. He will remain their symbol: loud, loose, talented, inconsistent, irreverent, unpredictable, unbridled, unfulfilled. Like the team he represented, Brown left unfinished plans. Up in Philadelphia, Brown's locker stall had been cleaned out and given to another player. It was time to move on. The Phillies won 23 of their first 30 games, the fastest start in franchise history. They were the talk of the town.

For one day, the old team was together again. Before the campers arrived on the field, they formed a loose circle, and talked and joked with each other. "So, Reggie, did God say exactly $17 million?" Joyner asked his former teammate. They all laughed. It was just like old times. The gang, including Jerome Brown, was all there.

"I know Jerome is here," White said. "He is still with us, in our hearts. He is the one who brought us all together down here."